# Mountains Are Mountains

## and

# Rivers Are Rivers

# MOUNTAINS ARE MOUNTAINS
## and
# RIVERS ARE RIVERS

*Applying Eastern Teachings to Everyday Life*

EDITED BY

# ILANA RABINOWITZ

FOREWORD BY JON KABAT-ZINN

HYPERION
NEW YORK

Library of Congress Cataloging-in-Publication Data

Rabinowitz, Ilana.
    Mountains are mountains and rivers are rivers : foreword by Jon
Kabat-Zinn.—1st ed.
    p. cm.
  ISBN: 0-7868-6476-1
  1.  Spiritual life—Psychology.  2.  Peace of mind—Religious
aspects.  3.  Buddhism—Doctrines.
  BQ4302 .R29 1999
  294.3'444—ddc21                                          98-56644
                                                              CIP

Designed by Laura Lindgren

FIRST EDITION

10  9  8  7  6  5  4  3  2  1

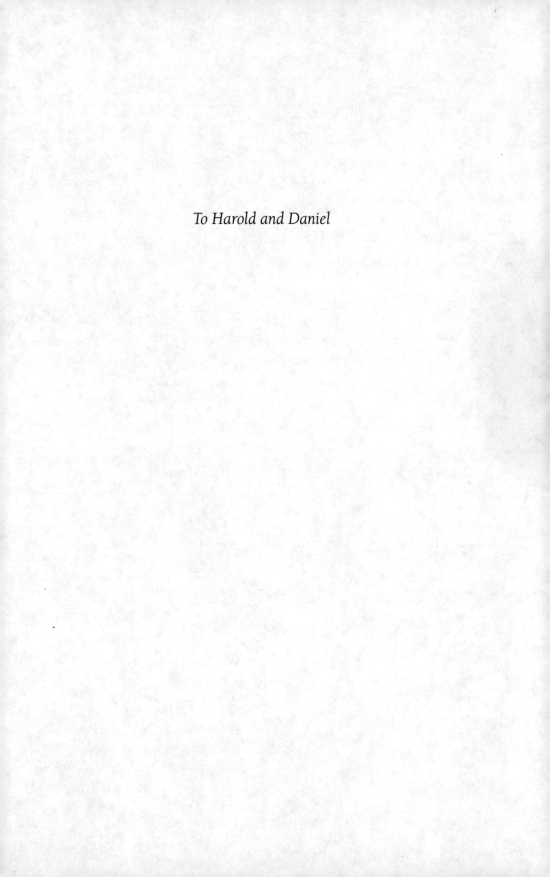

*To Harold and Daniel*

# CONTENTS

## Acceptance

## Harmony

## Meditation

# ACKNOWLEDGMENTS

I would like to thank Jennifer Lang of Hyperion, who has been a pleasure to work with, for her support of this book, and my agent, Alex Hoyt, for his work in finding such a good home for the book at Hyperion.

I am very grateful to my husband, Harold, for his invaluable editorial guidance and to his staff at The Reference Works for handling the permissions and the preparation of the manuscript.

A special word of thanks is due Jon Kabat-Zinn, who because of his uncompromising devotion to quality, offered his time, care, and attention beyond what I could have expected.

# FOREWORD

Any worthy anthology serves the important purpose of introducing new worlds to readers who might not otherwise be exposed to them. Once unearthed, these worlds afford undreamed of possibilities for delight and edification. When it comes to a meditation anthology such as this one, a positive experience of what lies within these pages goes well beyond delight and edification, to include the very real possibility of transformation and healing for the reader. Of course, this requires a personal commitment to take what is being pointed to, which is all that any words can accomplish, and attempt to embrace it in one's own life, in one's own way, so that it is neither mere imitation nor a mechanical pursuit of instructions, but an authentic adventuring and experimenting. The ancient Buddhist admonition not to mistake the finger pointing at the moon for the moon will come into play repeatedly as we drink in what is being pointed to in these chapters.

The writings included in this volume invite that kind of wholehearted participation and are, on the whole, impassioned enough to in turn ignite or amplify a passion for self-inquiry and understanding in the reader. Many are written by Westerners who have devoted their lives to the study, practice, and teaching of various forms of meditation, and who have found ways to speak about it through their own experience, ways that elucidate rather than obscure the heart of the subject and bring it to life. Other offerings are written by teachers who come from Asia, where these practices evolved and thrived for centuries before making their way to the West. These teachers are exquisitely articulate and impassioned in their voicing of what is deepest and best in their traditions. Together, the teachers featured here are among the vanguard of pioneering intermediaries of the past forty years who brought these teachings to the West and who have been able to translate what were, until recently, to us highly mysterious and, to a large extent, culture-bound practices into an idiom and into forms that people in the mainstream of Western culture can understand and engage in, thereby increasing the likelihood that these practices would take root in this new soil. Most of these teachers have their own centers and offer meditation retreats and instruction to those wishing to pursue this path, so the opportunities for exploration and adventuring beyond reading this book are extensive.

On the surface, it appears that these teachers represent different streams in the river of Buddhist meditation practice, and in a sense they do. But anyone familiar with the underlying essence of Buddhism will know that in order for Buddhism to be Buddhism, it has to be willing to let go of being Buddhist, since its unswerving commitment is to nonduality and nonclinging and therefore transcends Buddhism itself. All these streams and the river itself empty into a vast ocean, often spoken of as *the dharma*, which is truly universal, and ultimately simply human, beyond any notion of East or West, or for that matter, old or new. The contributions of other thinkers in this volume, who are not strictly speaking meditation teachers, round out an exploration of many salient features of this universe. While a book of this type can only whet the appetite of the reader, its value will be in part to encourage those who are touched by specific aspects to pursue their interests through reading the original sources from which these passages are excerpted and to read other works by the same authors and ultimately, to consider going to their centers and studying with them.

What unifies these contributors is their ability to capture this dharma universe in all its expanse and depth, while highlighting those aspects of it that speak most directly to our everyday lives. It is an honor for me to be included within these pages with teachers and thinkers whose work I hold in such high esteem, who are in some cases friends, and from whom I have learned so much. Finding myself, for the past twenty years, bridging the worlds of mindfulness meditation practice and its dharma elements on the one hand, with the worlds of Western medicine, science, health care, and society on the other, I am keenly aware, and reminded daily, of the huge subterranean yearning in people everywhere for authenticity and personal agency, for silence and stillness and peace of mind, for embodied experience, and for vehicles and methods that are equal to the task of helping us perceive and face the full extent of the human condition with integrity, freedom, wisdom, and compassion, including, importantly, self-compassion. The world seems hungry, if not starving, for the implementation of such explorations at work, in the family, in virtually every aspect of personal, professional, and institutional life. This anthology can provide both inspiration and nourishment to those drawn to explore and understand the healing power and the promise of mindfulness and of meditative perspectives on living. The broad spectrum of selections offered, with their different orientations and teaching styles, may be just what is needed to appeal to people with a wide range of different temperaments, motivations, and interests.

One of the first things I read in my earliest brushes with the Zen tradition, at a time when it was much harder to come by the kind of commonsensical and contemporary writings on meditation represented here, was an aphorism suggesting that at the beginning of Zen practice, mountains are mountains and rivers are rivers. As one gets more deeply into what was intimated to be a long and arduous relationship with meditation practices, it went on to say, mountains are no longer mountains and rivers are no longer rivers. But, when the long journey in the inner landscape of one's own heart/mind is fully completed, whatever that mysteriously meant, mountains are once again mountains and rivers once again rivers.

I found the paradox refreshing and inviting. As a student in my early twenties, it seemed to be pointing to something I had not considered before, something about perception and relationship, the experience of reality, and the shifting ground of the experiencer that might be vitally important in living our lives. It also pointed to a potential homecoming that I found nourishing to contemplate, a return to an original understanding lost, misplaced, or forgotten, and in its recovery somehow deepened and made real. This was enough for me to throw myself into a daily practice of meditation and to be on the lookout for teachers from whom I could obtain instruction, guidance, and direction for what else to read, where else to look, and where I might practice with like-minded people.

I soon found that practicing meditation enhanced the feeling that it was possible to come to know and inhabit our true nature as unique human beings, to realize that there really is nowhere to go, that we *already* belong, that we have always had a place in the larger whole, and what is more, that we ourselves are and have always been whole, although much of the time we may feel we are dwelling far from this actuality. Ultimately, the challenge of meditation, whatever the tradition and the method, comes down to living our lives authentically, awake to the moments and circumstances that present themselves to us as they are, not clinging to one limited view or another or noticing it when we inevitably do, embodying our undivided wholeness, each in our own unique way, and giving ourselves over to the world through our passion, through our longing, through our love and a desire to contribute in the service of the larger whole. This is the path of the dharma and of mindfulness, and the challenge of seeing mountains and rivers. All of it is accessible only in present moments, right here, right now. There simply are no other opportunities. But there are many doors into this world and into meditation practice, and part of the adventure, once they are pointed out, is finding our own ways in.

Dharma is a world that has found a place in modern discourse, yet its true meanings remain only vaguely understood. People know the term *dharma bum*—Jack Kerouac immortalized it in his writing—and they may know the term *dharma lion*—it has been used to describe one of the largest poetic figures of Kerouac's generation, Allen Ginsberg. While traditionally, dharma signifies teachings of the Buddha, encapsulated in the Four Noble Truths and the Eight-Fold Path, it can also be thought of as meaning something larger but still inclusive of and true to the Buddhist formulation, more along the lines of "the way things are," a universal lawfulness of name and form, cause and effect with great relevance for both our happiness and our suffering, a lawfulness that one can discover and confirm for oneself, but only by mobilizing one's own energies to look beneath the surface of appearances, in the world and within one's own mind.

The looking I am speaking of is not the one-shot glance, the tentative quick peek behind the curtain, but a sustained cultivation of penetrative seeing over a lifetime, fueled by a longing for freedom from our own vaguenesses and unexamined constricting mind habits, by our yearning for authentic experience, and perhaps by a growing desire in us, as we examine the unfolding nature of our lives, to slip free of the veiling patterns of thought and behavior that we sense unfailingly restrict and diminish the expressions of our innate human nature and cloud our capacity for living and acting with integrity, wisdom, and an openhearted selflessness. This is the work of meditation. It is the work of a lifetime.

Throughout history, each person who comes to be recognized by others as an authentic voice of dharma holds and expounds this universal lawfulness and its expressions through meditation practice in a unique and different way. This panoply of approaches enriches enormously the palette of colors and styles that attempt to capture the uncapturable, the formless, understandings that go beyond mere words, however skillfully strung together, to point to and embrace something larger, deeper, and yet unspeakably real and important to the unfolding of our nitty-gritty, everyday lives for anybody who is awake and listening.

Although just fragments of larger works, the writings assembled here individually and collectively provide the reader with engaging and luminous meditation teachings, each a skillful inducement to wake up from the slumbers of habitual unawareness and automaticity; to stop, look, and listen to the mountains and rivers of our inner and outer landscapes; and ultimately to see that there is no outer and no inner, no mountains and no rivers, simply an ongoing play of elements with nothing fixed or static, just the dynamic of things as they are, and an infinity of challenges to be present for our moments and live them with integrity, wherever and however we find ourselves.

Gary Snyder evokes this endless fluxing as he brings his poem of forty years, "Mountains and Rivers Without End," to its elegant conclusion:

> *Walking on walking,*
> *    under foot earth turns*
>
> *Streams and mountains never stay the same.*
>
> *    The space goes on.*
> *    But the wet black brush*
> *    tip drawn to a point,*
> *        lifts away.*

May this volume provide inviting glimpses into the world of meditation practice for many people and that, moonlike, it illuminate, in beauty and in surprising possibility, heart paths unwinding along, across, and within the mountains and rivers of our lives.

—Jon Kabat-Zinn
December 1998

# Mindfulness and the Art of Living

This book is fundamentally a collection of writings about paying attention—what Eastern teachers refer to as mindfulness. To be mindful or fully present as each moment of our lives unfolds is the foundation of the meditative mind. Mindfulness is also a challenge that the teachings of the East poses to our Western way of life, the challenge to see our lives and the world in a new way. This collection is about how writers and teachers who are speaking to us in the West have responded to this challenge, and what we have made of these valuable teachings so far, as the streams of Eastern and Western wisdom come together at the turn of the century and the millennium.

What is so important about mindfulness? Most of us make our way through life with more or less awareness of ourselves and our surroundings. We have families, careers, and perhaps satisfying lives. But without mindfulness and the attendant awareness it brings, the connection between us and what is truest in our lives may grow thin and weaken. For much of the time, we may be lost, even trapped, in daydreams and fantasies of our own devising, drifting in and out of the actuality of our lives. We forget that, as Jon Kabat-Zinn says, "This is it. When we let go of wanting something else to happen in the moment, we are taking a profound step toward being about to encounter what is here now."

In the course of practicing mindfulness, one discovers that much of the time the mind is traveling away from the scene: it relives and revises past experiences, worries or dreams about the future, and evaluates and analyzes the self and others. In fact, our thinking is typically so scattered that while we appear to be present, we often are not.

We can begin to fully appreciate how inattentive we are to what is happening in our lives when we to try to sit quietly and focus on something as simple as our own breathing. What we rapidly discover is that even though we may be alone in a quiet room with the television off and the windows closed, there is still a deafening din that is going on inside our heads. Added to the echoes of the sensory onslaught of modern culture is everything from personal and family issues, to politics and the urgently conveyed messages of modern media. Meditation can help us become aware of this. It can help us see what our particular patterns of thought are, and not be so trapped in them or mistake them for what is real. It can help us come to a deeper understanding of how our lives might be in greater harmony with the world in which we live.

But looking within can be uncomfortable, so we have become highly skilled at avoiding a developed awareness of ourselves. We accomplish this by creating distractions. We make phone calls, follow busy schedules, watch television, soothe ourselves with intoxicants, and work long hours. Over time, our highly personalized distraction strategies become habitual. When faced with an opportunity to quietly observe and experience a moment of time, we set ourselves in motion. We may play solitaire, eat chocolate, get into fights, or rearrange the furniture. (A friend of mine told me that since she has tried sitting quietly every day, her house has never been cleaner.)

My interest in meditation began with an interest in the literature of mindfulness. As a result of my reading, I discovered that mindfulness is a subject that cannot simply be studied as one would study, for example, anthropology or history. A book on the subject will only get you so far. Mindfulness is developed by meditating. As a relative newcomer to meditation, I approached it with the curiosity of a person with "beginner's mind." The lessons and values of mindfulness that I chose to illuminate in this book are a reflection of that curiosity.

When I first started to meditate, five minutes seemed like an eternity. I looked forward to meditating with a feeling somewhere between aversion and dread. But after a month or so, I approached my practice with the thought, "Let's see what is on my mind today. This should be interesting." Even if what was on my mind was difficult, it was actually a relief to become aware of the thoughts behind the way I was feeling at the time.

The path of mindfulness is not easy for anyone who chooses to walk it, and not just because of the discomfort of dealing with one's own thoughts. There are reasons why we might find the fit of Eastern teaching and our Western ethos challenging. In the first place, we may easily misinterpret the very language used to point to our potential for growth. We suspect that *openness* augurs uncertainty, when in fact, an open mind offers the possibility for creativity and learning that an attachment to a particular view precludes. We suspect that *acceptance* means acquiescence, when in fact, it simply means to acknowledge what is the case. Instead of observing a fact we don't like so that we can choose to deal with it or move away from it, we deny what is unpleasant and live with the consequences of what we have buried. We believe that *letting go* means giving up or quitting when it is this quality that allows for flexibility and change. The ability to let go is not a sign of weakness but a path to freedom. It means that we admit we do not have control over everything and everyone and we don't have every answer. It allows us to change—to let go of resentments and correct or avoid the mistakes that haunt us.

When we face a problem we tend to try to solve it by first answering the question, "What should I *do* about this? or "How can I change this?" To solve is to act. We often feel that the *more* we can do, the better we have done. But as the joke about Eastern teachings, and the title of a book by Sylvia Boorstein says, "Don't just do something, sit there." The writers in this collection offer teachings about how to pay attention to whatever is before us. The better the quality of attention, the more appropriate the response may be.

Meditation is a process that disciplines the mind to pay better attention through regular practice. The practice involves paying attention to, among other things, one's thoughts moment to moment, without judgment and without getting caught up in impulses or emotions. Just noting, just acknowledging: here is this thought and here is another thought—and better not get stuck on that one or I'll miss the next one. . . . Over time, this practice affects the way we pay attention to the world.

A meditation practice does not require the purchase of equipment, the making of an appointment, the changing of one's appearance, or changing or compromising one's religion. You don't need to shave your head, burn incense, or wear special clothing to meditate. It is an activity that can be done at no cost and at a time that is convenient. Unlike other ways we may have of relaxing, like getting a massage or being pampered at a spa or beauty salon, it is not something that is done *to* you. It is something you do to take care of yourself.

One of my teachers likened meditating to brushing one's teeth. It is best done regularly and at the same time every day. It best not to think we are doing anything special in practicing meditation since it is simply part of the work of attending to life unfolding, as it is, in its ordinariness. It is good to take care that our practice doesn't interfere with other people in the household so we don't make a fuss about telling people to accommodate us. Just as brushing is part of a daily regimen that helps us maintain our teeth, meditating is part of our daily regimen that may help us refine our ability to be in touch with our lives.

Meditation is the discipline that trains the mind to pay attention in each moment. Being mindful means giving priority to what is happening now. That is why when we fold the laundry, we can be mindful, and when we watch a sunset we can be mindful. If we only pay attention when we think something special is happening, a large portion of our lives will pass unnoticed.

The contributors in this book have examined the method and meaning of mindfulness in ways that are simple, straightforward, and understandable to a Western way of thinking. The lessons we learn by meditating may be exquisitely simple, yet they can transform our experience of the world and our relationships. This book is grouped into sections to highlight several of the qualities that may be developed through meditation practice. You may notice that these values are not entirely foreign to us, yet we are not accustomed to giving them a high priority or refining them in ourselves.

Meditation allows us to attend to the process of thought in such a way that four key elements of a balanced life are strengthened. The first four sections of this book address these values: Openness, Awareness, Acceptance, and Letting Go. Openness is practiced as we focus on our breathing and allow the root stillness and clarity of the mind to emerge. Awareness is practiced by learning to face our thoughts without enacting a distraction strategy; acceptance is gained as we recognize the thoughts when they enter our consciousness without judging them; and letting go entails being able to let the thoughts go without getting caught up in the process of reacting to them. The next two sections offer writing about Tranquility and Harmony. Through meditation, we may experience tranquility, which is the ability to relate to ourselves and others with patience and kindness, and eventually, harmony—the complete involvement in a task or awareness of another person as one with ourselves. The final section, Meditation, addresses the nature of meditation practice and offers some specific instructions to begin a practice on your own.

In selecting excerpts to be included in this collection, I searched for two types of presentations. One type of writing explains the psychology or philosophy of the qualities presented in each section of the book; although they do so simply and in a down-to-earth way, this writing is primarily theoretical. This group includes Shunryu Suzuki (on Openness), Eugene Herrigel (on Letting Go), and Pema Chodron (on Tranquility). The other group of writers share personal experiences that illuminate by example the qualities in each section of the book. When Sylvia Boorstein tells the story of being served broccoli at every meal on retreat, we may begin to understand the quality of Acceptance. When Jon Kabat-Zinn shares the thought process that begins with his annoyance at finding cat food dishes in the sink, we can understand how mindfulness may eventually lead to a feeling of Tranquility. Larry Rosenberg's description of his thoughts and feelings after getting a mosquito bite that he can't scratch provides us with another way of understanding Awareness.

In broad strokes, that is the road map of the journey we are about to take. The path has been charted by people who may have had to travel great distances, either on the map or in their minds, to obtain these teachings. They had to digest them and incorporate them into their own being, and finally present them in a way that we in the West can understand. It has not always been easy.

We end with a passage from *The Still Point*, by John Daido Loori, abbot of the Zen Mountain Monastery in Mount Tremper, New York, and a teacher of a form of meditation known as *zazen**. He here describes the

---

*Zazen*: sitting meditation.
   See Glossary for a description of technical terms throughout the book.

contemporary predicament with such clarity, and the path of meditation
with such allure, that one cannot help but feel that there is something
of value here, something relevant to us—something worth looking into.
It is my hope that this book may provide a lens through which we may
look and see ourselves reflected in our own hearts and minds:

> Most of us spend our time preoccupied. We are constantly carry-
> ing on an internal dialogue. While we are involved in talking to
> ourselves, we miss the moment-to-moment awareness of life. We
> look, but we don't see. We listen, but we don't hear. We eat, but
> we don't taste. We love, but we don't feel. The senses are receiving
> all the information, but because of our preoccupations, cognition
> is not taking place. Zazen brings us back to each moment. The
> moment is where our life takes place. If we miss the moment, we
> miss our life.
>
> Every other creature on the face of the earth knows how to be
> quiet and still. A butterfly on a leaf, a cat in front of a fireplace;
> even a hummingbird comes to rest sometime. But humans are
> constantly on the go. We seem to have lost the ability to just be
> quiet, to simply be present in the stillness that is the foundation
> of our lives. Yet, if we never get in touch with that stillness, we
> never fully experience our lives.
>
> When the mind is at rest, the body is at rest—respiration,
> heartbeat, and metabolism slow down. Reaching the still point is
> not something unusual or esoteric. It is a very important part of
> being alive and staying awake. All creatures on the earth manifest
> this stillness.
>
> In zazen, as you practice letting go of your thoughts and
> internal dialogue, and bringing your mind slowly back to the
> breath, the breath will slowly get easier and deeper, and the
> mind will naturally rest. The mind is like the surface of a
> pond. When the wind blows, the surface is disturbed. Then
> there are waves and ripples, and the image of the sun or the
> moon is broken up.
>
> When the wind quiets down, the surface of the pond becomes
> like glass. The stilled mind is like a mirror. It doesn't process, it
> just reflects. When there is a flower in front of it, it reflects a
> flower. When the flower is gone, the reflection is gone. When we

hear a fire engine go by, we hear a fire engine. When the fire engine is gone, its reflection is gone. The mind returns to that original smooth surface. A still mind is unobstructed—always open and receptive. It doesn't hold on or attach to anything. At any moment in time, it is free.

The search for the exotic, the strange, the unusual, the uncommon has often taken the form of pilgrimages, of turning away from the world, the "Journey to the East," to another country or to a different Religion. The great lesson from the true mystics, from the Zen monks, and now also from the Humanistic and Transpersonal psychologists—that the sacred is in the ordinary, that it is to be found in one's daily life, in one's neighbors, friends, and family, in one's backyard, and that travel may be a flight from confronting the sacred—this lesson can be easily lost. To be looking elsewhere for miracles is to me a sure sign of ignorance that everything is miraculous.

—Abraham H. Maslow

# Openness

The excerpts in this section point to the nature of an open mind and speak of some possible results of practicing and developing the quality of openness. When the mind is cluttered, it is difficult to pay attention. An open mind, free of assumptions, agendas, and demands is ready to accept what comes before it. As Shunryu Suzuki puts it in the prologue of *Zen Mind, Beginner's Mind*, "In the beginner's mind there are many possibilities, but in the expert's there are few."

Our ability to practice openness may be challenged by the importance we place on knowledge. We forget that knowledge changes constantly. What we now believe we know about the universe today makes our knowledge of a few years ago irrelevant, and fifty years from now much of what we know about the universe may be considered utter nonsense. We apply "tried and true" methods in business, even when cultural and economic trends argue for new approaches, and we may see our friends and family the same way we saw them ten years ago, even though both we and they have changed. We believe that it is important to have a grasp of what is true. With an open mind we can ask the question, What is true *now*?

Knowing the answers in advance may cloud our ability to see clearly. "On Questioning" is an edited version of a longer essay that appeared in *Shambhala Sun*. Questioning, says Zoketsu Norman Fischer in the essay, is "like a scouring pad or a torch, scrubbing or burning away the dross and scum of desire and confusion that covers ordinary activities." Questioning, he points out, makes life an adventure because mundane activities are not boring when we look at them as if seeing them for the first time.

Keeping an open mind in business is a particular challenge because it requires us to consider the possibility that we don't know the answers. In *Real Power*, James A. Autry and Stephen Mitchell point out that the temptation to educate new employees to operate according to our methods does not leave them room to find a way that may be better, and it deprives us of an opportunity to learn a more effective way of operating.

The importance of seeing "as if for the first time" is conveyed by Jon Kabat-Zinn in "Jack and the Beanstalk." In this excerpt, his son's open mind hears, even after the eighth telling of the same story, as if for the first time. He is able to experience the thrill anew at each telling.

In "Beginner's Mind" by Gary Zukav we see how creative thinking depends upon an open mind. Zukav reminds us that as children our minds were more open. As time goes on our minds may become closed because we surrender our thinking to the "obvious," the "commonsense," and the "self-evident," a belief echoed by Alan Watts in "A Cure for Education."

Openness means not being so determined to reach a goal or to adhere to a plan that we cannot change course when an unexpected opportunity presents itself. In "Airplane First Aid II: The Correction," Sylvia Boorstein revises her agenda to work on a cross-country flight, and instead listens to the passenger in the next seat. As a result, she is able to help another person, learn a lesson about compassion, and enhance the work she was trying to do. With an open mind, it is possible to give our full attention to each passing moment. An open mind provides a spacious place where mindfulness is possible.

# Prologue

from *Zen Mind, Beginner's Mind*

by Shunryu Suzuki

Beginner's mind: "In the beginner's mind there are many possibilities, but in the expert's there are few."

People say that practicing Zen is difficult, but there is a misunderstanding as to why. It is not difficult because it is hard to sit in the cross-legged position, or to attain enlightenment. It is difficult because it is hard to keep our mind pure and our practice pure in its fundamental sense. The Zen school developed in many ways after it was established in China, but at the same time, it became more and more impure. But I do not want to talk about Chinese Zen or the history of Zen. I am interested in helping you keep your practice from becoming impure.

In Japan we have the phrase *shoshin*, which means "beginner's mind." The goal of practice is always to keep our beginner's mind. Suppose you recite the Prajna Paramita Sutra only once. It might be a very good recitation. But what would happen to you if you recited it twice, three times, four times, or more? You might easily lose your original attitude towards it. The same thing will happen in your other Zen practices. For a while you will keep your beginner's mind, but if you continue to practice one, two, three years or more, although you may improve some, you are liable to lose the limitless meaning of original mind.

For Zen students the most important thing is not to be dualistic. Our "original mind" includes everything within itself. It is always rich and sufficient within itself. You should not lose your self-sufficient state of mind. This does not mean a closed mind, but actually an empty mind

and a ready mind. If your mind is empty, it is always ready for anything;
it is open to everything. In the beginner's mind there are many possibilities; in the expert's mind there are few.

If you discriminate too much, you limit yourself. If you are too demanding or too greedy, your mind is not rich and self-sufficient. If we
lose our original self-sufficient mind, we will lose all precepts. When
your mind becomes demanding, when you long for something, you will
end up violating your own precepts: not to tell lies, not to steal, not to
kill, not to be immoral, and so forth. If you keep your original mind, the
precepts will keep themselves.

In the beginner's mind there is no thought, "I have attained something." All self-centered thoughts limit our vast mind. When we have no
thought of achievement, no thought of self, we are true beginners. Then
we can really learn something. My beginner's mind is the mind of compassion. When our mind is compassionate, it is boundless. Dogen-zenji,
the founder of our school, always emphasized how important it is to
resume our boundless original mind. Then we are always true to ourselves, in sympathy with all beings, and can actually practice.

So the most difficult thing is always to keep your beginner's mind.
There is no need to have a deep understanding of Zen. Even though you
read much Zen literature, you must read each sentence with a fresh mind.
You should not say, "I know what Zen is," or "I have attained enlightenment." This is also the real secret of the arts: always be a beginner. Be
very very careful about this point. If you start to practice zazen, you will
begin to appreciate your beginner's mind. It is the secret of Zen practice.

# On Questioning

by Zoketsu Norman Fischer

Traditionally, the Zen stream in Buddhism is said to begin with Bodhi-dharma's strong words: a special teaching outside the scriptures, pointing directly to the human heart, without mediation. From the start then Zen presents itself as the essence of Buddhism, the kernel or core of it, with everything extra stripped away. Direct and experiential. Having nothing to do with faith or piety. And of course the style and tone of the literature of Zen throughout its long history bears this out. It's not that the Zen tradition is particularly reformist or iconoclastic; in fact throughout Zen there's a generalized respect for Buddhism per se, the Buddhism that precedes and runs parallel with Zen. It's just that all the schools of Zen understand the essence of Zen to be something deeper and wider than any particular school of Buddhism or even any particular religion, in-cluding Zen itself. You might say that Zen is the only one of the world's great traditions that explicitly makes going beyond itself the essence of what it is. Of course a lot of Zen people today and through the centuries forget about this and erect in Zen another temple to style or power or orthodoxy. But the teaching of Zen is clearly pointing to something else.

What then is the core of Zen, what is it that Zen advances as the core of Buddhism, the core of the religious quest?

And I would say it's questioning. The active, powerful, fundamental, relentless, deep and uniquely human act of questioning.

Questioning that leaves any possibility of or even notion of answering far behind. Questioning that produces a doubt so deep and so developed it eventually becomes indistinguishable from faith. Questioning that starts with language and concept but quickly burns language and concept to the ground. Questioning that brings humanness to its edge and pushes it off. So that being, existence itself, as manifested in a particular time and place and person becomes foregrounded.

In Zen there really aren't any doctrines. Zen isn't an ideology, it's an experience. But it isn't an experience either because experience is always something that begs description and explanation; experience understood as such, is ideology. Questioning takes us beyond even our experience.

When a child first learns speech it names. But soon after it gets the hang of naming, almost as soon as nouns give way to sentences, questioning begins. Where did Daddy go? Why is Mommy crying? Why can't I have more candy? When will we have to leave this place? And later, why must I speak nicely to her? Where did Grandma go when they put her in the ground? Why do I have to grow up?

The child's questioning begins with noticing that things in the world don't make sense, that we are given explanations that are bogus and conventional. This is why children always ask questions that are impossible for adults to answer. So adults laugh or smile or scratch their heads, which is a way of avoiding the issue entirely.

And, in fact, leaving childhood behind, growing up, turns out to be about putting aside these childish questions, which are after all expressions of wonderment, uncoverings of the boundaries of speech and thought. Growing up turns out to be about suspending questioning, burying it, so that we can get underway with the practical work of getting a living and cooperating with the existing arrangements of the world. Growing up is the submergence of questioning.

The questioning of course doesn't go away. It is still present with us, though below the surface. It manifests as anxiety in the middle of the night for no reason, or as a vague dissatisfaction with conditions as we find them, or as an out of scale feeling of anguish at instances of loss or defeat or disappointment. Somehow it is necessary for us to return to our questioning, but we don't know how. We don't even know that we need to do this.

On a discursive level questioning has no end. It seems disruptive and distracting. It causes us to hang back from our activity. It creates in us an inability to commit ourselves to anything. We can't seem to leave aside our concerns and doubts. They seem to plague us, to stand between us and a full blooded, full bodied, fully engaged life.

But this kind of discursive questioning is not the questioning of Zen. This kind of questioning flows from and goes only as deep as the personality: our history, our desires, our fears.

Zen drives questioning deeper than this. In Zen meditation we concentrate on the breath in the abdomen and on the posture, as a way of resting alertly and radically in the present moment. We eventually let all thinking fall away, but not by striving to eliminate it. Rather we simply allow thinking without becoming active in it. We let thinking think thinking, and in this way we bring it to rest. This powerful focus at a single point, with spaciousness, in the present moment with all its depth, hones down and develops questioning until it goes beyond language. Until the questioning is reduced to an intensity that burns up inquisitiveness and desperation. Life just is questioning and nothing but questioning. Everything else dissolves. Everything else seems partial or exaggerated.

This questioning is the essence of Zen, the essence of what is beyond Zen. No belief whatsoever, no doctrine. Only what is confirmed and sustained by what happens, and trusting this absolutely, even though moment after moment it disappears like smoke. And going deeper and deeper with questioning until there's no possibility of an answer one could repeat, define, or even precisely know. Instead the dawning of a certainty. And then the constant letting go of that certainty in the willingness to stand in the middle of uncertainty, because uncertainty is the only thing that has the rock solid feel of truth. Uncertainty is readiness. It is only a problem and a weakness when there lies underneath it the desire for a secure outcome. But in reality no outcome suffices, no outcome can rise to the level of this thoroughgoing questioning. No outcome can match the panoramic glory and color of the imagination. Uncertainty is pregnant with constant possibility. It's an endless adventure. Time is eternal because questioning drives time out of time. Questioning simply goes on.

I have perhaps given a false impression here if I have made questioning sound heroic. It is heroic in its essence, but of course it is also very ordinary, and Zen is nothing if not practical and grounded. In fact this is one of the cardinal aspects of Zen questioning: that its profundity and thoroughness is identical with ordinary everyday affairs. With everyday practice in the temple or out of the temple one gradually integrates questioning into chopping wood and carrying water so that the process of questioning purifies our everyday life. It's like a scouring pad or a torch, scrubbing or burning away all the dross and scum of desire and confusion that covers ordinary activities. With questioning when we walk we just walk, when we eat we just eat. Nothing extra can withstand the fire of questioning.

# The Wise Leader from *Real Power*

by James A. Autry and Stephen Mitchell

The ancient Master
didn't try to educate the people,
but kindly taught them to not-know.

When they think that they know the answers,
people are difficult to guide.
When they know that they don't know,
people can find their own way . . .

—from the *Tao Te Ching*

The most precious gift you can give to up-and-coming managers is to urge that they adopt an attitude of what Zen calls "don't-know mind." This is also called "beginner's mind." It is the mind that isn't limited by any ideas, the mind that is open to all possibilities. This is difficult to understand, and difficult to put into practice, yet it is the most creative space in the world. All the great works of science and art have come from letting go of preconceptions. Out of this mind has arisen everything from Newton's theory of gravity to Einstein's theory of relativity, Bach's work to Stravinsky's, Sappho's to Emily Dickinson's, Praxiteles' to Cezanne's.

There is no doubt that you, as a manager, will at some point become a mentor for new managers and leaders. Don't be confused by the idea of not-knowing. Resist the temptation to try to educate these up-and-coming people about how to do all the things you've learned to do over the years. Remember that the people you're mentoring are up-and-coming because they've proven that they're very good at doing what they do. They don't need more technical information, they don't need to know how you used to do things.

If you tell them what to do, they'll try it your way if you're senior to them in the organization. If you're their boss, they'll definitely try it your way. But there are two problems with your way: (1) It may be wrong for this time and this place; and (2) It will deprive you and the company of their creativity and new ideas.

What they do need is a sense that questions are more important than answers and that whatever answers exist now are answers to old questions. These answers may not work for tomorrow's questions; changing circumstances will dictate different questions and answers. They need you to guide them in finding their own answers, regardless of what changes may come throughout their careers. Thus, your emphasis should not be on what to do but on how to be.

It is essential to realize that the *Tao Te Ching* is not praising ignorance. Chapter I of the *Tao Te Ching* refers to darkness as "the gateway to all understanding." This means that the wise leader sees through the conventional definitions of light as good and darkness as bad. He knows that creative people in any field have always recognized and honored the darkness, not as something negative but as part of their creative process.

This is more practical than it may sound at first. Surely you've said at one time or another, "I'll sleep on that problem," and let your unconscious mind work on it. Often the solution will appear by itself, like magic.

In trying to understand "don't-know mind," reflect on your own career. You know that some of your most profound insights or creative solutions have not resulted from analysis but have just come to you, sometimes when you weren't even thinking about them. Every experienced manager can recall a time when answers came only after he had stopped thinking about the problem, or had even given up altogether.

There is a saying, popular in the 1970s and 1980s: "Keep your eye on the things you can't see." It was quoted often but probably not so often understood. Let's put it now in the form of a Zen koan, an enigma that can't be solved by the rational mind: "How will I know what I can't see?" Answer: "You'll know it when you can't see it."

Can anyone see how a sale is made? You can analyze and critique the information, the data, the sales calls, the presentation, the follow-ups, the leave-withs, and so on, but every experienced sales manager knows that none of that makes the sale. A person does. One sales rep can make a call, present the case, and the buyer says no, while another sales rep can then make a call on the same buyer, make the same case, and the buyer says yes. Why? No one knows. The fact is that all we can do is put together a list of the technical things most likely to work, then depend on what we call "chemistry." The mystery of a successful sale is one of those things we know is there but can't see.

The wise leader knows that mysteries can't be explained, but they can be used. By his example, he teaches those around him to live in the open space that comes from not-knowing.

# Beginner's Mind

from *The Dancing Wu Li Masters*

by Gary Zukav

The importance of nonsense hardly can be overstated. The more clearly we experience something as "nonsense," the more clearly we are experiencing the boundaries of our own self-imposed cognitive structures. "Nonsense" is that which does not fit into the prearranged patterns which we have superimposed on reality. There is no such thing as "nonsense" apart from a judgmental intellect which calls it that.

True artists and true physicists know that nonsense is only that which, viewed from our present point of view, is unintelligible. Nonsense is nonsense only when we have not yet found that point of view from which it makes sense.

In general, physicists do not deal in nonsense. Most of them spend their professional lives thinking along well-established lines of thought. Those scientists who establish the established lines of thought, however, are those who do not fear to venture boldly into nonsense, into that which any fool could have told them is clearly not so. This is the mark of the creative mind; in fact, this is the creative process. It is characterized by a steadfast confidence that there exists a point of view from which the "nonsense" is not nonsense at all—in fact, from which it is obvious.

In physics, as elsewhere, those who most have felt the exhilaration of the creative process are those who best have slipped the bonds of the known to venture far into the unexplored territory which lies beyond the barrier of the obvious. This type of person has two characteristics. The first is a childlike ability to see the world as it is, and not as it appears according to what we know about it. This is the moral of the (child's?) tale, "The Emperor's New Clothes." When the emperor rode naked through the streets, only a child proclaimed him to be without clothes, while the rest of his subjects forced themselves to believe, because they had been told so, that he wore his finest new clothing.

The child in us is always naive, innocent in the simplistic sense. A Zen story tells of Nan-in, a Japanese master during the Meiji era who received a university professor. The professor came to inquire about Zen. Nan-in served tea. He poured his visitor's cup full, and then kept on pouring. The professor watched the overflow until he no longer could restrain himself.

"It is overfull. No more will go in!"

"Like this cup," Nan-in said, "you are full of your own opinions and speculations. How can I show you Zen unless you first empty your cup?"

Our cup usually is filled to the brim with "the obvious," "common sense," and "the self-evident."

Suzuki Roshi, who established the first Zen center in the United States (without trying, of course, which is very Zen), told his students that it is not difficult to attain enlightenment, but it is difficult to keep a beginner's mind. "In the beginner's mind," he told them, "there are many possibilities, but in the expert's there are few." When his students published Suzuki's talks after his death, they called the book, appropriately, *Zen Mind, Beginner's Mind*. In the introduction, Baker Roshi, the American Zen Master, wrote:

> The mind of the beginner is empty, free of the habits of the expert, ready to accept, to doubt, and open to all the possibilities.

The beginner's mind in science is wonderfully illustrated by the story of Albert Einstein and his theory of relativity. That is the subject of this chapter.

The second characteristic of true artists and true scientists is the firm confidence which both of them have in themselves. This confidence is an expression of an inner strength which allows them to speak out, secure in the knowledge that, appearances to the contrary, it is the world that is confused and not they. The first man to see an illusion by which men have flourished for centuries surely stands in a lonely place. In that moment of insight he, and he alone, sees the obvious which to the uninitiated (the rest of the world) yet appears as nonsense or, worse, as madness or heresy. This confidence is not the obstinacy of the fool, but the surety of him who knows what he knows, and knows also that he can convey it to others in a meaningful way.

The writer, Henry Miller, wrote:

I obey only my own instincts and intuition. I know nothing in advance. Often I put down things which I do not understand myself, secure in the knowledge that later they will become clear and meaningful to me. I have faith in the man who is writing, who is myself, the writer.

The songwriter, Bob Dylan, told a press conference:

I just write a song and I know it's going to be all right. I don't even know what it's going to say.

# A Cure for Education

from *Talking Zen*

by Alan Watts

When a child begins to study arithmetic, he learns that two and two are absolutely and necessarily four. This is drummed into him with the weight of authority, since children are capricious creatures, and, if left to themselves, will discover all sorts of wayward answers for two plus two. But if—as is seldom the case—the child ever gets to the point where he can go rather more deeply into the mysteries of mathematics, he may discover, with some degree of concentration, that this absolute law of two plus two "ain't necessarily so." It depends on what kinds of things you are adding. Indeed, if he goes still further, he finds that nothing is absolutely so at all. He will discover whole systems of mathematics based on premises which seem to be completely absurd—as, for example, that four axes at right angles to one another can intersect at one point, giving us the mathematics of four dimensions, or, for that matter, as many dimensions as you like.

But this isn't going to be a talk about mathematics. I have mentioned these things as instances of the whole problem of unlearning, or, shall I say, of correcting necessary and unavoidable mistakes. To put it briefly, what we call upbringing or education is a way of making children conform to the conventions of society. This seems to be entirely necessary. But in the process, most children are—perhaps unavoidably—warped. They lose their innocence and their spontaneity, their unselfconsciousness. In psychological jargon, they develop all kinds of inner conflicts and complexities, and they do not seem to be able to recover from them in adult life without the expense of psychoanalysis or some similar kind of therapy. And even then, I am not quite sure how often they really recover.

If you persevere in the science of mathematics, you will eventually find out that the absolute rules which you learned in the beginning were strictly conventional and were not in any sense fixed laws of nature. But you can complete four years of college, become a parent, and reach the top of our business or profession, without ever "seeing through" the absolutes of conduct and feeling, of thinking and reasoning, which were so firmly implanted in you as a child. To put it another way, you can go through the whole of life without ever getting out of the splints and crutches, the spectacles and hearing aids, which were used to train your mind in the beginning. The result is that the conventional disciplines do not become the mere instruments of free minds; they become the very structure of the mind itself, so that for all our boasting about living in the "land of the free," we are no more free than Dr. Pavlov's dogs.

This may be the inevitable price of civilization and culture. What you gain upon the roundabout you lose upon the swings, or, as Ogden Nash put it:

> *The trouble with a kitten is THAT*
> *Eventually it becomes a CAT*

, It may be that the refreshing naturalness of the child is something which the civilized adult loses as irreplaceably as the cat its kittenishness. But I do not think this is a proper analogy. I have lived a lot with cats, and I much prefer them to kittens. Furthermore, I have from time to time met with adults—highly sophisticated and cultured adults—who have somehow regained, or perhaps never lost, their unaffected spontaneity. It does not seem to me to be a necessary law that an advanced culture requires the loss of these natural qualities.

I am not trying in any way to idealize the child. With five of them, I know better than that! The point is that children begin to develop certain virtues which, as a result of their upbringing, they do not continue to develop. Social conventions require them to develop their orderliness and skill rather than their simplicity and unaffectedness, since the two types of virtue seem to be mutually exclusive at a young age. If this is the cost of civilization, there is a serious question as to whether the cost is not much too great, as to whether—indeed—it may not eventually be fatal to civilization.

Perhaps I can try to define, or at least to suggest, the qualities which we are losing. These are qualities which the child exhibits in a rather primitive and embryonic form, and which one finds more fully developed only in the most exceptional people. To use psychological jargon again, we say that people of this rare type are integrated. That's to say, they are not at cross-purposes with themselves; they do not get in their own way and stand in their own light. They are what the Gospels call "single-eyed," for "if thine eye be single, thy whole body shall be full of light." We call this trait sincerity—the virtue of not being self-deceived, of not thinking one thing and feeling another, or of not feeling one thing and trying to feel another. It is, furthermore, the marvelous quality of un-selfconsciousness—the quality of the man who can think, act, and live without anxious side-glances at himself, which spoil the directness and effectiveness of his action. And this lack of self-consciousness involves something else besides, of a still deeper order. A truly unselfconscious person feels related to his environment, or rather, integrated with his environment. To put it another way, he does not experience any gulf or gap between his own inner workings—his thoughts and feelings—and the natural processes going on around him. And thus he has a kind of unaggressive but nonetheless unshakable assurance, which at a deep level is religious faith, or at its deepest level a kind of metaphysical certainty. I do not mean by this that he is certain as to the truth of some idea or proposition. What I call a metaphysical certainty cannot really be put into words at all, for it is more nearly a feeling, shall I say a feeling of the inescapable naturalness and rightness of everything that one feels and does, even when it is perfectly clear that, from a relative standpoint, one is in the wrong.

# Jack and the Beanstalk

## from *Everyday Blessings*

### by Myla Kabat-Zinn and Jon Kabat-Zinn

Children want total attention and engagement on the part of adults at key times; at other times they want and can be left to their own devices or with their friends.

For adults, it is hard to give total attention, especially over a sustained period of time. We have drifted from that capacity. Adult minds, as a rule, are filled with conflicting impulses and thoughts, which compete for attention even within ourselves. We have multiple responsibilities. We're very busy. A child may want us to play or to read, and we may do it, but we may do it with only a fraction of our mind, and they sense that easily. Many a time I (JKZ) have caught myself reading to one of my children, but thinking about the next telephone call I have to make as soon as the child is asleep. Or reading a story and realizing that I was getting through the story but that I had no idea what it was about. I was thinking universes of thoughts in between each line, if not each word.

Once, when I was so tired I could hardly keep my eyes open, I was telling my daughter a story about a lion, making it up as I went along. But five minutes later, in my tiredness, the lion had become a rabbit. She noticed. We have had many a laugh about that one.

When our son was about four, Jack and the Beanstalk was a favorite of his. He wouldn't just let me read it once or twice and then move on to another story. He wanted to hear it over and over again at the same sitting. I loved the story too, but it was hard for me to read it for the seventh or eighth time. Then I realized that he was hearing it each time as if for the first time: the deep theme of the milk running out and having to sell the cow; the tension of hiding from the giant in his castle and observing his covetousness; the challenge of stealing the giant's gold and magic hen and singing harp; the thrill of being chased down the bean-stalk, and of getting the ax from his mother just in time to cut it down and destroy the giant—these were real for him every time. His body would tense when the giant came in, and he would smile gleefully as Jack tricked the giant every time.

Seeing the story through his eyes taught me that I, too, could try to be fully present each time I read it, even though part of my adult mind was resisting like crazy. Letting go of that, the story became like a piece of music, repetition of the essence. It is the same each time it is told or read, but it is also never the same. Realizing this expanded my world. Jack and the Beanstalk became part of my meditation practice for quite some while, and taught me to be present when I didn't want to be present anymore. Once again, the child becomes the parent's teacher. Fee fi fo fum . . . we lumber about.

# Airplane First Aid II: The Correction

from *It's Easier Than You Think*

by Sylvia Boorstein

Settled in my seat on United flight 33, Boston–San Francisco, I was looking forward to six hours of writing time, since I was only weeks away from the manuscript due date for this book. The woman next to me seemed clearly uncomfortable, fidgeting in her seat, eager to engage in conversation. She told me she bruised her coccyx in a recent fall and sitting was painful for her. She explained she was worried because the flight would be too long for her to be comfortable without smoking a cigarette.

I allowed some time for conversation, hoping she would settle down so I could write without seeming impolite. I shuffled my papers in a way that suggested I wanted to work. Each time we concluded a topic and I began to turn away, she started in on a new subject.

Lunch came and went. I had hoped our mealtime conversation would allow me to resume writing in earnest, but that didn't happen. The longer the flight wore on, the more uncomfortable she became. Her back hurt and she missed smoking.

It was actually she, and not I, who caught me before I had made a mistake. We had mentioned our respective jobs, and she asked a long string of questions about what I did as a meditation teacher: Whom did I teach? Was what I taught good for people with stress? Was it hard to learn? How could she learn? Eagerly, she had me write down names of books she could read, tapes she could buy, places she might go to study.

Finally, I got it. I said, "Would you like me to teach you to meditate right now? It might make you feel better."

"Yes, I would," she said. "I really would."

I put down the writing. I gave some meditation instructions. She sat quietly for a while. Then we talked about her experience.

She said she felt more relaxed. We talked about how feeling a little better made her feel much better, because now she was sure she would survive the trip. We talked about how the mind takes pain and blows it up bigger than it really is.

I began to realize I was having a good time. It occurred to me that it was totally ludicrous to be writing a book about the joys of selfless acts of kindness, about relating with compassion every chance we get, while trying to ignore a person in pain sitting next to me. During the last half hour of the flight she fell asleep, and I wrote something really good.

# Awareness

In the words of Sharon Salzberg and Charlotte Joko Beck, awareness is the "heart of mindfulness." As such, it encompasses other values of mindfulness presented in this book—openness, acceptance, and the ability to let go. These values help develop our ability to see clearly and to give our undivided attention to the present moment.

In "Attention Means Attention," Charlotte Joko Beck makes it clear that the ultimate priority is awareness—that it is "the secret of life"—because awareness means that every moment of life is important.

Both Stephen Batchelor in "Awareness" and Joseph Goldstein in "Bare Attention" develop the connection between acceptance and the ability to be aware. Batchelor shows how the measure of control we have over our lives begins with our awareness of our lives, which requires acceptance. Joseph Goldstein defines bare attention, an Eastern term for awareness, as "observing things as they are, without choosing, without comparing, without evaluating"—in other words, with acceptance.

In Sharon Salzberg's "The Heart of Practice" we see a nonevaluating approach to hearing a sound. Salzberg suggests that just listening without reacting to a sound or labeling it as unpleasant or pleasant, means that we will not tune out certain sounds. Here again, awareness encompasses acceptance because mindfulness is wholly inclusive.

In three selections—"Vait a Minute, Vait a Minute" by Sylvia Boorstein; "Softball Breaks Through the Gloom" by Myla Kabat-Zinn and Jon Kabat-Zinn; and "The Listening Mind" by Ram Dass and Paul Gorman, we see how satisfying it may be when someone truly attends to us. Focusing our mind on another person by truly listening and being present for that person can enhance and even transform a relationship. Jon Kabat-Zinn discovers in "Softball Breaks Through the Gloom" that simply being with his daughter in an activity that validated her interest—playing softball—did more to open up their relationship than all of the questioning and verbal expressions of interest could ever have accomplished.

The depth and multifaceted qualities of awareness are captured by Larry Rosenberg in "When the Student is Ready, the Teacher Bites." In this brief, humorous story, the mosquito is the teacher who shows the author the varied and changing nature of an itch. "It's a process. It grows more intense, then less so, disappears altogether for a few seconds, returns with a vengeance . . . it is impersonal. It comes from nowhere, goes nowhere . . ." Rosenberg also shows us how the thoughts and emotions he attached to the itch made him lose awareness of the actual sensation while at the same time making the itch into something more catastrophic than it was.

The story told by Thich Nhat Hanh, "Three Wondrous Answers," asks the questions, what should we do, what is the best time to do it, and with whom should we do it? The message of this story is that the answers to all of those questions are the same: live in the present moment.

One sees that Sylvia Boorstein's speaking with the person who sat next to her on the airplane, Jon Kabat-Zinn's playing softball with his daughter, or Larry Rosenberg's attending to an itch, meant getting off the agenda treadmill and living in the moment, thereby transforming a moment of life.

# Attention Means Attention

from *Nothing Special: Living Zen*

by Charlotte Joko Beck

There's an old Zen story: a student said to Master Ichu, "Please write for me something of great wisdom." Master Ichu picked up his brush and wrote one word: "Attention." The student said, "Is that all?" The master wrote, "Attention. Attention." The student became irritable. "That doesn't seem profound or subtle to me." In response, Master Ichu wrote simply, "Attention. Attention. Attention." In frustration, the student demanded, "What does this word *attention* mean?" Master Ichu replied, "Attention means attention."

For attention, we could substitute the word awareness. Attention or awareness is the secret of life, and the heart of practice. Like the student in the story, we find such a teaching disappointing; it seems dry and uninteresting. We want something exciting in our practice! Simple attention is boring; we ask, is that all there is to practice?

When students come in to see me, I hear complaint after complaint: about the schedule of the retreat, about the food, about the service, about me, on and on. But the issues that people bring to me are no more relevant or important than a "trivial" event, such as stubbing a toe. How do we place our cushions? How do we brush our teeth? How do we sweep the floor, or slice a carrot? We think we're here to deal with "more important" issues, such as our problems with our partner, our jobs, our health, and the like. We don't want to bother with the "little" things, like how we hold our chopsticks or where we place our spoon. Yet these acts are the stuff of our life, moment to moment. It's not a question of importance; it's a question of paying attention, being aware. Why? Because every moment in life is absolute in itself. That's all there is. There is nothing other than this present moment; there is no past, there is no future; there is nothing but this. So when we don't pay attention to each little this, we miss the whole thing. And the contents of this can be anything. This can be straightening our sitting mats, chopping an onion, visiting someone we don't want to visit. It doesn't matter what the contents of the moment are; each moment is absolute. That's all there is and all there ever will be. If we could totally pay attention, we would never be upset. If we're upset, it's axiomatic that we're not paying attention. If we miss not just one moment but one moment after another, we're in trouble.

Suppose I'm condemned to have my head chopped off in a guillotine. Now I'm being marched up the steps onto the platform. Can I maintain attention to the moment? Can I be aware of each step, step-by-step? Can I place my head in the guillotine carefully so that I serve the executioner well? If I am able to live and die in this way, no problem arises.

Our problems arise when we subordinate this moment to something else, to our self-centered thoughts; not just this moment, but what *I want*. We bring to the moment our personal priorities, all day long. And so our troubles arise.

Another old story concerns a group of thieves who broke into the study of a Zen master and told him that they were going to slice off his head. He said, "Please wait until morning; I have some work to complete." So he spent the night completing his work, drinking tea, and enjoying himself. He wrote a simple poem, comparing the severing of his head to a spring breeze, and gave it to the thieves as a present when they returned. The master understood practice well.

We have trouble comprehending this story because we are so attached to keeping our heads on our shoulders. We don't particularly want our heads severed. We're determined that life go as we want it to go. When it doesn't, we're angry, confused, depressed, or otherwise upset. To have such feelings is not bad in itself, but who wants a life dominated by such feelings?

When attention to the present moment falters and we drift into some version of "I have to have it *my* way," a gap is created in our awareness of reality as it is, right now. Into that gap pours all the mischief of our life. We create gap after gap after gap, all day long. The point of practice is to close these gaps, to reduce the amount of time that we spend being absent, caught in our self-centered dream.

We make a mistake, however, if we think that the solution is that *I* pay attention. Not "*I* sweep the floor," "*I* slice the onions," "*I* drive the car." Though such practice is okay in the preliminary stages, it preserves self-centered thought in naming oneself as an "I" to which experience is present. A better understanding is simple awareness: just experiencing, experiencing, experiencing. In mere awareness there is no gap, no space for self-centered thoughts to arise.

At some Zen centers, students are asked to engage in exaggerated slow-motion actions, such as slowly putting things down and slowly picking them up. Such self-conscious attention is different from simple awareness, just doing it. The recipe for living is simply to do what we're doing. Don't be self-conscious about it; just do it. When self-centered thoughts come up, then we've missed the boat; we've got a gap. That gap is the birthplace of the troubles and upsets that plague us.

Many forms of practice, commonly called concentrative meditation, seek to narrow awareness in some way. Examples include reciting a mantra, focusing on a visualization, working on Mu (if done in a concentrated way), even following the breath if that involves shutting out the other senses. In narrowing attention, such practices quickly create certain pleasant states. We may feel that we have escaped from our troubles because we feel calmer. As we settle into this narrow focus, we may eventually go into a trance, like a drugged and peaceful state in which everything escapes us. Though at times useful, any practice that narrows our awareness is limited. If we don't take into account everything in our world, both mental and physical, we miss something. A narrow practice does not transfer well to the rest of our life; when we take it into the world, we don't know how to act and may still get quite upset. A concentrative practice, if we're persistent (as I used to be), may momentarily force us through our resistance, to a glimpse of the absolute. Such a forced opening isn't truly genuine; it misses something. Though we get a glimpse of the other side of the phenomenal world, into nothingness or pure emptiness, there's still *me* realizing that. The experience remains dualistic and limited in its usefulness.

In contrast, ours is an awareness practice that takes in everything. The "absolute" is simply everything in our world, emptied of personal emotional content. We begin to empty ourselves of such self-centered thoughts by learning more and more to be aware in all our moments. Whereas a concentrative practice might focus on the breath, but block out the sound of cars or the talking in our minds (leaving us at a loss when we allow any and all experience back into consciousness), awareness practice is open to any present experience—all this upsetting universe—and it helps us slowly to extricate ourselves from our emotional reactions and attachments.

Every time we have a complaint about our lives, we're in a gap. In awareness practice, we notice our thoughts and the contraction in our body, taking it all in and returning to the present moment. That's the hardest kind of practice. We'd rather escape this scene entirely or else stay immersed in our little upsets. After all, our upsets keep us in the center of things, or so we think. The pull of our self-centered thoughts is like walking through molasses: our feet come out of the molasses with difficulty and then rapidly get stuck again. We *can* slowly liberate ourselves, but if we think it's easy, we are kidding ourselves.

Whenever we're upset, we're in the gap; our self-centered notions, what *we* want out of life, are dominant. Yet our emotions of the moment are no more important than is replacing the chair at the table or putting the cushion where it should be.

Most emotions do not arise out of the immediate moment, such as when we witness a child hit by a car, but are generated by our self-centered demands that life be the way we want it to be. Though it's not bad to have such emotions, we learn through practice that they have no importance in themselves. Straightening the pencils on our desk is just as important as feeling bereft or lonely, for example. If we can experience being lonely and see our thoughts about being lonely, then we can move out of the gap. Practice is that movement, over and over and over again. If we remember something that happened six months ago and with the memory come upset feelings, our feelings should be looked at with interest, nothing more. Though that sounds cold, it's necessary in order to be a genuinely warm and compassionate person. If we find ourselves thinking that our feelings are more important than what is happening at the moment, we need to notice this thought. Sweeping the walk is reality; our feelings are something we've made up, like a web we have spun in which we catch ourselves. It's an amazing process that we put ourselves through; in a way, we are all crazy.

When I see my thoughts and note my bodily sensations, recognize my resistance to practicing with them, and then return to finishing the letter I'm writing, then I've moved out of the gap into awareness. If we are truly persistent, day after day, we gradually find our way out of the gooey mess of our personal lives. The key is attention, attention, attention.

Writing a check is just as important as the anguished thought that we won't see a loved one. When we don't work with the gap created in inattention, everyone pays the price.

Practice is necessary for me, too. Suppose I hope that my daughter will visit me at Christmas, and she calls to say she's not coming. Practice helps me to continue to love her, rather than becoming upset that she's not doing what I want. With practice, I can love her more fully. Without practice, I would simply be a lonely and cantankerous old lady. In a sense, love is simply attention, simply awareness. When I maintain awareness, I can teach well, which is a form of love; I can place fewer expectations on others and serve them better; when I see my daughter again, I don't have to bring old resentments into the meeting and am able to see her with fresh eyes. So the priority is right here and now. In fact, there's only one priority, and that's attention to the present moment, whatever its content. Attention means attention.

# Awareness

from *Buddhism Without Belief*

by Stephen Batchelor

I open the refrigerator to discover that I have no milk and so decide to go down to the store to get some. I shut the door behind me, turn left into the street, follow the sidewalk for two blocks, turn left and left again, enter the store, snatch a carton of milk from the shelf, pay for it at the checkout, leave the store, turn right and right again, go back along the sidewalk for two blocks, turn right, unlock the door, and go back into the kitchen.

The only evidence I have that any of this has happened is the cold carton of milk now clutched rather too firmly in my hand.

As I try to reconstruct those ten vanished minutes, I recall being engrossed in a memory of something S said to me yesterday that I have been shrugging off ever since. It irked me and has become lodged as a stab of disquiet somewhere in the upper part of my stomach. I can re-member that as I walked along, I was absorbed in what I should have said when the remark was made and what I would say were it repeated. The exact words of my response escape me. But I recall feeling gratified by their sharp blend of insouciance and cruelty, confirmed, in my imag-ination, by the look of fear on S's face as he is pinned to a rough wooden floor.

As for the first chill hint of winter in the gust of wind that sent the last withered leaves scratching along the sidewalk before me as I pulled my warm collar tight against the skin of my neck, I have no recollection. And although I was staring intently in S's direction, I failed to notice the waving arm of my friend perched on his bicycle across the street, his call and whistle, his smile as he rode off when the light turned green.

Much of our time is spent like this. As we become aware of it we begin to suspect that we are not entirely in control of our lives. Much of the time we are driven by a relentless and insistent surge of impulses. We notice this in quiet moments of reflection, but usually just get carried along on the crest of its wave. Until, that is, we crash once more onto the rocks of recriminatory self-consciousness, and from there into moods and depressions.

One of the most difficult things to remember is to remember to remember. Awareness begins with remembering what we tend to forget. Drifting through life on a cushioned surge of impulses is but one of many strategies of forgetting. Not only do we forget to remember, we forget that we live in a body with senses and feelings and thoughts and emotions and ideas. Worrying about what a friend said can preoccupy us so completely that it isolates us from the rest of our experience. The world of colors and shapes, sounds, smells, tastes, and sensations becomes dull and remote. Even the person who offers sympathy appears alien and out of reach. We feel cut off and adrift.

To stop and pay attention to what is happening in the moment is one way of snapping out of such fixations. It is also a reasonable definition of meditation.

While meditation may be cultivated as a formal practice once or twice a day for half an hour or so, the aim is to bring a fresh awareness into everything we do. Whether walking or standing still, sitting or lying down, alone or in company, resting or working, I try to maintain that same careful attention. So when I go to get milk, I will notice the scratching sound of the leaves on the sidewalk as well as my anger and hurt at what S said.

Awareness is a process of deepening self-acceptance. It is neither a cold, surgical examination of life nor a means of becoming perfect. Whatever it observes, it embraces. There is nothing unworthy of acceptance. The light of awareness will doubtless illuminate things we would prefer not to see. And this may entail a descent into what is forbidden, repressed, denied. We might uncover disquieting memories, irrational childhood terrors. We might have to accept not only a potential sage hidden within but also a potential murderer, rapist, or thief.

Despite the sense I might have of myself as I caring person, I observe that I want to punch S in the face. What usually happens to this hatred? I restrain myself from expressing it, not out of any great love for S but because of how it would affect other people's view of me. The attachment to self-image likewise inclines me to shy away from and forget this viciousness. In one way or another I deny it. I do not allow it into the field of awareness. I do not embrace it.

Or I may play it out as a fantasy, either in my imagination or on the analyst's couch. This may temporarily relieve the symptoms of rage and frustration, but will it make a difference when S presents me with his next barbed remark? Probably not. Such fantasies might even reinforce the kind of emotions they seek to assuage. As the hatred rears up again, something in me knows immediately how to relieve it. This becomes a habit that demands ever larger doses of anger to enjoy relief from. I could develop a subtle taste for violence. I might even end up by hitting S.

But to embrace hatred does not mean to indulge it. To embrace hatred is to accept it for what it is: a disruptive but transient state of mind. Awareness observes it jolt into being, coloring consciousness and gripping the body. The heart accelerates, the breath becomes shallow and jagged, and an almost physical urge to react dominates the mind. At the same time, this frenzy is set against a dark, quiet gulf of hurt, humiliation, and shame. Awareness notices all this without condoning or condemning, repressing or expressing. It recognizes that just as hatred arises, so will it pass away.

By identifying with it ("I really am pissed off!"), we fuel it. Not that we consciously choose to do so. The impulsive surge has such an abrupt momentum that by the time we first notice the anger, identification has already occurred. Suddenly we realize that we are perspiring, the heart is beating faster, hurtful words are choking in the throat, and our fists are clenched. By that time there is little we can do but watch the anger buffet and batter us. The task of awareness is to catch the impulse at its inception, to notice the very first hint of resentment coloring our feelings and perceptions. But such precision requires a focused mind.

Focused awareness is both calm and clear. Just as calmness is prevented by restlessness and distraction, so clarity is undermined by boredom and lethargy. Drifting between these two poles, we spend much of our time either slightly hyper or slightly depressed.

Restlessness is like a monkey swinging from branches and crashing through foliage. When in its grip, we suffer a compelling urgency to be elsewhere: if I am in, I want to go out; if I am out, I want to come in.

We feel imprisoned. Even if we manage to settle down physically, the mind runs amok. No sooner have we started meditating than we're off chasing chimeras. Instead of contemplating life and death, I struggle to remember the name of Led Zeppelin's drummer.

Distraction drugs us into forgetfulness. Even when we yearn to be focused on something meaningful, it erupts again. We cannot switch it off—and the more frustrated we get, the worse it becomes.

Instead of fighting it, embrace it. Accept that this is how things are right now: I am compulsively distracted. Acceptance might even lead to understanding what it is that we're running from. Instead of giving in to irritation, gently and patiently keep bringing the attention back. Then we may suddenly notice that the turmoil has stopped, as though a storm has passed. There might still be an occasional gust, but—for the time being, at least—it is calm.

Of course no sooner does calm establish itself than the doldrums are likely to set in. Distraction is replaced by boredom. Instead of an excess of energy, we feel drained. We want to collapse somewhere, lie down, doze, and sleep. Our thoughts are fuzzy, unwieldy, trapped in a mental fog. This might be just physical exhaustion, in which case a nap would do the trick. But if it doesn't, then this sleepiness might be the dark shadow of restlessness: another strategy of evasion. It's easy to tell: when the phone rings or lunch is announced, such tiredness suddenly vanishes.

No amount of meditative expertise from the mystical East will solve this problem, because such restlessness and lethargy are not mere mental or physical lapses but reflexes of an existential condition. Focused awareness is difficult not because we are inept at some spiritual technology but because it threatens our sense of who we are. The apparently unthreatening act of settling the mind on the breath and observing what is occurring in the body and mind exposes a contradiction between the sort of person we wish to be and the kind of person we are. Restlessness and lethargy are ways of evading the discomfort of this contradiction.

At such times, it may be futile to try to force the attention back to the object of meditation. Instead, we need to clarify the resolve that underpins dharma practice. We need to reflect on our motive, asking ourself: "Why I am doing this?" Or we may consider the certainty of death and the uncertainty of its time, concluding with the question: "What should I do?" Such reflections can help ground us in the very reality that restlessness and lethargy are so keen to avoid.

When centered in a clear and firm resolve, remembering to be aware can lead to a focused awareness that permeates every aspect of experience. What started as occasional moments of recollection develops into moment-to-moment mindfulness. This is not to say we never suffer from bouts of excitement or lethargy, but it is possible for consciousness to become increasingly wakeful.

# Bare Attention

from *The Experience of Insight*

by Joseph Goldstein

There is an ancient prophecy which says that twenty-five hundred years after the Buddha's death a great revival and flourishing of the Dharma will take place. We are presently experiencing the truth of this in the renaissance of spiritual practice now happening. In order to have an appreciation of the breadth and scope of the prophecy it is helpful to understand what the word "Dharma" means. Dharma is a Sanskrit word and its most general meaning is the law, the way things are, the process of things, the Tao, and more specifically, the teachings of the Buddha: all of this is the Dharma. It also means each of the individual psychic and physical elements which comprise all beings. The elements of mind: thoughts, visions, emotions, consciousness, and the elements of matter, individually are called "dharmas." The task of all spiritual work is to explore and discover these dharmas within us, to uncover and penetrate all the elements of the mind and body, becoming aware of each of them individually, as well as understanding the laws governing their process and relationship. This is what we're doing here: experiencing in every moment the truth of our nature, the truth of who and what we are.

There is one quality of mind which is the basis and foundation of spiritual discovery, and that quality of mind is called "bare attention." Bare attention means observing things as they are, without choosing, without comparing, without evaluating, without laying our projections and expectations on to what is happening; cultivating instead a choiceless and noninterfering awareness.

This quality of bare attention is well expressed by a famous Japanese haiku:

*The old pond.*
*A frog jumps in.*
*Plop!*

No dramatic description of the sunset and the peaceful evening sky over the pond and how beautiful it was, just a crystal clear perception of what it was that happened. "The old pond; a frog jumps in; Plop!" Bare attention: learning to see and observe, with simplicity and direct- ness. Nothing extraneous. It is a powerfully penetrating quality of mind.

As the quality of bare attention is developed it begins to effect certain basic changes in the way we live our lives. The watchwords of our time are "be here now"—living in the present moment. The problem is how to do it. Our minds are mostly dwelling in the past, thinking about things that have already happened, or planning for the future, imagining what is about to happen, often with anxiety or worry. Reminiscing about the past, fantasizing about the future; it is generally very difficult to stay grounded in the present moment. Bare attention is that quality of aware- ness which keeps us alive and awake in the here and now. Settling back into the moment, experiencing fully what it is that's happening.

There is a Zen story about living in the moment. Two monks were returning home in the evening to their temple. It had been raining and the road was very muddy. They came to an intersection where a beautiful girl was standing, unable to cross the street because of the mud. Just in the moment, the first monk picked her up in his arms and carried her across. The monks then continued on their way. Later that night the second monk, unable to restrain himself any longer, said to the first, "How could you do that?! We monks should not even look at females, much less touch them. Especially young and beautiful ones." "I left the girl there," the first monk said, "are you still carrying her?" As the quality of bare attention develops, noticing what's happening in and around us, we begin to experience and respond to the present with greater sponta- neity and freedom.

Bare attention also brings the mind to a state of rest. An untrained mind is often reactive, clinging to what is pleasant and condemning what is unpleasant, grasping what is liked, pushing away what is disliked, reacting with greed and hatred. A tiring imbalance of mind. As bare attention is cultivated more and more, we learn to experience our thoughts and feelings, situations and other people, without the tension of attachment or aversion. We begin to have a full and total experience of what it is that's happening, with a restful and balanced mind.

The awareness of bare attention is not limited to a certain time of sitting in the morning and evening. To think that sitting meditation is the time for awareness and the rest of the day is not, fragments our lives and undermines a real growth of understanding. Mindfulness is applicable and appropriate in each moment, whether we are sitting, standing, lying down, talking or eating. We should cultivate the state of bare attention on all objects, on all states of mind, in all situations. Every moment should be lived completely and wholeheartedly. There is a story of a man fleeing a tiger. He came to a precipice and catching hold of a wild vine, swung down over the edge. The tiger sniffed at him from above while below another tiger growled and snapped waiting for him to fall. As he hung there two mice began to gnaw away the vine. Just then he saw a big wild strawberry growing nearby. Reaching out with his free hand he plucked the strawberry. How sweet it tasted!

Another quality of bare attention is that when developed through a period of training it becomes effortless, it starts to work by itself. It's similar to the process one undergoes when learning to play a musical instrument. We sit down, take a few lessons, and are given certain exercises. We begin to practice, and at first the fingers don't move very easily; they hit a lot of wrong notes and it sounds terrible. But every day we practice, and gradually the fingers start to move more easily, the music starts to sound more beautiful. After a certain period of time, a proficiency develops so that the playing becomes effortless. At that time there is no difference between playing and practice; the playing itself is the practice. In just the same way, as we practice awareness, we start out very slowly, aware of the movement of each step, "lifting," "moving," "placing," aware of the breath, "rising, falling," or "in, out." In the beginning great effort is required. There are many gaps in the mindfulness. There are a lot of struggles and hindrances. But as the mind becomes trained in being aware, in being mindful, it becomes increasingly natural. There is a certain point in the practice when the momentum of mindfulness is so strong that it starts working by itself, and we begin to do things with an ease and simplicity and naturalness which is born out of this effortless awareness.

Bare attention is very much learning how to listen to our minds, our bodies, our environment. Perhaps at some time you have sat quietly by the side of an ocean or river. At first there is one big rush of sound. But in sitting quietly, doing nothing but listening, we begin to hear a multitude of fine and subtle sounds, the waves hitting against the shore, or the rushing current of the river. In that peacefulness and silence of mind we experience very deeply what is happening. It is just the same when we listen to ourselves; at first all we can hear is one "self" or "I." But slowly this self is revealed as a mass of changing elements, thoughts, feelings, emotions, and images, all illuminated simply by listening, by paying attention.

# The Heart of Practice

from *A Heart as Wide as the World*

by Sharon Salzberg

The first retreats we had for families at the Insight Meditation Society were specifically designed for parents of our students. Introducing them to the practice was a way to dispel their concerns about their children's strange new hobby. One student, apprehensive about her mother coming to learn how to meditate, said, "My mother is the kind of woman who would say 'The goddamn birds kept me up all night.' " In fact, her mother said exactly that after her first night here! But by the end of the week, she was listening in a whole different way. She had begun to simply hear, letting go of the judgments that might attach themselves to sounds like birds in the middle of the night.

There are so many ways to hear a sound. We might hear a certain noise and become reactive and upset, finding it unpleasant. If we think the sound is a pleasant one, we might want it to go on and on. If the sound strikes us as neither pleasant nor unpleasant, however, we may only "half hear" it. Or, we can hear a sound directly, without judgment or conceptual elaboration—simply as a sensory event—and the whole world can open up before us. To experience the phenomena of the world in this direct way is the essence of mindfulness.

Mindfulness is a quality of awareness that sees directly whatever is happening in our experience and meets it face to face, without the intrusion of bias, without adding such forces as grasping, aversion, or delusion to the experience. Conditioned to live in a state of grasping, we make futile attempts to keep pleasant experiences going on forever. Conditioned to live in anger and fear, we recoil from painful experiences as though we could prevent them from happening. Conditioned to live in delusion, we "space out" and become disconnected from the moment when an experience is not strikingly pleasant or unpleasant.

If we add together all of the times when we do not experience life fully because desire and attachment keep us from being present; and all the times that we try to separate from what is, out of anger or fear; and all of the times that we are spaced out, we end up with a pretty big pile of moments. What is left over is a tiny parcel of mindful moments when we are fully alive, not lost in clinging, resisting, or disconnecting. This is a shockingly limited way to live.

It is possible to be awake and present with balance, serenity, and understanding, whether our experience is pleasant, unpleasant, or neutral. This is the power of mindfulness. Mindfulness is a penetrative and profound awareness characterized by nonsuperficiality. Traditionally, the quality of mindfulness is illustrated by comparing what happens if you throw a cork into water versus what happens when you throw a rock. Superficial awareness is like the cork that floats on top of the water. The rock, in contrast, sinks right to the bottom.

Another way of understanding this quality of awareness is to consider what happens if we pour water into a cup. The water doesn't stay in one place—it fills whatever space there is. In the same way, mindfulness suffuses the object of attention, spreading over it entirely. When we are mindful, we suffuse our experience with awareness. When we hear a sound, our awareness moves deeply into the moment of hearing.

When we are mindful, when we can meet what is happening directly, then there is great vitality in our world. Rather than seeing through the filters of our conditioned hopes and fears, we can be with things as they are. When we are mindful, we look with meditative vision, or as the Sufis say, with "eyes unclouded by longing."

Seeing in this way might be likened to what happens when we get to know someone new. When we first meet a person, we might want them to be a certain way, and we might be careless in our observations so that we create a fabrication of who they are based on their surface appearance. Slowly, as our projections lessen, we pay more attention and can see through the elements of the facade. We come closer and closer to the actual, living reality of that person. In the same way, when we are being mindful, we come closer to the actual living reality of our experience.

Mindfulness can go anywhere. It is not limited to any particular experience. You might say, as did our student's mother, "Well, I couldn't be mindful because it was too noisy." But that would be a misperception of mindfulness. We can be mindful of quiet; and we can be mindful of noise. We can be mindful of tremendously resenting the noise.

We can be mindful of everything in our experience. Mindfulness is an infinitely inclusive quality of mind.

It is said that awareness does not take the shape of its object, which means that we can be mindful of pleasure in one moment, of sadness in the next moment, and then of boredom, and the nature of mindfulness does not alter. Whatever we are being aware of, the nature of the awareness itself is spacious, open, and free.

Practicing mindfulness is like taking a journey or unraveling a great mystery. There are countless times every day when we lose mindfulness and become lost in reaction or disconnected from what is happening. But as soon as we recognize that we have lost it, we can begin again. In fact, the moment we recognize that we have lost mindfulness, we have already regained it, because the recognition is itself a function of awareness.

When we are willing to continually begin again, the power of mindfulness reveals itself. The practice reaches fruition in each arising moment as well as in future moments. Mindfulness is not something abstract or far away; it comes alive for each of us the moment we begin, and as we begin again. This is the very heart of the practice.

# Vait a Minute, Vait a Minute

from *Don't Just Do Something, Sit There*

by Sylvia Boorstein

## A SLOTH AND TORPOR STORY

From time to time, the mind runs out of steam. Lacking energy, it feels confused, it daydreams, it falls asleep. Especially after lunch. Paying closer attention to every moment of experience—the Buddha called it "aiming the mind"—is, itself, the antidote to lack of clarity.

My friend Martha's ethnic roots are different from mine, and so she never had a grandfather who said, "Vait a minute," but she uses that phrase with me a lot. I use it often to signal lack of clarity. It's shorthand for "Let's slow down. Too much data is happening at one time. I am on overload. I am confused."

Focusing on one thing at a time cultivates clarity. Slowing down, doing less, makes it possible to aim the mind with precision.

My grandfather moved slowly, and he did one thing at a time. When he was very old, he came to live for a while in my home, and my children took him to school for show-and-tell. No one else had a ninety-five-year-old great-grandfather. He was a big help in our household. His health was wonderful, and he enjoyed chores.

His only limitation was his hearing loss, which was considerable. He needed to concentrate fully to understand what anyone was saying. That's where the "Vait a minute" password originated.

My grandfather might have been, for example, standing at the sink peeling potatoes. I would approach and begin talking. He would be concentrating on peeling, and besides, the water would be running. "Vait a minute! Vait a minute!" he would say. He would turn off the water, put down the paring knife, turn to face me fully, and say, "Now. What?" *That* is aiming.

# Softball Breaks Through the Gloom

## from *Everyday Blessings*

### by Myla Kabat-Zinn and Jon Kabat-Zinn

Sunday of a three-day weekend—the start of school vacation week. I (JKZ) have been away so much of late that when I'm home, I feel like a stranger. Myla and the girls develop their own rhythms in my absence. To reconnect, I sometimes ask dumb questions, like "What are you talking about?" when they are speaking together.

They don't like this. It feels intrusive. I stand in the doorway to my daughter's room while Myla is having a conversation with her. I'm seeking closeness, but it feels off to them, like I'm waiting for something to happen, filled with unvoiced expectations. In such moments, I feel like a stranger in my own home.

My practice in such moments is to be present without imposing myself and my needs. It is not easy. In fact, it's quite a struggle. Just being present, doing what I need to do, but not succumbing to resentment or isolating myself further by leaving the breakfast table early, or working, or being on the phone, these are my challenges. If I do these things, it feels like I'm still traveling, fundamentally away, even though my body is around.

The morning was gloomy with low clouds, a mid-April chill, communications with distant family, and the need to catch up on work. But rather than isolate myself in my study, I came in and out of the kitchen, making sure that I was around and not giving in to the impulse to pick up the Sunday paper.

Trying to get my daughter out of the house is not easy, but I try again today, in the late afternoon. At this age (eleven), she usually rejects anything I propose we do together. But her softball coach had called a few days earlier and told her she should play catch to prepare for the team's first practice. After dinner, she agrees to play in the backyard with me. We go outside. The setting sun is shining now beneath the clouds which have kept the day gray and gloomy, matching my mood. Now low evening light from the west floods the side yard, setting everything aglow.

We start throwing the ball back and forth. At first, we can't find a left-handed glove for her, so she throws rightie, claiming to be ambidextrous. And she is. She can throw accurately with her right arm and catch beautifully with her left hand. We play with intensity, the ball rocketing back and forth. I direct my throws first to one side of her, then to the other, so she will have to backhand a fair number of balls. Then we expand to include pop-ups and low line drives, mixing up everything.

She catches about 90 percent of everything I throw, this after a year of not playing at all. We are in synch. I can feel her enjoyment of this, and her recognition of her own grace and mastery. She is good, a natural. But I know she should have the one left-handed glove we have somewhere. We take a break and I look for it in the one place I haven't looked yet, and find it.

Now her catching is shakier for a time, as she adjusts to the new glove and the opposite positioning. But her throwing, competent with her right arm, is three times more powerful and accurate with her left. Back and forth, back and forth, high, low, catching backhand, catching on the open side. I haven't done this in ages. I am fast revisiting ancient rhythms from my own childhood. The pattern hasn't entirely disappeared in forty years. It amazes me that the glove knows where the ball is so much of the time.

She is warming to this. Her cheeks turn red. She is fine in the chill air without a coat. She is also warming to me. I feel it. Finally, finally, we are doing something together out of doors that involves some exertion, something we can both enjoy and talk easily around.

I have waited months for such a moment. I have invited her to bike ride together. "No." To rollerblade. "No." To go for a walk. "Are you crazy?" To drive someplace nice and sit by a pond. "No way." Yet right now, it is happening, and I feel that the effects of my having been absent are being washed away. Right now we are truly together, doing something that is rare for us and that we can come back to all spring if she likes.

Now that we are on Daylight Saving Time, we can play after I come home from work.

We are also rediscovering that it is still possible for us to have fun together. I feel her strength as the ball goes back and forth, and see her experiencing her own strength in the most natural of ways. I am enjoying this playing catch immensely, and can feel the same from her. And the enjoyment is richer for bringing father and daughter back to closeness. We dwell so much apart, and in such different worlds, that we can become estranged from each other. But here is at least one way, at least in this moment, where we are being shown that we are still deeply connected, and can enjoy doing something together. As we throw the ball back and forth and listen to the thud in the gloves, and the sharp crack when it goes over my head and hits the wooden fence behind me, it feels as if we've been doing this forever. Time falls away.

I am careful not to find ways to stop or interrupt these moments for anything. I know they will not last. The light is fading. She is expecting a phone call from her friend about when the friend and her mom will be coming by to pick her up for a sleepover. The phone call comes. She must get ready. But we have met once again, she and I, and that counts for a lot with both of us.

Afterward, we sit around waiting for the doorbell to ring. We are alone in the house. Out of the blue, she offers (this never happens, I can hardly believe that it is happening now) to tell me how she made the larger-than-life sketch of herself in her art class. She explains that the exercise was to do the whole thing without lifting the pencil from the paper, looking in the mirror and only rarely at the drawing. I could have asked her a hundred probing questions and never gotten her to talk about something like this. She doesn't answer probing questions. But she does respond to presence. I see that it is my job to know this and to be accessible, even when it seems like there are light-years between us.

# The Listening Mind

from *How Can I Help?*

by Ram Dass and Paul Gorman

Much of our capacity to help another person depends upon our state of mind. Sometimes our minds are so scattered, confused, depressed, or agitated, we can hardly get out of bed. At other times we're clear, alert, and receptive; we feel ready, even eager, to respond generously to the needs of others. Most of the time it's really not one extreme or the other. Our minds are . . . well . . . they're just our minds. Like old cars, typewriters, or appliances, we put up with their idiosyncrasies with a shrug. What can we do about it anyway?

Perhaps we settle for too little. Our mind, after all, is our most potentially powerful tool. With it we have harnessed fire, devised technology, extended our ability to grow and process food, developed ways to protect ourselves from the elements, discovered means to cure illness and extend our life span.

Our mind is not only the source of ideas, a tool for gathering data, an instrument of training and technique, or a repository of experience and memory. Because the mind's capacity to think is so brilliant, we tend to be dazzled by it and fail to notice other attributes and functions. There is more to the mind than reason alone. There is *awareness itself* and what we sometimes think of as the deeper *qualities* of mind. Most of us know how supportive it is merely to be in the presence of a mind that is open, quiet, playful, receptive, or reflective. These attributes are *themselves* helpful. Moreover, there is something we frequently experience—perhaps we can call it intuitive awareness—that links us most intimately to the universe and, in allegiance with the heart, binds us together in generosity and compassion. Often it leaps to vision and knowledge instantaneously. "My understanding of the fundamental laws of the universe," said Albert Einstein, "did not come out of my rational mind."

This resource of awareness can give us access to deeper power, power to help and heal.

◆   ◆   ◆

The phone rings. We turn from the checkbook we were balancing to answer. It's someone seeking counsel. Even as the person begins to speak, our minds are conflicted. We don't quite want to leave that column of figures unadded, and yet we know that we have to let go of our bookkeeping to listen carefully to the problem.

The voice on the other end tries to find words to describe suffering: "I'm just feeling so . . . it's like I . . . I really don't know, but . . ." Painstaking work, But sometimes even as it starts, our mind may begin to wander. "This is going to be a tough one. . . . Am I up to this? . . . What about dinner? . . . I'd better circle that place where I think the bank screwed up."

At a certain stage, personal judgments may start competing for attention. "He's really romanticizing it a lot. . . . He ought to be done with this one by now. . . . He's not hearing what I mean." We may get a little lost in evaluating—"Is it working? Am I helping?" Or we could as easily turn the evaluation on ourselves: "I don't care that much. I really don't like him."

Sometimes we catch ourselves in distraction and rejoin the person on the other end of the phone. Now it's better. Something's beginning to happen. Then we take an intentionally audible in-breath—we've got something helpful to say—but the signal goes by; he keeps right on talking. Off goes the mind to utterly unrelated topics: "Call Dad. . . . That picture on the wall is crooked. . . . I'm tired. . . . I have to feed the cat."

This mental chatter goes on and off. Sometimes we really get lost, and by the time we're back, we realize we've missed a key point, and it's too late to ask for it to be repeated. At other times we can take quick note of our reactions and still stay with it. Perhaps we just let it all rain off, it's not something we even notice—it fades into the background like film-score music we're hardly aware is there.

Then the call is over. The voice on the other end says "Thank you." We reply "You're welcome." But how welcome was he? How much room did the mind give him? How much did we really hear? How much did he feel heard? Maybe we sit back in the chair and reflect on that for a moment. Or perhaps we get up, walk to the kitchen, and savor the "thank you" along with a sandwich. Perhaps we simply turn back to the check-book.

Reckoning, judging, evaluating, leaping in, taking it personally, being bored—the helping act has any number of invitations to reactiveness and distraction. Partly we are agitated because we so intensely want to help.

◆ ◆ ◆

If we continue to observe our mind over some time, we notice that it's not always distracted and busy. For all of us, there are times when our minds become concentrated, sharp and clear. Perhaps we are doing a crossword puzzle, playing a video game, reading a mystery story, cleaning house or cooking. For some, it's the simple tasks that engage us in ways that allow our mind to be composed and focused; for others, it's complex problem solving.

Many times, however, the needs of others are what bring us to a state of sharp concentration. Whether it's because we feel very secure with those we're with or because we are functioning under conditions of extreme crisis, we find that in this state of intense concentration helpful insights arise on their own, as a function of our one-pointedness. In these experiences we meet a resource of remarkable potential. While we may be frustrated in not having access to it all the time, these experiences lead us to inquire whether there might be something we could do more regularly and formally to quiet the mind, strengthen its concentration, make available the deeper insights that often result, and bring them into closer attunement with the empathy and compassion of our heart. How immeasurably this might enhance our ability to help others.

Traditionally, one such way to begin this investigation is through meditation, systematically observing the mind itself and becoming more familiar with the ways in which we are denied the experience of full concentration. When we do this, with even a simple exercise like focusing our attention on our breath or on a candle flame, we begin to see that there is a continuous stream of thoughts going on all the time. Meditation may be frustrating if we think we can stop this process right away. We can't. But by penetrating and observing it, we can free ourselves from being carried away by our thoughts.

Our thoughts are always happening. Much like leaves floating down a stream or clouds crossing the sky, they just keep on coming. They arise in the form of sensations, feelings, memories, anticipations, and speculations. And they are all constantly calling for attention: "Think of me." "Notice me." "Attend to me." As each thought passes, either we attend to it or we don't. While we can't stop the thoughts themselves, we can stop our awareness from being snared by each one. If you are standing by a river and a leaf floats by, you have your choice of following the leaf with your eye or keeping your attention fixed in front of you. The leaf floats out of your line of vision. Another leaf enters . . . and floats by.

But as we stand on the bank of the river and the leaves float by, there is no confusion as to whether or not we are the leaves. Similarly, it turns out that there is a place in our minds from which we can watch our own mental images go by. We aren't our thoughts any more than we are the leaves.

If we imagine that our mind is like the blue sky, and that across it pass thoughts as clouds, we can get a feel for that part of it which is other than our thoughts. The sky is always present; it contains the clouds and yet is not contained by them. So with our awareness. It is present and encompasses all our thoughts, feelings, and sensations; yet it is not the same as them. To recognize and acknowledge this awareness, with its spacious, peaceful quality, is to find a very useful resource within. We see that we need not identify with each thought just because it happens to occur. We can remain quiet and choose which thought we wish to attend to. And we can remain aware behind all these thoughts, in a state that offers an entirely new level of openness and insight.

♦   ♦   ♦

For one who has not examined the mind and has always identified completely with passing thoughts, the possibility of being able to rest in awareness free of thought may be a bit disconcerting. It's a little like the caterpillar pointing up at the butterfly and saying, "You'll never get me up in one of those things."

♦   ♦   ♦

In the clarity of a quiet mind, there is room for all that is actually happening and whatever else might also be possible. Though we may be mindful of myriad details, our attention never wavers from the specific situation or person in need. The intimacy of our attention becomes a heart-to-heart lifeline made firm and fast; no one need fall from the edge.

The quiet appreciation of the total situation and its inherent possibilities steadily moves things toward resolution; we find ways to step back. In a spirit of compassion and reverence for life, these various skills flourish and combine appropriately.

Such feats might seem to be the result of crisis. Many of us have experienced rising to the occasion under such conditions. The intensity of the situation keeps the mind from wandering. For most of us, fortunately or unfortunately, our helping work doesn't entail the intensity that brings forth these heightened faculties. But whatever the circumstances, and however extensive the training and experience, it's important to recognize that the faculties of awareness being called into play are exactly those we have been cultivating and discovering in the practice of meditation and the investigation of awareness. General laws are operating under particular circumstances.

Why, for example, if one was tightly attentive to a single object—a man on the edge of a roof—wouldn't everything else disappear from awareness? Because, as we've discovered, it is possible to notice a single thought, sensation, or situation arise, but not get totally lost in identifying with it. We observe the cloud but remain focused on the sky, see the leaf but hold in vision the river. We are that which is aware of the totality. And our skills develop with practice. First, we have to appreciate the value of such qualities of mind and desire to develop them. Next, we have to have faith in the possibility that we can indeed make progress. Finally, we have to explore and practice appropriate techniques. Twenty minutes a day of such practice can lead to results and the incentive to go deeper still. Continuous practice brings about great transformation of mind and leads to a new quality of service.

When we function from this place of spacious awareness rather than from our analytic mind, we are often surprised to find solutions to problems without our having "figured them out." It's as if out of the reservoir of our minds which contains everything we know and everything we are sensing at the moment, all that could be useful rises to the surface and presents itself for appropriate action. Sudden flashes of memory, past experience, or understanding seem to get expressed: "I can't explain it." "It just came to me." "It all suddenly became clear." "I forgot I even knew that."

We often call this quality of mind "intuition" but often we don't trust or honor it. Unlike our thinking mind, which arrives at solutions through a linear process of analysis which we can follow, the intuitive mind seems to leap to a solution. Perhaps the process is going on outside the range of our consciousness; perhaps we are delving into regions of the mind where thinking, in the conventional sense, is not necessary. Whatever, it is still an important resource of our minds and worthy of more than incidental attention.

Ultimately, this kind of listening to the intuitive mind is a kind of surrender based on trust. It's playing it by ear, listening for the voice within. We trust that it's possible to hear into a greater totality which offers insight and guidance. Ultimately, but really ultimately, we trust that when we are fully quiet, aware, and attentive, boundaries created by the mind simply blur and dissolve, and we begin to merge into All That Is. And All That Is, by definition, includes answers as well as questions, solutions as well as dilemmas.

When we have been used to knowing where we stand at every moment, the experience of resting in awareness without any specific thoughts to hold on to and trusting our intuition, turns out to be a refreshing and exciting adventure. In this choiceless spacious awareness, we don't necessarily know from moment to moment how everything is going to come out. Nor do we have a clear idea of what is expected of us. Our stance is just one of listening . . . of fine tuning . . . trusting that all will become apparent at the proper time.

To rest in awareness also means to stand free of the prejudices of mind that come from identifying with cherished attitudes and opinions. We can listen without being busy planning, analyzing, theorizing . . . and especially judging. We can open into the moment fully in order to hear it all.

As we learn to listen with a quiet mind, there is so much we hear. Inside ourselves we can begin to hear that "still small voice within," as the Quakers call it, the voice of our intuitive heart which has so long been drowned out by the noisy thinking mind. We hear our skills and needs, our subtle intentionalities, our limits, our innate generosity.

In other people we hear what help they really require, what license they are actually giving us to help, what potential there is for change. We can hear their strengths and their pain. We hear what support is available, what obstacles must be reckoned with.

♦   ♦   ♦

The more deeply we listen, the more we attune ourselves to the roots of suffering and the means to help alleviate it. It is through listening that wisdom, skill, and opportunity find form in an act that truly helps. But more than all these, the very act of listening can dissolve distance between us and others as well.

◆   ◆   ◆

There are so many ways in which we listen to one another. "I hear you," we say to one another. Such a message would be welcome indeed if, for example, it came in the words of a trapped coal miner or a deaf person who had just undergone corrective ear surgery. In most helping situations, however, "I hear you" reflects a much deeper message: "I understand. I'm with you." Such a message can be immensely reassuring for a person who has felt isolated or alone in their pain and suffering. The reassurance does not come from the words themselves, of course, but from what the words represent. It comes if the person indeed feels heard.

It may not be that a particular story from one's life is so important. But sharing it is a way of being together heart to heart. In those moments we are no longer alone with our fear; we are reminded that we are not forgotten.

To reach its full potential, however, this hearing from the heart requires that we remain alert to entrapments of the mind. Seeking to help others, we may start out open and receptive, but after a short time being with them seems to bring us down rather than lift them up. Somehow their suffering, self-pity, despair, fear, or neediness begins to get to us. It's a little like trying to pull someone out of quicksand and feeling ourself suddenly starting to sink. As reassuring as it may be for one depressed person to be heard by another depressed person, the relationship doesn't really open the door to escape from depression. Empathy is not enough.

Here, once again, our ability to remain alert to our own thoughts as they come and go serves us in our relations with others. We hear into their pain . . . they feel heard . . . we meet together inside the confusion. And yet we ourselves are able to note, perhaps even to anticipate, that moment when another's entrapment of mind might be starting to suck us in. We are as alert to what is happening within us as we are to what is happening in them.

The ability to avoid being entrapped by one another's mind is one of the great gifts we can offer each other. With this compassionate and spacious awareness, and the listening it makes possible, we can offer those we are with a standing invitation to come out from wherever they are caught, if they are ready and wish to do so. It is as if we are in the room of experience with them, but also standing in the doorway, offering our hand, ready to walk out together.

# When the Student Is Ready,
## the Teacher Bites
### from *Breath by Breath*
### by Larry Rosenberg

Some years ago, my first Buddhist teacher got permission for me to do a retreat in Korea that is usually only attended by monks. I was the only layperson there, an American at that, and we took a vow not to move while sitting. (At our center, we ask just that meditators keep movement to a minimum, and to change posture mindfully if they decide to do so. That is a valuable way to practice, but it is also instructive not to move at all.) There was a great deal of ego involved. I felt as if I were sitting there holding the flag. The official American meditator of the Olympic games.

At the beginning of one morning sitting, after the first minute or so, I was bitten by a mosquito. This is a rather ordinary event, but it marked a major turning point in my practice. I am actually deeply grateful to that Korean mosquito. She was just doing her job, of course. She was being a mosquito. But the bite really started to itch. I didn't think I could stand it. There I sat, with fifty-eight minutes between me and the opportunity to scratch.

Right practice, of course, was just to feel the sensation. Forget about mosquitoes, the nature of insect bites, the word itch. Just feel exactly what the sensation is on your skin at that moment. The breath is very helpful in that regard. It helps you stay with the object; it nourishes your mindfulness; it cuts down on unnecessary thinking.

You can also become absorbed in the breath to take your mind off the powerful urge to scratch.

It's quite varied, this thing we call a mosquito bite: If you look closely, you see that the itch isn't one feeling but a whole host of feelings, coming and going. It's not solid; it's a process. It grows more intense, then less so, disappears altogether for a few seconds, returns with a vengeance.

Sustained awareness perceives this truth; without awareness, it's just a solid sheet of itch. Awareness also sees that the itch is impersonal. It comes from nowhere, goes to nowhere. You don't own it, and it isn't you. It's a phenomenon of the natural world. You're a part of that natural world. It begins to lose its power when you see what it really is.

But if you lose your mindfulness for even a second, all kinds of thoughts rush in: "Who made this rule about not moving anyway? Who are they to tell me not to move. I hate this practice. I hate this country. I'm just going to go ahead and scratch. They'll have to find a way to deal with it. . . ."

Those thoughts kept rushing in for me—it was a difficult morning—and at some point I had a major realization. I was a highly educated man, had been a college professor; I'd read a great many books, even Dharma books, but I was making this itch into one of the worst catastrophes in human history. If someone had said, "It could be worse. You could be in a Stalinist labor camp," I would have said, "What do you mean? This is worse than any torture Stalin inflicted." My mind had become that deluded, all from—to say the least—a rather trivial stimulus. Imagine what it would have done with a more serious problem.

If you go back to the original feeling, as I did when I was mindful, it still isn't pleasant: nobody wants to itch. But you eliminate an enormous amount of suffering by concentrating on the suffering that is actually present instead of creating more with your thinking. It is the difference between discomfort and torment.

That is a good, if trivial, example of aversion. I have an even more humiliating one of craving. I have always had a great love for anything Indian. The Buddha's teaching comes from India, and I began inner work with yoga, which also originated in that country. I've benefited a great deal from Indian culture.

I also love the taste of Indian food, but, unfortunately, it doesn't agree with me. Years ago I would go through a repeating cycle of taking great enjoyment from an Indian meal, and then an hour later being extremely uncomfortable. "That's it," I'd think. "I'm never going to that restaurant again." A week later somebody would ask me to dinner, and I'd say, "Indian food? Sure. I love it."

You know what will happen if you eat that food, but the craving keeps growing until you say, "I don't care what happens. I've just got to have that taste." Fine. But that is the same decision people make with all kinds of harmful behavior: overeating, drinking, drug use, sexual misconduct. The list could go on and on.

Everything begins with feelings, all the difficult mind states that people get themselves into. The closer you are able to get to that original sensation, the more clearly you can see it.

# Three Wondrous Answers

from *The Miracle of Mindfulness*

by Thich Nhat Hanh

Let me retell a short story of Tolstoy's, the story of the Emperor's three questions. Tolstoy did not know the emperor's name . . .

One day it occurred to a certain emperor that if he only knew the answers to three questions, he would never stray in any matter.

*What is the best time to do each thing?*

*Who are the most important people to work with?*

*What is the most important thing to do at all times?*

The emperor issued a decree throughout his kingdom announcing that whoever could answer the questions would receive a great reward. Many who read the decree made their way to the palace at once, each person with a different answer.

In reply to the first question, one person advised that the emperor make up a thorough time schedule, consecrating every hour, day, month, and year for certain tasks and then follow the schedule to the letter. Only then could he hope to do every task at the right time.

Another person replied that it was impossible to plan in advance and that the emperor should put all vain amusements aside and remain attentive to everything in order to know what to do at what time.

Someone else insisted that, by himself, the emperor could never hope to have all the foresight and competence necessary to decide when to do each and every task and what he really needed was to set up a Council of the Wise and then to act according to their advice.

Someone else said that certain matters required immediate decision and could not wait for consultation, but if he wanted to know in advance what was going to happen he should consult magicians and soothsayers.

The responses to the second question also lacked accord.

One person said that the emperor needed to place all his trust in administrators, another urged reliance on priests and monks, while others recommended physicians. Still others put their faith in warriors.

The third question drew a similar variety of answers.

Some said science was the most important pursuit. Others insisted on religion. Yet others claimed the most important thing was military skill.

The emperor was not pleased with any of the answers, and no reward was given.

After several nights of reflection, the emperor resolved to visit a hermit who lived up on the mountain and was said to be an enlightened man. The emperor wished to find the hermit to ask him the three questions, though he knew the hermit never left the mountains and was known to receive only the poor, refusing to have anything to do with persons of wealth or power. So the emperor disguised himself as a simple peasant and ordered his attendants to wait for him at the foot of the mountain while he climbed the slope alone to seek the hermit.

Reaching the holy man's dwelling place, the emperor found the hermit digging a garden in front of his hut. When the hermit saw the stranger, he nodded his head in greeting and continued to dig. The labor was obviously hard on him. He was an old man, and each time he thrust his spade into the ground to turn the earth, he heaved heavily.

The emperor approached him and said, "I have come here to ask your help with three questions: When is the best time to do each thing? Who are the most important people to work with? What is the most important thing to do at all times?"

The hermit listened attentively but only patted the emperor on the shoulder and continued digging. The emperor said, "You must be tired. Here, let me give you a hand with that." The hermit thanked him, handed the emperor the spade, and then sat down on the ground to rest.

After he had dug two rows, the emperor stopped and turned to the hermit and repeated his three questions. The hermit still did not answer, but instead stood up and pointed to the spade and said, "Why don't you rest now? I can take over again." But the emperor continued to dig. One hour passed, then two. Finally the sun began to set behind the mountain. The emperor put down the spade and said to the hermit, "I came here to ask if you could answer my three questions. But if you can't give me any answer, please let me know so that I can get on my way home."

The hermit lifted his head and asked the emperor, "Do you hear someone running over there?" The emperor turned his head. They both saw a man with a long white beard emerge from the woods. He ran wildly, pressing his hands against a bloody wound in his stomach. The man ran toward the emperor before falling unconscious to the ground, where he lay groaning. Opening the man's clothing, the emperor and hermit saw that the man had received a deep gash. The emperor cleaned the wound thoroughly and then used his own shirt to bandage it, but the blood completely soaked it within minutes. He rinsed the shirt out and bandaged the wound a second time and continued to do so until the flow of blood had stopped.

At last the wounded man regained consciousness and asked for a drink of water. The emperor ran down to the stream and brought back a jug of fresh water. Meanwhile, the sun had disappeared and the night air had begun to turn cold. The hermit gave the emperor a hand in carrying the man into the hut where they laid him down on the hermit's bed. The man closed his eyes and lay quietly. The emperor was worn out from a long day of climbing the mountain and digging the garden. Leaning against the doorway, he fell asleep. When he rose, the sun had already risen over the mountain. For a moment he forgot where he was and what he had come here for. He looked over to the bed and saw the wounded man also looking around him in confusion. When he saw the emperor, he stared at him intently and then said in a faint whisper, "Please forgive me."

"But what have you done that I should forgive you?" the emperor asked.

"You do not know me, your majesty, but I know you. I was your sworn enemy, and I had vowed to take vengeance on you, for during the last war you killed my brother and seized my property. When I learned that you were coming alone to the mountain to meet the hermit, I resolved to surprise you on your way back and kill you. But after waiting a long time there was still no sign of you, and so I left my ambush in order to seek you out. But instead of finding you, I came across your attendants, who recognized me, giving me this wound. Luckily, I escaped and ran here. If I hadn't met you I would surely be dead by now. I had intended to kill you, but instead you saved my life! I am ashamed and grateful beyond words. If I live, I vow to be your servant for the rest of my life, and I will bid my children and grandchildren to do the same. Please grant me your forgiveness."

The emperor was overjoyed to see that he was so easily reconciled with a former enemy. He not only forgave the man but promised to return all the man's property and to send his own physician and servants to wait on the man until he was completely healed. After ordering his attendants to take the man home, the emperor returned to see the hermit. Before returning to the palace the emperor wanted to repeat his three questions one last time. He found the hermit sowing seeds in the earth they had dug the day before.

The hermit stood up and looked at the emperor. "But your questions have already been answered."

"How's that?" the emperor asked, puzzled.

"Yesterday, if you had not taken pity on my age and given me a hand with digging these beds, you would have been attacked by that man on your way home. Then you would have deeply regretted not staying with me. Therefore the most important time was the time you were digging in the beds, the most important person was myself, and the most important pursuit was to help me. Later, when the wounded man ran up here, the most important time was the time you spent dressing his wound, for if you had not cared for him he would have died and you would have lost the chance to be reconciled with him. Likewise, he was the most important person, and the most important pursuit was taking care of his wound. Remember that there is only one important time and that is now. The present moment is the only time over which we have dominion. The most important person is always the person you are with, who is right before you, for who knows if you will have dealings with any other person in the future? The most important pursuit is making the person standing at your side happy, for that alone is the pursuit of life."

Tolstoy's story is like a story out of scripture: it doesn't fall short of any sacred text. We talk about social service, service to the people, service to humanity, service for others who are far away, helping to bring peace to the world—but often we forget that it is the very people around us that we must live for first of all. If you cannot serve your wife or husband or child or parent—how are you going to serve society? If you cannot make your own child happy, how do you expect to be able to make anyone else happy? If all our friends in the peace movement or of service communities of any kind do not love and help one another, whom can we love and help? Are we working for other humans, or are we just working for the name of an organization?

## SERVICE

The service of peace. The service of any person in need. The word service is so immense. Let's return first to a more modest scale: our families, our classmates, our friends, our own community. We must live for them— for if we cannot live for them, whom else do we think we are living for?

Tolstoy is a saint—what we Buddhists would call a Bodhisattva. But was the emperor himself able to see the meaning and direction of life? How can we live in the present moment, live right now with the people around us, helping to lessen their suffering and making their lives happier? How? The answer is this: We must practice mindfulness. The principle that Tolstoy gives appears easy. But if we want to put it into practice we must use the methods of mindfulness in order to seek and find the way.

I've written these pages for our friends to use. There are many people who have written about these things without having lived them, but I've only written down those things which I have lived and experienced myself. I hope you and your friends will find these things at least a little helpful along the path of our seeking: the path of our return.

*Acceptance*

To the Western mind, acceptance often means acquiescence. When we hear, "just accept it," we may believe we have to be resigned to something we do not really want, or that we cannot be discriminating. Acceptance here means that we simply note or acknowledge what is true. It means facing what there is to face—not looking away; not trying to change, hold on to, or judge it. The writers excerpted in this section show how the process of constant evaluation screens out the truth and clouds our vision. They show us why we tend to think this way, and how our outlook may change if we practice acceptance.

In "This Is It" Jon Kabat-Zinn teaches us that in meditation, we may learn to accept what happens. We learn not to dismiss or ignore anything or to want something better to happen. Wanting something better to happen is a common pitfall of meditating. To have relaxation or enlightenment as a goal defeats the purpose of simply observing. We may well become relaxed and perhaps we will even see more clearly, but neither are likely if we stay busy blocking out thoughts that we think conflict with our desire for a "result."

The excerpts "Judging" by Sharon Salzberg, "Discover What Is Asking for Acceptance" by Jack Kornfield, and "Loving Whatever Is Incomplete" by John Tarrant, each speak of the ways in which practicing the value of acceptance helps us experience greater love and compassion, both for ourselves and others. By not becoming caught in the inevitable judgments we make, we may discover a greater generosity of spirit in ourselves. Acceptance means being inclusive. It allows for greater intimacy as we remove the barriers of judgment we place between ourselves and our experience.

We may tend to reject any unpleasantness because we feel that once we accept it we are stuck with it. We forget that things change. Sylvia Boorstein reminds us in "The Limited Menu of Disturbing Mind States" that nothing goes on forever. She also points out that we may have difficulty with acceptance because we fear that if we acknowledge something painful we will not be able to tolerate it. In "Restlessness," she explains that our frenzied efforts to fight, deny, or change the painful truth are themselves painful. In "The Broccoli Phenomenon" she shows us how practicing acceptance allows us to experience the pains and disappointments that are an unavoidable part of our lives. We cannot make them go away by ignoring them but paying attention with an open mind and accepting mind gives us the option of choosing *how* to respond—an option we are deprived of if we are not even aware of the conflict we create for ourselves.

There may be unexpected benefits to accepting what we normally reject, as Bernard Glassman shows us in "How to Cook." Using cooking as a metaphor, he urges us to include all of the ingredients at our disposal—to work with what we have. "If you can work with what you reject, it turns out that you're working with yourself, with those parts of yourself that you've rejected." We may be surprised to find new options and opportunities open up to us when we include what we normally reject. Our world certainly becomes wider when we stop chipping away at it.

# This Is It

from *Wherever You Go, There You Are*

by Jon Kabat-Zinn

*New Yorker* cartoon: Two Zen monks in robes and shaved heads, one young, one old, sitting side by side cross-legged on the floor. The younger one is looking somewhat quizzically at the older one, who is turned toward him and saying: "Nothing happens next. This is it."

It's true. Ordinarily, when we undertake something, it is only natural to expect a desirable outcome for our efforts. We want to see results, even if it is only a pleasant feeling. The sole exception I can think of is meditation. Meditation is the only intentional, systematic human activity which at bottom is about not trying to improve yourself or get anywhere else, but simply to realize where you already are. Perhaps its value lies precisely in this. Maybe we all need to do one thing in our lives simply for its own sake.

But it would not quite be accurate to call meditation a "doing." It is more accurately described as a "being." When we understand that "This is it," it allows us to let go of the past and the future and wake up to what we are now, in this moment.

People usually don't get this right away. They want to meditate in order to relax, to experience a special state, to become a better person, to reduce some stress or pain, to break out of old habits and patterns, to become free or enlightened. All valid reasons to take up meditation practice, but all equally fraught with problems if you expect those things to happen just because now you are meditating. You'll get caught up in wanting to have a "special experience" or in looking for signs of progress, and if you don't feel something special pretty quickly, you may start to doubt the path you have chosen, or to wonder whether you are "doing it right."

In most domains of learning, this is only reasonable. Of course you have to see progress sooner or later to keep at something. But meditation is different. From the perspective of meditation, every state is a special state, every moment a special moment.

When we let go of wanting something else to happen in this moment, we are taking a profound step toward being able to encounter what is here now. If we hope to go anywhere or develop ourselves in any way, we can only step from where we are standing. If we don't really know where we are standing—a knowing that comes directly from the cultivation of mindfulness—we may only go in circles, for all our efforts and expectations. So, in meditation practice, the best way to get somewhere is to let go of trying to get anywhere at all.

> If your mind isn't clouded by unnecessary things, this is the best season of your life.
>
> —Wu-Men

Try: Reminding yourself from time to time: "This is it." See if there is anything at all that it cannot be applied to. Remind yourself that acceptance of the present moment has nothing to do with resignation in the face of what is happening. It simply means a clear acknowledgment that what is happening is happening. Acceptance doesn't tell you what to do. What happens next, what you choose to do, that has to come out of your understanding of this moment. You might try acting out of a deep knowing of "This is it." Does it influence how you choose to proceed or respond? Is it possible for you to contemplate that in a very real way, this may actually be the best season, the best moment of your life? If that was so, what would it mean for you?

# Judging

## from *A Heart as Wide as the World*
### by Sharon Salzberg

Early in my practice I got the idea that really good meditators were continuously being bathed in a flood of white light. No one ever told me I had to experience this white light; somehow I just imagined that it was a sign of good practice. And I had a sneaking suspicion that as soon as I finally experienced white light, my teachers would bestow the truth upon me: "Finally," they would say, "we had almost given up hope that you would ever get here."

But I didn't experience any white light. I mostly had knee pain. As time went on and my practice deepened, I had many different experiences, but none of them were white light, and I really wanted that white light. No matter what I experienced, it wasn't good enough for me. "Where is the light? Why isn't it here?" This was my inner incantation. I felt contemptuous of my practice and judged it constantly, comparing it with what I thought should be happening. The heartache was tremendous.

In meditation practice, as in life, we might judge our difficult experiences—such as restlessness, negative mind-states, physical pain, and so on—as not being right, as being somehow out of place or worthless. We often try to prolong pleasant experiences, as though they are the only ones worth having. But with increased patience and insight, meditation practice can take us beyond these conditioned reactions.

When we meditate, we view whatever arises with acceptance and a spirit of generosity, with a mind that is open and spacious. The purpose of this acceptance is not to develop passivity but to get as close to our experience as we can. When we are free of our conditioned reactions, we are able to have an intimate, personal vision of what is true. The full range of what a human being can know and feel and want and fear is within each of us: the entire display of a human life. No matter what we are experiencing, being aware of it is the path to wisdom.

Once when I was sitting with U Pandita, I began to notice a recurring pattern in our interviews. Whenever I told him about a meditation experience that I thought was wonderful and impressive, his response was: "Did you note it?" In his tradition of practice, "noting" refers to placing a mental label on each experience, so as to know it more directly. But I would sit there and think, "What does he mean, 'Did you note it?' It was glorious; how could I have just noted it like everything else?" Other times I went to see him with doleful accounts of painful meditation experiences. He looked at me and said each time, "Did you note it?" I would think, "What does he mean, 'Did you note it?' It was awful; can't he understand that?" It took a while for me to appreciate the simplicity, and importance, of U Pandita's approach: he was asking me if I had been aware of each experience with spaciousness and clarity of mind. He was far less concerned with what was happening than with the quality of awareness I was bringing to it. What we want in practice is to understand the nature of our lives, and this does not demand a particular experience but a quality of awareness that excludes nothing.

Meditation is like going into an old attic room and turning on the light. It is not the fantastic white light that I had so much desired but the common, average, liberating light of awareness. In that light we see everything. We see all of the beautiful treasures that engender awe and gratitude for our ability to discover them. We see all of the dusty, neglected corners that inspire us to say, "I'd better clean that up." We see all of the unfortunate relics of the past that we thought we had rid ourselves of long ago. We see it all with an open and loving awareness.

The inclusiveness and intimate nature of mindfulness mirrors the nature of love. We discover the fact that awareness can go anywhere, and that we are capable of having a loving heart in any circumstance. This discovery is the wellspring of joy that meditation can bring into our lives. Loving awareness contains a strength that the judging mind can never give us.

The truth is everywhere, in all of our experiences. We do not have to fitfully try to have a sublime, magical experience and, in this effort, disdain what is actually happening. We do not have to struggle to find the truth. Every single moment is expressive of the truth of our lives, when we know how to look. As Saint Augustine said, "If you are looking for something that is everywhere, you don't need travel to get there; you need love."

# Discover What Is Asking for Acceptance

## from *A Path with Heart*

### by Jack Kornfield

This may sound like a very complicated and busy way to meditate, but in practice it is very simple. The general rule is simply to sit and be aware of what arises. If there are repeated patterns, expand the field of aware-ness. Then sense what is asking for acceptance. This is the third principle. Repeated patterns remain because of some level of resistance: an aversion, fear, or judgment locks them in. This contraction is built out of fear. To release it, we must acknowledge what is present and ask our heart, "How am I receiving this?" Do we wish it to change? Is there a difficult feeling, belief, or sensation we have contracted around that we want to be over or go away? Is there some attachment, some fear?

The Dalai Lama has pointed out that communism worldwide did not work because it was not based on compassion and love; it was based on class struggle and dictatorial control, which in the end just doesn't work. Struggle and dictating doesn't work in our inner life either. So we must inquire what aspect of this repeated pattern is asking for acceptance and compassion, and ask ourself, "Can I touch with love whatever I have closed my heart to?" This doesn't mean solving it or figuring it out—it is simply asking, "What wants acceptance?" In difficult patterns of thought, emotion, or sensation, we must open to feel their full energy in our body, heart, and mind, however strongly they show themselves. This includes opening to our reactions to this experience as well, noticing the fear, aversion, or contraction that arises and then accepting it all. Only then can it release.

In my earliest practice as a celibate monk I had long bouts of lust and images of sexual fantasy. My teacher said to name them, which I did. But they often repeated. "Accept this?" I thought. "But then they'll never stop." But still I tried it. Over days and weeks these thoughts became even stronger. Eventually, I decided to expand my awareness to see what other feelings were present. To my surprise I found a deep well of loneliness almost every time the fantasies arose. It wasn't all lust, it was loneliness, and the sexual images were ways of seeking comfort and closeness. But they kept arising. Then I noticed how hard it was to let myself feel the loneliness. I hated it; I resisted it. Only when I accepted this very resistance and gently held it all in compassion did it begin to subside. By expanding my attention, I learned that much of my sexuality had little to do with lust, and as I brought an acceptance to the feeling of loneliness, the compulsive quality of the fantasies gradually diminished.

# Loving Whatever Is Incomplete
## from *The Dark Within the Light*
### by John Tarrant

Soul and spirit, like other opposites, tend to express their own separate natures. At first in our journey, for the sake of clarity, we have to recognize and even encourage this division. At that time, we are like Psyche sorting the seeds. As we go on, though, there is something suspect about such opposition. For, as well as a fissile pressure, soul and spirit have a natural companionship, a predilection for conversation, a shared delight in the unfolding moment.

After traveling their long-separate paths, soul and spirit draw toward each other again because each has what the other lacks. They seem now to want to mingle, and when they do, the experience is deeply ecstatic. Illuminating each other, they are beautiful but difficult lovers. Secretly, spirit wants embodiment, wants to sink down and be mortal, to bleed, to struggle with high blood pressure and menstrual cramps and cold toes. Without these pains, spirit is ghostlike, vague, adrift without links to the earth. And the soul, which knows more than it needs to about the fragility of the body, secretly loves weightlessness, the voice of the soprano, rising like the lark vertically above the tussocks at dawn. We need both realms. We are at once vast and tiny, intensely personal and at peace.

Honoring what is incomplete, we must love our lives in their details: the puzzling marriage and the child who likes to read, the smell of melting asphalt in summer, the wistful pleasure in the autumn mist that gives its nobility to the procession of cars. Soul and spirit hold their conversation within these moments, and their conjunction is the embodiment of enlightenment. By holding soul and spirit together, we rescue love for the spiritual world and allow earth to be enlivened by Heaven. The ingredient of soul in the compound permits the outpouring of compassion. Heaven, in turn, is given weight and zest and the terrifying beauty of mortality. When the two interpenetrate, then there is a harmonious state of affairs; the child plays, the summer afternoon goes on and on.

In the *I Ching,* it is not a good condition when Heaven is above earth. Each realm recedes from the other into its own pure nature, and less and less becomes possible. The spirit flies up and the soul plunges. Then we have to wait, and worry out the time until it changes. This is the hexagram of Standstill, in which there is no intermingling. On the other hand, when earth is above Heaven, we find the situation of Peace. The heavy earth sinks and Heaven rises through it. They interpenetrate and inform each other. Nothing is perfect or pure, but all things are right.

A woman had her bathroom remodeled by a Japanese-trained carpenter. It was slow, precise work, requiring bent wood and odd angles, and each detail was perfect, it seemed. But when he had finished, he took her into the room and asked her to bend down and look into a dark corner. He had left a flaw in the skirting board, a slight and deliberate error. This is an ancient idea. It stops the gods from being envious and acknowledges that in our human realm, imperfection allows life to flow in, making a path for happiness and human uses. In such a gap, uncertainty becomes a surprise, a wonder. We are ready to fall into it, as if into happiness itself.

# The Limited Menu of Disturbing Mind States

from *It's Easier Than You Think*

by Sylvia Boorstein

In traditional Buddhist texts the five energies of Lust, Aversion, Torpor, Restlessness, and Doubt are called "Mind Hindrances." They are called hindrances of the mind because they obscure clear seeing, just as sandstorms in the desert or fog on a highway can cause travelers to get lost. They hinder the possibility of us reconnecting with the peaceful self that is our essential nature. They confuse us. We think they are real. We forget that our actual nature is not the passing storm. The passing storm is the passing storm. Our essence remains our essence all the time.

Five different energies seem like a limited menu, but they present themselves in an infinite variety of disguises. Ice-cream sundaes are different from pizzas are different from sex, but fundamentally they are all objects of the lustful desire. The same energy of aversion fuels our annoyance with our neighbor for playing a radio too loud and our annoyance with our president for not running the country better. Grumbly mind is grumbly mind; sleepy mind is sleepy mind; restless mind is restless mind; doubtful mind is doubtful mind.

The fact that it's in the nature of minds for storms to arise and pass away is not a problem. Living in a place where the weather changes frequently is not a problem. It does, however, require having clothing to suit different climate challenges and the wisdom to stay indoors when the weather gets bad. It also helps in keeping the spirits up to remember that the weather is going to change. Our difficult mind states become a problem only if we believe they are going to go on forever. Then, because they are uncomfortable energies, they start to frighten us.

We have two kinds of fears. One is a fear that whatever is going on is going to go on forever. It's just not true—nothing goes on forever. The other is the fear that, even if it doesn't go on forever, the pain of whatever is happening will be so terrible we won't be able to stand it. There is a gut level of truth about this fear. It would be ridiculous to pretend that in our lives, in these physical bodies, which can hurt very much, and in relationships that can hurt very much, there aren't some very, very painful times. Even so, I think we underestimate ourselves. Terrible as some times may be, I believe we can stand them.

Because we become frightened as soon as a difficult mind state blows into the mind, we start to fight with it. We try to change it, or we try to get rid of it. The frenzy of the struggle makes the mind state even more unpleasant.

The familiar image is a children's cartoon character, like Daffy Duck, walking along freely and suddenly stepping into taffy. In a hasty, awkward attempt to extricate himself, he might fall forward and backward and eventually be totally stuck in the taffy. Even children see a better solution.

The best solution would be the nonalarmed recognition, "This is taffy. I didn't see it as I stepped into it, but I felt it after I got stuck. It's just taffy. The whole world is not made out of taffy. What would be a wise thing for me to do now?"

# Restlessness

## from *It's Easier Than You Think*

### by Sylvia Boorstein

If aversion is the mind looking for a fight and torpor is the mind falling asleep, restlessness is the mind scanning the horizon for the next impending catastrophe. Energetically, it is the polar opposite of torpor. Torpor is low-energy mind, and restlessness is high-energy mind.

Sometimes restlessness manifests as fidgety body, but that only becomes a problem in meditation situations where protocol requires sitting quietly to avoid disturbing other people. What is more problematic is fidgety mind, mind unable to remain calm. It is as if the mind, with energy to spare, looks around for potential sources of worry. People with restlessness as their predominant hindrance become habitual fretters, and, although they are often embarrassed to admit it ("Worrying about things you can't change is so silly."), restlessness is a particularly difficult mind habit to change.

I know more about restlessness than any other hindrance, because it has been my predominant hindrance. My mind has the capacity and the tendency to take essentially neutral data and spin it into worry.

## SCENARIO

I am on a street corner in a foreign country where my husband and I have agreed to meet at five o'clock. It is two minutes before the hour. I have the thought, "What if he doesn't arrive in the next two minutes? That will surely mean he has been mugged or even killed! Or held hostage somewhere. Or had a heart attack! I wonder where the American embassy is. If he doesn't arrive, I'll go to the embassy. . . ." This thought takes three seconds, during which time adrenaline fills my body, my heart beats rapidly, and I start to sweat. The adrenaline burst intensifies the worry, and more worries arise: "Who do I know in this country? How can I phone our children?" At five o'clock he arrives. I am relieved, and I am tired.

In the mind of a habitual fretter, this type of scenario is commonplace. Only the place names and characters change to suit each particular situation. The sense of restless mind prowling around looking for material to write a story about remains constant.

As a result of my practice, I am a recovering worrier. My mind still makes up terrifying stories, but I am much less apt to believe them. Sometimes I can catch the story-making machine in the act of churning up a new story, and sometimes I can even laugh at it. If I could disengage the worry machine entirely from my mind, I would surely do it. I don't like it at all. But I was born with it, for whatever karmic reasons, and I'm stuck with it. I've come to think of it, and myself, with compassionate affection. I treat it as if it were an unpleasant neighbor who lives in the apartment next door to me and plays loud music in the middle of the night. If I am obliged to remain in my apartment, I have two choices. I can relax and say, "These are very unpleasant neighbors. Perhaps some day they will move out." Meanwhile, I will buy earplugs or a Walkman and tapes I like! Or I can fume and call the landlord, send letters to the tenants' association, and get more frenzied about it. It's when I recognize what's going on that I get to choose.

# The Broccoli Phenomenon

from *Don't Just Do Something, Sit There*

by Sylvia Boorstein

The Broccoli Phenomenon, a classic illustration of the malleability of the mind, is reported to me regularly on retreats. Probably plenty of people who attend mindfulness retreats aren't crazy about broccoli. You might be one of them. The soup served for supper on the first evening is full of broccoli bits. "Hmm," you might think, "I'm not sure I'll be happy here. I hope this is the last of the broccoli." You begin to practice mindfulness, sitting still for certain periods, walking slowly for other periods, feeling your breath as you sit or your feet as you walk.

You begin to calm down. Breakfast is no problem. No scrambled eggs, no sweet rolls, nothing very interesting, but nevertheless okay. Then lunch: A huge stew appears, full of assorted vegetables, *including* broccoli. And steamed rice. "Uh-oh. How should I do this? Should I just eat rice? No, I'll be hungry. I guess I'll put the stew over the rice and pick out the broccoli. I hope they don't do this to me again!"

They do. The mind devotes an inordinate amount of air time to the dreaded broccoli:

"*Where* do they get these cooks?"

"When I get home, I'm sending them a collection of *good* cookbooks!"

"What if a person were *allergic* to broccoli?"

"Maybe I should leave a note for the cooks. They have no idea."

"I bet if I saw their shopping list, *broccoli* would be the main item!"

"If they are *determined* to serve so much broccoli, they could at least cook it separately, as a side dish, and not mix it into everything else."

Days pass, meals pass, and between bouts of culinary criticism that temporarily cause mind storms, you continue to develop composure. Sitting, walking, breathing, stepping—hour by hour, gradually, while you are busy concentrating, your mind smoothes itself out. It happens steadily, but usually unremarkably, so sometimes you don't realize it's happening.

The Broccoli Phenomenon is how you can tell the practice is working. You enter the dining hall, broccoli is again prominently featured, and you experience nothing much in the way of a reaction. The mind accommodates. Maybe you even smile. Maybe you even have the thought, "Now I hope they don't leave out the broccoli at any meal because, if they do, I won't have nearly as good a story to tell when I get home."

If mindfulness meditation worked only with broccoli, it wouldn't be as valuable as it is. Mindfulness meditation addresses the broccolis of life, the inevitable pains of the body and disappointments of mind that are continually and fundamentally our experience.

The point of practice is not to be finished with pain forever, because we can't be. Nor is it to get over being pleased and then being displeased, liking and not liking, because these are natural responses to life. Mindfulness practice smoothes out the mind so that it sees clearly and responds wisely.

I seem to myself wiser on some days than I do on other days. My level of wisdom is more a reflection of my degree of mindfulness than of external life circumstances. The mind, when it is relaxed, makes sounder judgment calls.

Shanti, the head cook on many of the meditation retreats at which I teach, told me the advice she got from Mrs. Hammond, her third grade teacher, about overcoming aversion to arithmetic. "Listen," Mrs. Hammond said. "You are going to have to do some sort of arithmetic every day for the rest of your life. You might as well enjoy it!"

Joining the ranks of Mrs. Hammond, I add, "We are going to experience some sort of broccoli every day for the rest of our lives." Some will be trivial, minor unpleasantnesses, and some will be very, very hard.

Shanti doesn't use too much broccoli in her cooking. Even if she did, that wouldn't be a problem for me. I rather like broccoli. It's celery that's my problem.

# How to Cook

## from *Instructions to the Cook*
### by Bernard Glassman with Rick Fields

### TRANSFORMATION

Cooking, like life, is about transformation. When we cook, we work directly with the elemental forces of fire and heat, water, metal, and clay. We put the lid on the pot and wait for the fire to transform the rice, or we mix the bread with yeast and put it in the oven to bake. There is something hidden, almost magical about it.

This kind of transformation involves a certain amount of faith. We work hard to prepare the food. We wash the rice, knead the bread, and break the eggs. We measure the ingredients carefully. We mix, stir, blend. But then we have to wait. We have to let fire and water transform the food we've prepared.

But we also have to keep an eye on things. We have to be aware of what is going on. For the Zen cook the old adage "A watched pot never boils" is only half true. We leave the lid on the pot most of the time. But we also lift the lid every once in a while to taste the food.

The Zen cook follows the middle way. We have faith that the soup is coming along—but we still check now and then.

The accomplished Zen cook is something of an alchemist. He or she can transform poisons into virtues.

The Zen cook doesn't do this by adding a secret ingredient but by leaving something out. The Zen cook leaves out our attachment to the self.

For example, anger is considered a poison when it is self-motivated and self-centered. But take that attachment to the self out of anger, and the same emotion becomes the fierce energy of determination, which is a very positive force. Take the self-centered aspect out of greed, and it becomes the desire to help. Drop the self-orientation from ignorance, and it becomes a state of unknowing that allows new things to arise.

## INGREDIENTS

How do we find the ingredients? We simply open our eyes and look around us. We take the materials that are at hand, right in front of us, and prepare the best meal possible. We work with what we have in each and every moment.

Our body is an ingredient. Our relationships are ingredients. Our thoughts, our emotions, and all our actions are ingredients.

The place we live, the leaves that fall, the haze around the moon, the traffic in the city streets, the corner market—all these are also our ingredients. In order to see the ingredients in front of us, we have to open our eyes. Usually we create our own boundaries, our own small view, our own territory, and that's the only place we look. With practice, our territory expands, and all the objects of the world become our ingredients.

As we see ourselves as the world, as we see the oneness of life, the whole world becomes available. Then the Zen cook knows that every aspect of life is an ingredient of the supreme meal.

## USE EVERYTHING

Our natural tendency is not to use ingredients we think might ruin our meal. We want to throw them away or maybe move them way back on the shelf, out of sight, behind everything else. But Dogen instructs us to take the ingredients we think are going to ruin our meal and figure out how to use them so that they improve it.

If something doesn't seem to work as a main course, for example, it might become an appetizer or a dessert. You can't just say, "I don't want it to be like that. I'll leave it out." That's a kind of denial. It's going to be there, whether you like it or not.

Take a group of people starting a new company. Their first step might be to take an inventory of their gifts. But if you decide you don't want the gifts one person has, you could be creating a problem, because his or her gifts are part of the company. In any case, that person's gifts will wind up getting used because they are part of the person. The question is how to use them. If you don't find a way, the person will end up jealous or resentful or bored. The unused gifts will wind up working to rot the company from the inside.

Let's say, for example, that someone is aggressive. But that energy might be just what's needed for certain difficult jobs—dealing with re-calcitrant bureaucrats, for example. Or perhaps someone is so preoccu-pied with details that they are unable to see the larger picture. You wouldn't put that person on your five-year-planning committee. But they might be perfect as an accountant keeping track of daily receipts.

Sometimes it might seem that we can't find a way to use someone's particular qualities, which may seem toxic or harmful to our goal. In that case, we make a clear decision not to use their particular ingredient in the meal we are cooking. But we don't ignore or deny the ingredient. We acknowledge it, we're aware of it, we may even appreciate it in another context. But we just decide to use zero amount of it at the moment.

## NONREJECTION

No matter who we are, we tend to reject someone or something.

When we first moved to the East Coast, before we began our bakery in Yonkers, we ran the food concession at the exclusive Riverdale Yacht Club. Some Zen students thought cooking gourmet meals and learning to set the table properly didn't really constitute traditional samu, or work practice, as did weeding the monastery garden or chopping wood. Many of our members said, "How can you serve the rich? What kind of a thing is that for a Zen center to do?"

Rejection can take many forms. We should not exclude the rich just because we think it is somehow nobler or more spiritual to work with the poor. The Zen student who rejects the rich person has the same problem as the rich person who rejects the Zen student. If you can work with what you reject, it turns out that you're working with yourself, with those parts of yourself that you've rejected. If I can learn to work with a rich person whom I've rejected, for example, then I can begin dealing with the richness rather than the poverty in myself.

The same principle holds true for businesspeople who reject their competitors or social activists who reject working with the government. In every area, working with what you habitually reject is one of the best ways to facilitate growth and transformation. Try to connect with the person you are rejecting or who seems to be rejecting you. When you try to see the world through your opponent's eyes, you have taken the first step toward turning enemies into friends or even allies.

When we first started Greyston Inn, Jack Meehan, who was in charge of a large private foundation, said to me, "Don't get involved with government. Get all your money from private sources. Then you can do whatever you want." But to me, the government was one of the ingredients. Even if they were an obstacle, I needed to learn how to cook with them.

Some people said, "Don't get involved with the politicians. They'll mess everything up." But to me, the politicians were also one of the ingredients, and I had to learn how to cook with them, too, as tough and difficult to work with as they might be.

I don't try to change the ingredients, though. I'm not trying to change conservatives into liberals or liberals into conservatives. Dogen says that every meal has to include a harmony of the six tastes—bitter, sour, sweet, hot, salty, and plain. None of these is better or more important than the others. Each ingredient has a different taste and a different reason for being part of the meal. They're all important.

# Letting Go

We may question the value of letting go because we may be afraid that letting go means giving up. The importance we place on determination—we sometimes call it stick-to-it-iveness—means we hold on to a cherished goal like a dog with a bone. Letting go, however, does not mean indiscriminately giving up. It is part of a process that allows us to choose how long we embrace something. We may be able to understand this value better by thinking of it as flexibility.

"True Nature" by Les Kaye and "Drifting Clouds, Flowing Water" by Kyogen Carlson address common misperceptions about letting go, particularly as they apply to life in the business world. For Les Kaye, letting go involves giving up grasping or trying to get something for ourselves. It does not mean living aimlessly, or irresponsibly. It simply means that we keep our mind on what we are doing and trust the result.

Kyogen Carlson responds to the question of an entrepreneur who wonders how he can reconcile the idea of nonattachment with the idea of commitment. Confusing letting go with not caring, the businessperson believes that letting go will endanger his life savings and put the people who depend on him at risk. But Carlson teaches that letting go involves commitment—a commitment to give of ourselves, to our work and to others, as we become unattached to getting something for ourselves. For Carlson, letting go means doing your best and trusting that the result will come of itself rather than focusing so exclusively on the end result that the process is ignored.

James A. Autry and Stephen Mitchell also apply the attitude of letting go to a business environment. In "Giving Up Control" they describe the predetermination of results as the "tyranny of expectation" that may lead people in business to act in ways that represent compliant behavior but may have little to do with being productive.

In "Meditation" psychiatrist Mark Epstein tells of a patient who is a horseback rider and was not able to master a new set of hurdles because she was too focused on achievement. Her horse felt the tension and could not clear the hurdles. When she learned to let go of her need to force the end result, she was able to "surrender to the connection with her horse," and the jump went smoothly—once she was involved in what she was doing, and not focused exclusively on the goal.

Eugen Herrigel had a similar experience studying archery. Archery is an ironic metaphor for letting go since we expect archery to be focused on a goal—hitting the bull's-eye. In the excerpt from *Zen in the Art of Archery*, Herrigel talks of the years he spent with a Zen master learning how to draw the bow "spiritually." The lesson he learned is "purpose-lessness and aimlessness." What he discovered is that the more he tried to shoot for the sake of hitting the target, the less he succeeded. He learned to trust himself and let go of his fixation on the result. When he became involved in the shot, it became effortless. Letting go is a process that develops trust in ourselves and others.

Because the process of letting go begins with acceptance, it is not surprising that the twelve-step programs for letting go of addictions begin with acknowledging that there is a problem. In "Suffering Ends by Letting Go of Attachment to Desire: Learning to Let Things Be," Ronna Kabatz-nick urges us to look closely at the unpleasant feelings that we have—feelings of deprivation, of hate, of lust—in essence to acknowledge or accept them. "It's hard to let go," she says, "unless you know what you need to let go of."

# True Nature

## from *Zen at Work*

### by Les Kaye

I had a very short career as an IBM salesman. After I had been in the sales office for just over a year, I was asked to "prospect," to visit businesses in one of San Jose's older neighborhoods to identify and gain the interest of potential IBM customers. During the previous several months, I had completed IBM's sales and systems engineering training program, one of the most successful in the world. But despite my new marketing skills and the backing of IBM's reputation, I had a hard time lining up prospects.

I was troubled by the idea of actively trying to sell a product or a service to another person. I did not trust aggressive selling, feeling that it is intrusive, that it manipulates people through clever words, taking advantage of their weaknesses and their insecurities. I felt that people should be left alone to recognize for themselves what they need without having to be told or sold.

Yet I knew that there is nothing inherently wrong with selling. I recognized that it is a vital element of any cohesive community. In the marketplaces of earlier societies, in the modern department store, or in private, face-to-face negotiations, selling continues to be a fundamental way for people to exchange and share, to support each other with what they have to offer. I knew that selling can be creative and beneficial, if approached with integrity and thoughtfulness.

As a result of my conflicting feelings, I had trouble getting started as a salesman. I was aware that I had something to resolve.

During my first week of "prospecting," I got nowhere with the small companies in the pre–World War II industrial section of town. I couldn't get past the reception desks. I didn't know if my lack of success was caused by my resistance and fear of selling, poor technique, or simply being at the wrong place at the wrong time. For several days, I was discouraged, until finally, one morning, the office manager of a family-owned paving and gravel company accepted my offer to survey his business procedures to determine if automation would save time and money.

During the next week, the clerks and foremen showed me how their company manually handled its finances, its inventory, and the status of its jobs. I developed a new set of procedures for managing their information, based on the use of IBM's punch card equipment. Problem solving was the easy and enjoyable part—creating procedural flow diagrams and the analysis that showed time and dollar savings. But in the back of my mind was a nagging anxiety about making a "sales pitch."

First of all, there was fear, which I supposed was natural for a beginning salesman. I was afraid they wouldn't accept my proposal; I didn't like the prospect of being turned down, of hearing the dreaded no. But my anxiety didn't make logical sense. People at the paving company were pleased that I was studying their procedures and looked forward to my presentation. I knew that my fears were irrational and that it would be a mistake to give in to them, to run away, for example, by pleading to my sales manager, "I'm not a salesman, I'm an engineer! Get a more experienced guy to make the pitch!"

So I simply continued what I was doing, deciding that the best way to overcome my fear was to go into as much detail as was needed to convince myself that the system I was developing would really benefit the company. I learned something very interesting about fear: it arose only when I thought about the possible negative impact on me—will I fail? will I make a fool of myself?—rather than about the work and the potential positive effect on the company. As long as I kept my mind on what I was doing, I was OK.

I noticed something else about my reluctance. I was developing my analysis and sales approach from a single viewpoint: my own. On paper, I was sure that I could demonstrate how the use of IBM equipment would result in cost savings. But this would be the company's first venture into automation. I didn't know how they felt emotionally about such a major change. So I started to spend more time with the office manager and his staff, trying to understand their feelings about the business and its future. As I modified my sales approach to include their expectations and concerns, my anxiety diminished almost completely. I looked forward to making my sales pitch.

It almost worked. My sales presentation confidently demonstrated increased efficiency, better service, and money in the bank for this company. Everyone was pleased, with one exception. Until the day of my presentation, I had not met the key decision maker, the owner of the company, a man in his eighties who rarely came into the office because of a disability. Despite the logic of my analysis, his "gut feel" told him something else: the time was not right for a change. In my inexperience and eagerness to make the presentation, I had not recognized the necessity, the wisdom, of understanding the minds and gaining the confidence of everyone, without exception.

So I didn't close the sale. I felt disappointed not to succeed after all my struggles, another encounter with discouragement and the workings of my mind. However, the seeds were planted. Within a few years, the company began an extensive program of automation with IBM.

## WORLD WITHOUT BOUNDARIES

Our inherent nature, what is known in Buddhism as our true nature, is without limit, so vast that it includes everything. It means that we, ourselves, include everything and at the same time that we are included in everything. But it is impossible to appreciate our lives in this way by just thinking about them with our rational minds. If we use only our analytic capacity to try to understand our lives and the world we live in, we will overlook the vastness of our true world, the world of our true nature. The limitless world, the world without boundaries, cannot be reached by thinking.

The thinking mind constantly comes up against the limits of what it knows at some particular moment. As we make our efforts in daily life to understand situations and solve various problems, we increase our knowledge and push back the boundaries of what we know about our everyday world. And as our knowledge and experience grow wider, the limits expand. Yet even as the thinking mind expands the limit of what it knows, it comes up against boundaries. And because that is its everyday experience, it believes that the entire world inherently has boundaries. But a world of boundaries is a made-up world, created by the limitations of our rational minds.

When we envision a world of boundaries, we logically presume that it must have a center. The small mind—the ego—then tries to make itself the center of this world. But it is impossible to stand in the center of a made-up world. When we try to stand in this imaginary center, we feel off balance and anxious. We attempt to relieve our anxiety by filling our made-up world with material and emotional things. We may even try to obtain enlightenment. However, enlightenment does not exist in a world of boundaries, a made-up world. Enlightenment exists in the world without limits, the vast world that shows itself when we are not trying to be at the center. The point of Zen practice is to let go of ideas about boundaries and to feel our limitless true nature. When we express our limitless true minds, we understand that there are no boundaries and no center. Then we are no longer concerned about being the center.

When we first feel limitless mind, we may also feel various emotions, such as anger, sadness, or discouragement. These feelings are just the small mind trying to be the center. Our egos do not want to give up their world of boundaries because they do not want to give up ideas about themselves. So if we feel discouraged, it is just the stubbornness of our thinking minds. Even if we feel stubbornness, the best thing to do is to continue mindfulness and stay aware of what we are feeling. There is no need to turn away from limitlessness because we feel some emotion. We only need to continue with confidence and let ourselves drop into the world of no limits.

In the limitless world, we do not know where we are going. But this is not a problem because inherently we have nowhere to go. When we feel our limitlessness, we just move in the direction of Big Mind, the mind that includes everything. In the limitless world, we just let Big Mind be our guide.

Big Mind can appear when our hearts start to open and our concerns turn from ourselves to others. Then our true nature can express itself. When we feel our minds turn from "inside" to "outside," we should move in that direction, toward compassion and the relief of suffering. To do so, we have to make an effort not to become sidetracked by ideas of comfort or pleasure or desire. Otherwise, we will create a limited, made-up world again.

Desires are very strong. Like drugs, they promise us excitement and comfort, but they fool us, so that we want to make our efforts only for ourselves. A life driven by desire creates serious problems for us and for others. So when desire appears, we continue observing the thinking mind trying to fool itself. We watch how it tries to create boundaries and establish itself as the center. When we become aware of what our mind is doing, we should make an effort to let go of the boundaries and of ourself as the center of some small world. Our spiritual practice is to let the mind be wide so that it can resume its vastness. Then we can express our true selves and give ourselves to life and to others.

## NOTHING TO CATCH

In Zen practice, we do not try to obtain anything, not even peace of mind. Trying to obtain something for our minds actually disturbs our peace of mind. Ironically, by trying to obtain peace of mind, we lose it. Only when we do not try to obtain it can we have peace of mind.

It is impossible to obtain what we already possess. Similarly, we cannot express what we already possess if we are trying to obtain it. So if we feel discouraged in our practice, it is an indication that we are trying to obtain something for our minds rather than expressing what we already have. Zen practice expresses what we inherently possess.

Inherently, every one of us has complete wisdom. But because we do not understand our fundamental nature, we strive to obtain wisdom and concern ourselves with having some experience of it. The point of our practice is simply to give inherent wisdom a chance. We begin by trusting it. And in order to trust inherent wisdom, we first have to trust ourselves. Practice must begin with deep trust in ourselves. If we emphasize obtaining something for our minds, it means that we do not trust ourselves or our inherent wisdom. So we practice zazen to let go of self-oriented ideas. This is the basis for trusting ourselves and for giving inherent wisdom a chance.

Inherent wisdom is real; it is Reality itself. However, it cannot come from emphasizing something substantial, something material that we can recognize with our rational, everyday minds. Everyday mind is limited to things of the phenomenal world, things of form and color and sound and feelings. By contrast, the basis of wisdom is our true nature, which everyday mind cannot reach. If we try to obtain wisdom or happiness, we are attempting to grasp something that cannot be held like a physical object. This kind of effort leads only to disappointment.

Imagine a child trying to catch a soap bubble. After playing with bubbles for a short time, the child learns their nature. He understands that they are insubstantial and gives up trying to catch them. He understands the nature of bubbles without thinking about it. He doesn't say to himself, "I understand. These bubbles have no permanent nature." Just watching and playing with them, the child understands and enjoys them as they are. But if the child cannot understand the nature of bubbles through his experience, he will continue to try to catch them and will become unhappy when he cannot.

It is fruitless for us to try to grasp wisdom or peace of mind. We should simply let practice be the basis of our lives. Then our inherent wisdom can reveal itself. Then we can realize our inherent completeness and we can see that there is no need to obtain or grasp anything. That is how we learn to appreciate and enjoy bubbles.

Giving up grasping does not mean giving up the activities of our daily lives. And it does not mean that we live aimlessly by not taking care of things and the responsibilities that we have to each other and the world. It simply means that we let our lives be living continuations of activities. An activity is alive for us when we give ourselves up in its midst, just letting ourselves be the activity without trying to obtain something for our minds. When we do that, we feel the joy of doing something free from desire. Then we feel enlivened and refreshed. That is real freedom.

Our lives do not belong to us. We are just taking care of them. So our practice is to give up our self-oriented view of life, to give up trying to obtain things for our minds, and to understand how to truly take care of whatever comes along. Then we can enjoy the bubbles.

# Giving Up Control

## from *Real Power*

### by James A. Autry and Stephen Mitchell

If you want to be a great leader,
you must learn to follow the Tao.
Stop trying to control.
Let go of fixed plans and concepts,
and the world will govern itself.

The more prohibitions you have,
the less virtuous people will be . . .

–from the *Tao Te Ching*

The more rules you make, the less people will do things on their own and the more effort they will put into circumventing your rules. Most companies operate on the principle that if employees are given half a chance they'll do something wrong. A culture of prohibition derives from two common management shortcomings: the compulsion to control and the desire to manage people in groups rather than one at a time. Typically, if an employee is doing something that is counterproductive, the manager will avoid confronting the employee directly and will instead send a memo or write a policy prohibiting everyone from doing what only one employee is doing.

Most people will do the right thing when left to use their own judgment. And most of the time, an appeal to common sense will suffice. In one sales and marketing company, it became clear that a pattern of excessive attendance at trade shows had developed over the years. Too many people from the company were spending too much time and money covering the trade shows. The attendance list had grown as the company had prospered and more people were hired. No one had ever questioned the number.

As a remedy, the senior vice president of sales might have said to his department heads, "Listen, folks, we have over fifty people attending the such-and-such show at a cost of almost a hundred thousand dollars, twice a year. Figure out a way to cut this down and still get the show covered." That's it. It would have been done as a matter of common sense and good planning.

Instead, the senior VP devised a complicated formula for determining who should attend trade shows, and when. In addition, he required trip and call reports and a narrative of each day's activities. The result was a burdensome chore for the salespeople and a chore for the VP's staff in reviewing and filing all this paperwork. It took all flexibility out of the selection process, which in turn stimulated a lot of creative attempts to qualify for attendance.

The company should state clearly that it will operate within the letter and the spirit of the law, and according to the highest moral standards. Nothing more needs to be said. Rules should be limited to three categories: (1) what the law requires and what procedures the company has instituted in order to comply with the law; (2) policies that guide people in techniques or procedures about the work flow and efficiency, operational and accountability matters, purchasing, budgeting, approvals, and so on (some of which is connected to legal compliance); (3) policies and guidelines about hiring, appraisals and evaluations, compensation (some of which is also connected to legal compliance)—and of course, there should be manuals and other explicit employee materials explaining benefits.

It's not the policies listed above that cause the problems; it's the ad hoc policies of individual departments. A manager might say, "I think too many people are surfing the Internet instead of doing their jobs. Let's have a policy against that." This assumes that if the employee is doing anything not specifically in the job description, he must not be working. In earlier days, a favorite target was talk sessions at the watercooler. And some managers still mentally clock their employees in and out for lunch breaks.

But what's the appropriate way to evaluate work? By results or by appearances? Who says that surfing the Net can't be a productive way to get good ideas? Who says that playing computer games for a while isn't better for relaxation than an approved coffee break? Who really knows the source of people's creativity? If you focus on appearances instead of results, you are creating an environment in which people invest their energy in appearances rather than results. If your employees are achieving good results and behaving with respect for one another, so what if they aren't doing it according to the rules?

The more you try to tell people exactly how to do their work, the less they'll bring their creativity to it. The more you try to control, the less influence you'll have. The wise leader knows that nothing good can be compelled from people; it can only be elicited from them. By letting go of the need for control, both he and the employees are liberated from the tyranny of expectation, and the workplace becomes a center of creativity, commitment, passion, and productive activity.

# Drifting Clouds, Flowing Water

## from *Zen in the American Grain*

### by Kyogen Carlson

"Here's a question for you. How can I manage to practice nonattachment when everything I have is invested in this business? In this situation, everything I have worked for, and that others have worked for too, could be lost tomorrow. Just one false move and we'd all be out of work." I was being asked, in effect, "How can I be responsible in a really tough situation like this if I remain unattached, and don't care about how things turn out?" The man asking this question was one who had had a career working for government agencies and was in the process of starting his own company. It was at that critical, fledgling stage of beginning to take off, but in need of constant care and feeding. The pressures on him were tremendous and unrelenting, for one miscalculation and his savings and life's work could be lost, and that of others as well. But in terms of practice, he was far from alone in this predicament. The specifics of his situation may have been different, but this question is the same one asked by Buddhists for centuries. It has always been the case that responsible people, at home as well as at work, find that others depend upon them, sometimes a great deal. It can seem that every way they turn there are commitments and responsibilities. In addition, this man was at an age when he could see the many options of youth dropping away. As we recognize this happening, it becomes clear how the choices we make can have profound, long-term consequences. Therefore, they require very careful consideration. What does nonattachment mean in these situations? And how in the world does nonattachment harmonize with the idea of commitment?

The word for a Buddhist monk in Sino-Japanese is "Unsui," literally "cloud, water." It comes, originally, from the phrase "gyounryusyu," or "drifting clouds, flowing water." Neither clouds nor water insist upon any particular form, for they take shape according to conditions. Clouds attach to nothing, and so drift freely across the sky. Water twists and turns on its way downhill in complete accord with the path it must follow. The flowing of the water has the strength to move mountains, while the drifting of the clouds is utterly free. In these qualities we have a perfect description of the Zen mind. Just as clouds cling to nothing, floating free and changing with the wind, acceptance of change is the essence of nonattachment and expresses the perfect freedom of meditation. Flowing water follows its course naturally, without resistance or hesitation. This lack of resistance describes the willingness at the heart of a true commitment to Zen practice, which like water, has the strength to move mountains. To become a monk, an Unsui, requires ordination. By its very nature, ordination means a deep commitment to the form of practice we call Zen Buddhism. It also means a commitment to a teacher, and to a Sangha, or community of fellow trainees. Ordination means a commitment to a life of training in nonattachment, so right from the very beginning, the concepts of nonattachment and commitment are present together in Zen teaching.

What exactly does nonattachment in Zen practice mean? First of all, it does not imply a lack of feeling, or a quietistic unconcern. Basically, nonattachment means all-acceptance with willingness and positivity of mind. All-acceptance means complete willingness to admit that things are exactly as they are. This implies absolutely nothing about whether or not they can or should be changed, but it does mean seeing things clearly. After all, we can't understand something that is right in front of us if we do not first accept that it is. When we see things clearly with an all-accepting mind, we stand a much better chance of acting wisely. All-acceptance means to drop the "self," with all its preferences, opinions, and attachments, whenever it arises, remembering our own free, natural mind of meditation.

In the practice of all-acceptance, one of the toughest things to do is to drop attachment to the results of our most carefully planned actions. Because we usually have strong expectations about how our efforts should turn out, we often can't accept the results we actually get. Wisdom will be quickly lost, despite our good intentions, if we are unable to live in nonattachment while in the midst of endeavors we care very much about. Nonattachment does not, therefore, mean we can indulge in the selfish "freedom" of dropping responsibility, but rather that we make a vow to drop self-centeredness in the midst of responsible action.

Now what about commitment? Commitment, of course, always implies taking on responsibility. If "resolve" is the effort we bring forth at each moment, commitment is the willingness to keep at something over time. Commitment in Zen practice means to try to do our best in all situations to make our lives an expression of that practice. A job, marriage, family ties, relationship to a temple, as well as becoming a monk, can all be expressions of practice if we make a commitment to ourselves to make it so. Commitment means a willingness to be relied upon, time and time again, in specific ways. As a parent, spouse, or friend it is in sharing ourselves with others, as in giving and receiving emotional and physical support. As a worker, it is in giving our best effort and being part of the team. As a man or woman on the path of Zen, it is in making all actions expressions of that practice. You can make the whole world your monastery, and all living things your Sangha if you are sincere in this. It is through this practice that we come to see the Truth appearing everywhere. Whether or not those around us also practice does not matter if we concentrate hard on making our own lives expressions of practice. It can be done, but it takes real commitment to do it.

While it is true that living and practicing as a monk are different from lay life and practice, some things are not so different as many people think. The entrepreneur with his life savings at stake has no more invested in his enterprise than a monk does in his practice. Some years ago, while still living at the monastery, I faced knee surgery. This was no great matter medically, but with it came the realization that I had no financial resources whatsoever of my own. The monastery could not help me, and I found that I had to seek public assistance. I was just about thirty years old at the time, and I had spent the previous eight years in the monastery. I had worked very hard and learned a great deal, but my rewards were not in the least bit financial. It was then that it occurred to me that with each passing year doors were closing behind me. I realized with great clarity that it is very difficult to consider another career when just about your entire work experience is as a Zen monk. Not that I would ever want to, fortunately, but the seriousness of the decision I made in my early twenties became vividly clear. A monk invests his life in developing selflessness, and he forgoes other things. Yet, in a very real sense, he is just as tied to this commitment, if not more so, as a layman is to his career and family. The true freedom of the Unsui, it turns out, is realized when he fully embraces the depth of commitment the life demands, willingly following the course of training without resistance, like flowing water. It is definitely not found in a "carefree" nonattachment. It is in this commitment to selflessness that the deepest meaning of Zen training is found, and it is in commitment that the practice of nonattachment has its deepest form.

Nonattachment and commitment meet in willingness. The willingness to accept things as they are, and the willingness to let things go; this is the essence of nonattachment. The willingness to give of ourselves, to be depended upon, and the willingness to keep at a form of practice over time; this is the essence of commitment. Willingness is the mind bright and positive, the will flexible, the ability to bow; what could better sum up Zen practice?

Zen training is sometimes referred to as stillness within activity, and activity within stillness. In compassionate all-acceptance we find the life of Kanzeon Bosatsu*: stillness, the quiet of meditation, the essence of nonattachment. In responsibility we find the life of Fugen Bosatsu: loving action, transcendence of the opposites, the true meaning of commitment. Stillness and activity, nonattachment and commitment, are the clouds and water of the Unsui. Together they lead to the life of Monju, wisdom itself. A life of nonattachment without commitment is like a tree without its roots in the ground. It will grow progressively weaker, so how could this be true freedom? Nonattachment within commitment brings peace of mind when you know that you can bow no matter how things turn out, even should your business fail; for then you can know that you have done your very best. In the life of a Zen trainee, success at the deepest level is found in this willingness to accept all things positively, the willingness to bow, and it is not measured by any external yardstick. You can make your own life an expression of this practice by embracing your many responsibilities within nonattachment. The duties of daily life can be transformed into a commitment to practice if you vow to perform

---

*The three Bodhisattvas of Kanzeon, Fugen, and Monju (Avalokitesvara, Samantabhadra, and Manjusri in Sanskrit) represent the Buddha's compassion, loving kindness, and wisdom, respectively. They are three aspects of enlightenment that exist within each of us.

them compassionately and with all-acceptance, drop attachment to re-sults, and vow to keep going each day and to do your best for all con-cerned. This requires the willingness to accept things as they are, and the willingness to be depended upon. It requires keeping the mind bright and positive, the will flexible, and the ability to bow; what could better sum up Zen training?

# Meditation

from *Going to Pieces Without Falling Apart*
by Mark Epstein

There is an expression in horseback riding circles that one is supposed to ride with "soft eyes," letting the world go by without focusing on any one thing too specifically. I learned about it from a patient who was having a problem doing complicated jumps with her horse, but I was interested in the broader applications of what she discovered. My patient, a young woman named Marilyn, was an accomplished rider, but, as she described it, she was "too involved" when it came to mastering a new set of hurdles. She was too focused on achievement, she told me, to permit her "soft eyes" to develop. Unable to relax into the jump, her tension and her desire for success interfered with the horse's capacity to navigate the obstacles cleanly. Like an actor stumbling over her lines, Marilyn grew more and more unsure of herself, and her performance became more and more self-conscious.

One of her riding instructors showed Marilyn a way to distract herself from her worried anticipation. He urged her to imagine that an additional turn took place after the final leap. He gave her a method of getting her mind out of the way. This mental trick worked beautifully. Rather than becoming fixated on the jump as the culmination of her efforts, Marilyn was able to set the jump up and then move on. As she was visualizing the imaginary turn, her horse soared perfectly into the air. Because her mind was at ease, Marilyn was able to sit back and enjoy the fruits of her efforts.

As Marilyn told me her story, I realized that she had been resisting that critical moment when her self fell away, when she and the horse and the jump became one. By worrying over how well she was doing, she was perpetuating the hold of her ego, refusing to allow it to fade back into transparency. Her ambition had been interfering with her success. Her riding instructor's efforts to show Marilyn her "soft eyes" were attempts to bring forward her capacity for unintegration, to allow her to surrender into the connection with her horse that the jump demanded. What was interesting was that Marilyn needed a trick to make this natural thing happen. Telling her to have "soft eyes" was not enough; she needed something to do with her mind to get it out of the way. This is the function of meditation practice: It provides a method of getting the mind out of the way so that we can be at one with our experience.

While I have never been much of a horseback rider, I could relate to Marilyn's predicament, and to her solution. When I was in elementary school, I developed something of a stammer, especially when I had to introduce myself or say my own name. My anticipation of having to speak, like Marilyn's anticipation of having to jump, created such a reaction within me that I became immobilized. My parents finally took me to a speech therapist, a kindly gray-haired woman named Mrs. Stanton whose musty office I remember was up a long and dusty flight of stairs in downtown New Haven. We played board games, which I enjoyed, and while we played we would talk. She told me once about a man with a stutter who had a particularly difficult time with words that began with the letter w. He would always have trouble when he had to introduce his wife at a party. I remember laughing together, with some horror on my part, over the plight of this poor gentleman, struggling to introduce his w-w-w-wife. In the midst of these games and discussions, Mrs. Stanton taught me how to distract myself when the stammering was imminent. By stamping my foot lightly, or touching the table in front of me, I could create enough space for the words to come. Just as Marilyn had learned how to get out of the way so that she could jump, I learned how to let go so that I could speak.

Years later, when I would get stuck in a therapy session, my therapist would urge much the same strategy. "Speak without thinking," he would tell me. I was always surprised to find that I would say just the right thing. The lesson was similar. Speech does not always have to be thought out beforehand. We discover what we need to say when we get out of the way of ourselves.

# Zen in the Art of Archery

## by Eugen Herrigel

To be able to draw the bow "spiritually" after a year, that is, with a kind of effortless strength, is no very startling achievement. And yet I was well content, for I had begun to understand why the system of self-defense whereby one brings one's opponent to the ground by unexpectedly giving way, with effortless resilience, to his passionately delivered attack, thus turning his own strength against him, is known as "the gentle art." Since the remotest times its symbol has been the yielding and yet unconquerable water, so that Lao-tzu could say with profound truth that right living is like water, which "of all things the most yielding can overwhelm that which is of all things most hard."* Moreover, the saying of the Master went round in school that "whoever makes good progress in the beginning has all the more difficulties later on." For me the beginning had been far from easy: was I not entitled, therefore, to feel confident in the face of what was to come, and the difficulties of which I was already beginning to suspect?

The next thing to be learned was the "loosing" of the arrow. Up to now we had been allowed to do this haphazardly: it stood in parentheses, as it were, on the margin of the exercises. And what happened to the arrow was even more a matter of indifference. So long as it pierced the roll of pressed straw which served the double purpose of target and sandbank, honor was deemed to have been satisfied. To hit it was no great feat, since we were only ten paces away from it at most.

---

*The Way and Its Power, tr. by Arthur Waley, London 1934, ch. XLIII, p. 197.

Hitherto I had simply let go of the bowstring when the hold at the point of highest tension had become unendurable, when I felt I had to give way if my parted hands were not forcibly to be pulled together again. The tension is not in any sense painful. A leather glove with a stiffened and thickly padded thumb guards against the pressure of the string becoming uncomfortable and prematurely shortening the hold at the point of highest tension. When drawing, the thumb is wrapped round the bowstring immediately below the arrow, and tucked in. The first three fingers are gripped over it firmly, and at the same time give the arrow a secure hold. Loosing therefore means: opening the fingers that grip the thumb and setting it free. Through the tremendous pull of the string the thumb is wrenched from its position, stretched out, the string whirrs and the arrow flies. When I had loosed hitherto, the shot had never gone off without a powerful jerk, which made itself felt in a visible shaking of my whole body and affected the bow and arrow as well. That there could be no possibility of a smooth and, above all, certain shot goes without saying: it was bound to "wobble."

"All that you have learned hitherto," said the Master one day when he found nothing more to object to in my relaxed manner of drawing the bow, "was only a preparation for loosing the shot. We are now faced with a new and particularly difficult task, which brings us to a new stage in the art of archery." So saying, the Master gripped his bow, drew it and shot. Only now, when expressly watching out for it, did I observe that though the right hand of the Master, suddenly opened and released by the tension, flew back with a jerk, it did not cause the least shaking of the body. The right arm, which before the shot had formed an acute angle, was jerked open, but ran gently back into full extension. The unavoidable jerk had been cushioned and neutralized.

If the force of the discharge did not betray itself in the sharp "thup" of the quivering bowstring and in the penetrative power of the arrow, one would never suspect its existence. At least in the case of the Master the loose looked so simple and undemanding that it might have been child's play.

The effortlessness of a performance for which great strength is needed is a spectacle of whose aesthetic beauty the East has an exceedingly sensitive and grateful appreciation. But ever more important to me—and at that stage I could hardly think otherwise—was the fact that the certainty of hitting seemed to depend on the shot's being smoothly loosed. I knew from rifle-shooting what a difference it makes to jerk away, if only slightly, from the line of sight. All that I had learned and achieved so far only became intelligible to me from this point of view: relaxed drawing of the bow, relaxed holding at the point of highest tension, relaxed loosing of the shot, relaxed cushioning of the recoil—did not all this serve the grand purpose of hitting the target, and was not this the reason why we were learning archery with so much trouble and patience? Why then had the Master spoken as if the process we were now concerned with far exceeded everything we had practiced and accustomed ourselves to up till now?

However that may be, I went on practicing diligently and conscientiously according to the Master's instructions, and yet all my efforts were in vain. Often it seemed to me that I had shot better before, when I loosed the shot at random without thinking about it. Above all I noticed that I could not open the right hand, and particularly the fingers gripping the thumb, without exertion. The result was a jerk at the moment of release, so that the arrow wobbled. Still less was I capable of cushioning the suddenly freed hand. The Master continued undeterred to demonstrate the correct loose; undeterred I sought to do like him with the sole result that I grew more uncertain than ever. I seemed like the centipede which was unable to stir from the spot after trying to puzzle out in what order its feet ought to go.

The Master was evidently less horrified by my failure than I myself. Did he know from experience that it would come to this? "Don't think of what you have to do, don't consider how to carry it out!" he exclaimed. "The shot will only go smoothly when it takes the archer himself by surprise. It must be as if the bowstring suddenly cut through the thumb that held it. You mustn't open the right hand on purpose."

There followed weeks and months of fruitless practice. I could take my standard again and again from the way the Master shot, see with my own eyes the nature of the correct loose; but not a single one succeeded. If, waiting in vain for the shot, I gave way to the tension because it began to be unendurable, then my hands were slowly pulled together, and the shot came to nothing. If I grimly resisted the tension till I was gasping for breath, I could only do so by calling on the arm and shoulder muscles for aid. I then stood there immobilized—like a statue, I mocked the Master—but tense, and my relaxedness was gone.

Perhaps it was chance, perhaps it was deliberately arranged by the Master, that we one day found ourselves together over a cup of tea. I seized on this opportunity for a discussion and poured my heart out.

"I understand well enough," I said, "that the hand mustn't be opened with a jerk if the shot is not to be spoiled. But however I set about it, it always goes wrong. If I clench my hand as tightly as possible, I can't stop it shaking when I open my fingers. If, on the other hand, I try to keep it relaxed, the bowstring is torn from my grasp before the full stretch is reached—unexpectedly, it is true, but still too early. I am caught between these two kinds of failure and see no way of escape." "You must hold the drawn bowstring," answered the Master, "like a little child holding the proffered finger. It grips it so firmly that one marvels at the strength of the tiny fist. And when it lets the finger go, there is not the slightest jerk. Do you know why? Because a child doesn't think: I will now let go of the finger in order to grasp this other thing. Completely unself-consciously, without purpose, it turns from one to the other, and we would say that it was playing with the things, were it not equally true that the things are playing with the child."

"Maybe I understand what you are hinting at with this comparison," I remarked. "But am I not in an entirely different situation? When I have drawn the bow, the moment comes when I feel: unless the shot comes at once I shan't be able to endure the tension. And what happens then? Merely that I get out of breath. So I must loose the shot whether I want to or not, because I can't wait for it any longer."

"You have described only too well," replied the Master, "where the difficulty lies. Do you know why you cannot wait for the shot and why you get out of breath before it has come? The right shot at the right moment does not come because you do not let go of yourself. You do not wait for fulfillment, but brace yourself for failure. So long as that is so, you have no choice but to call forth something yourself that ought to happen independently of you, and so long as you call it forth your hand will not open in the right way—like the hand of a child. Your hand does not burst open like the skin of a ripe fruit."

I had to admit to the Master that this interpretation made me more confused than ever. "For ultimately," I said, "I draw the bow and loose the shot in order to hit the target. The drawing is thus a means to an end, and I cannot lose sight of this connection. The child knows nothing of this, but for me the two things cannot be disconnected."

"The right art," cried the Master, "is purposeless, aimless! The more obstinately you try to learn how to shoot the arrow for the sake of hitting the goal, the less you will succeed in the one and the further the other will recede. What stands in your way is that you have a much too willful will. You think that what you do not do yourself does not happen."

"But you yourself have told me often enough that archery is not a pastime, not a purposeless game, but a matter of life and death!"

"I stand by that. We master archers say: one shot—one life! What this means, you cannot yet understand. But perhaps another image will help you, which expresses the same experience. We master archers say: with the upper end of the bow the archer pierces the sky; on the lower end, as though attached by a thread, hangs the earth. If the shot is loosed with a jerk there is a danger of the thread snapping. For purposeful and violent people the rift becomes final, and they are left in the awful center between heaven and earth."

"What must I do, then?" I asked thoughtfully.

"You must learn to wait properly."

"And how does one learn that?"

"By letting go of yourself, leaving yourself and everything of yours behind you so decisively that nothing more is left of you but a purpose-less tension."

"So I must become purposeless—on purpose?" I heard myself say.

"No pupil has ever asked me that, so I don't know the right answer."

"And when do we begin these new exercises?"

"Wait until it is time."

# Suffering Ends by Letting Go of Attachment to Desire: Learning to Let Things Be

from *The Zen of Eating:*

*Ancient Answers to Modern Weight Problems*

by Ronna Kabatznick

The third Noble Truth presents the solution to the problem and cause of emotional hunger. It states: Suffering ends by letting go of attachment to desire. Letting go of suffering is a process. It involves learning how to dissolve the source of suffering that drives you to eat but never feel satisfied. You let go of the "I've got to (need to, have to, love to, hate to, want to, don't want to)" feelings that lie at the heart of suffering/emotional hunger, and that bond you to the objects of desire (lose weight, eat more cookies, exercise, etc.). When there's no grasping, there's a spacious feeling of acceptance with the way things are. It's this experience that offers the nourishment you've been looking for.

Letting go doesn't mean annihilating, rejecting feelings, or pretending that you don't have strong feelings. There's no point in saying, "I'm not into losing weight; I've let go of that," when you're really lusting after a slim body. It's equally absurd to deny being angry when you're so enraged that you can hardly contain yourself. This is fooling yourself, not letting go. Letting go means learning how to become intimate with the lust and rage and learning how to relate to these attachments without grasping, acting out, or repressing them. This is a lifelong task that takes a lot of practice, patience, and compassion for yourself.

## MARILYN'S PATTERN OF REJECTION
## AND LETTING GO OF IT

Marilyn, a clothing designer in her late thirties, wanted to reshape her eating habits because she had gained a lot of weight. Very few of her elegant clothes fit her anymore. During the process of losing weight, Marilyn regularly had images about being rejected. When she was nine, Marilyn was rejected by a school friend and was distraught about it for months. She was an only child and he was her only friend. Marilyn depended on walking to school with him and playing together on weekends. She concluded that there was something bad about her that caused her only friend to leave. Her rational mind kept saying, "It's ridiculous to be upset about something that happened so long ago," but her behavior told a different story. She was driven by the fear of rejection and that fear had become an integral part of her self-image. Marilyn was terrified of people leaving her. She anticipated rejection wherever she went. She ate and overate to compensate for intense feelings of loneliness.

Marilyn decided to pay attention to how this childhood experience was impacting her adult life. That decision initiated her into the letting-go process. It's hard to let go unless you know what you need to let go of. Letting go for Marilyn meant learning to become intimate with the fear of rejection: how she anticipated rejection and even initiated it, both with others and within herself.

Marilyn observed these patterns the way she would watch an actress on a movie screen. This offered her a sense of detachment so that she could be more objective about what she was seeing.

Marilyn began noticing many things: her aloof attitude, her preference to stay uninvolved, the amount of time she spent worrying about being rejected, anticipating how much it was going to hurt, and the feelings of relief when she was alone.

Rather than getting upset or frustrated by what she observed, Marilyn acknowledged the presence of these feelings. She watched them and realized that they all changed at one point or another. She was surprised to find that the more familiar she became with feeling rejected, the more open she was to others, and the more others opened to her. Her relationship to food also changed. The more she allowed those feelings to come and go, the less she needed to cut off that process by overeating.

Investigating her relationship to rejection was the doorway to freedom. In other words, Marilyn let go of her fear of rejection through her willingness to experience all the facets of that fear without grasping or clinging. She realized how much suffering she had perpetuated within herself by avoiding those feelings. When she felt these feelings instead of rejecting them, she was no longer re-creating the conditions for rejection that were based on her early childhood experience.

## LETTING GO IS LETTING BE

The key to letting go of attachment to desire is to acknowledge and feel the experiences of grasping and clinging within you. This isn't easy. If you don't like the feeling of rejection, there's grasping. You want to get rid of rejection. As Marilyn learned, rejecting rejection only intensified the fear of it, her loneliness, and her habit of overeating.

There's nothing inherently wrong with fear or hatred or even aggression. But when you're attached to them and take them personally or act them out mindlessly, you create suffering by cutting off the nourishment supply they offer. It's impossible to connect with your own vulnerability, compassion, and gentleness when you're caught up in hating yourself or wanting to be right in an argument or having to be the best cook in town.

Marilyn realized that her painful pattern of behavior was related to early experiences of rejection, but that understanding wasn't enough to end the suffering. Letting go is not an intellectual exercise to see how smart you are. You can come up with all the rational reasons in the world to explain away attachments to desire, but if you don't actually let go of them, they'll continue to be a source of suffering.

By staying with the raw feelings of grasping (hatred, love, self-righteousness, boredom, or whatever) you open up to awareness itself. Your willingness to stay with these feelings transcends your attachment to them because in the moment of awareness, those concepts disappear. There's not even a you there; there's just acceptance. When your mind is free from attachments to desire, it assumes a natural state of balance and a spacious feeling of nourishment. The deep nourishment that comes from letting go serves as lasting food for your mind and heart.

This creates space for new possibilities and choices that otherwise would not be available. You can still have a strong desire to lose weight, but when you're not attached to that desire, you also have the freedom to choose how to respond to it. You don't feel compelled to latch on to the latest weight-loss gimmick or meal replacement bar. You can make a reasonable decision about the best way to go about it, depending on the circumstances of your life and what you know about yourself.

In fact, Marilyn continued to experience fear of rejection, but it no longer had the grip that it once had on her. She was familiar with the many facets of it. When these feelings came up within her, she allowed them to arise and pass away without interference. They didn't cut her off from opportunities to enjoy herself, like going to parties or taking walks with friends.

You can practice letting go of anything: feeling deprived, beliefs about your self-image, the desire to be thin, wanting dessert every day, or needing to feel desirable at the expense of your self-respect. Letting go of an attachment to hatred is no different from letting go of an attachment to love. Letting go of attachment to anything allows a spacious feeling of peace to expand and breathe within you.

Letting go doesn't mean any of these desires disappear. It means that they no longer have control over you. Your response to them changes from feelings of a requirement, to realizing there are options. You can be lonely and not overeat. You can feel anxious without judging yourself. You can be a bagel expert or have strong opinions about proper table manners and eating habits and not create suffering for yourself or others. In short, you are no longer a slave to your desires, to your Hungry Ghost or to that inner authority that's constantly telling you to look for happiness where it can't be found. Above all, you don't have to be beholden to patterns of behavior that don't serve you well.

## NASRUDIN'S NEIGHBOR

Nasrudin was eating a simple meal of chick-peas and bread at the same time his neighbor was dining on a sumptuous meal provided by the emperor. His neighbor suggested, "If you would learn to flatter the emperor, then you wouldn't have to eat chick-peas and bread." Nasrudin replied, "If you would learn to let go of those sumptuous meals and live on chick-peas and bread, then you wouldn't have to flatter the emperor."

Nasrudin and his neighbor had different relationships toward eating well. His neighbor was attached to eating well. He needed to eat a certain kind of meal in order to be happy with it. But his need to eat a certain way meant he was beholden to his desires. He wasn't free to enjoy a simple meal; he needed sumptuous ones. He was compelled to flatter the emperor; he wasn't free to behave in a more authentic way.

On the other hand, Nasrudin wasn't attached to eating well. He had let go of it. Nasrudin could enjoy the simplicity of his meal and didn't have to flatter anyone. Unlike his friend, Nasrudin could preserve his dignity instead of compromising it. He wasn't beholden to a pattern of behavior that didn't serve him well or that created a sense of suffering within him. He didn't need sumptuous meals to support an image of himself in this way. He was free of that.

## A CLOSER LOOK AT LETTING GO

Let's look at a familiar experience and go through the process step by step. Let's say you want to let go of mindless eating. You hate feeling that you can't eat whatever you want, whenever you want it. It makes you feel deprived. Here's what to do:

*Step One:* Identify the cause of suffering (the attachment to desire). The feeling of hatred is your attachment to the desire to eat mindlessly. It's what binds you to this desire and causes suffering. That feeling of hatred is the focus of the letting-go process.

*Step Two:* Explore how the attachment feels within you. Make the effort to become familiar with hatred. What's it like to hate? Where do you feel hatred in your body? What thoughts do you have about it in your mind? Is it comfortable or painful to hate?

*Step Three:* Explore your relationship to the attachment. Learn about how you relate to the attachment. This is what binds you to it and keeps the suffering alive. Do you like or dislike the feeling of hatred? Do you want it to stay or do you want to make it go away? If you don't like the feeling of hatred, there's usually resistance to feeling it. Resistance to hatred uncovers another layer of attachment, another source of suffering. There's hatred toward mindless eating (your attachment) and there's also a feeling of hatred toward the hatred (your relationship to the attachment). You don't like the idea of being someone who hates.

*Step Four:* Become intimate with the attachment and your relationship to it. Explore what resisting hating feels like. Where is it in your body? What thoughts do you have about it in your mind? What actions are you tempted to take? Your intimacy with hatred and hating hatred lie at the heart of the letting-go process. Your ability to make peace with these experiences is what helps release you from the hold they have on you.

*Step Five:* Notice what happens. Your attachments give you the opportunity to develop patience and kindness toward them, and the grasping melts away. Then you are free to choose the best response to the situation: what's really best for you and also for others.

When you pay attention to the way hatred works (and the way hating hatred works), there's no struggle, there's no grasping, there's no clinging. If there's no struggle, there's no suffering. If there's no suffering, there's no problem. You are free to receive nourishment from hatred (or any other attachment) because the nourishment comes from your willingness to be fully in the present moment, no matter what it is.

## BARRIERS TO LETTING GO

From birth, you are conditioned to relate things to yourself. You learn your name, where you live, who your parents are, and which toys are yours. These are important things to know in life because they help create the concept of who you think you are. You continuously add new concepts to who you imagine yourself to be: "I'm overweight," "I'm physically fit," "I'm a good cook," or "I'm a vegetarian," for example. Once the concepts become me, there's also the need to defend them, because that's who you think you are.

If you think you are a gourmet cook, you worry about how everything tastes. If you believe you're physically fit, you spend your time trying to stay that way. If you believe you're frightened of gaining weight, you obsess about what you put in your mouth.

But these descriptions of me are only concepts, and they survive only

because you cling to them. The truth is they're not who you are because who you are is constantly changing. If you don't understand the temporary and fleeting nature of these descriptions, you struggle to make them permanent. This struggle to make these descriptions permanent is what makes letting go so difficult. You don't want to give up the idea of being someone who needs dessert after every meal, or give up the image of yourself as someone who makes the best apple crisp in town.

But the truth is that you don't really lose anything when you let go. Letting go of these concepts is like removing something that is imaginary. You can't lose these things because they weren't ever really yours. There is nothing that you own or possess for very long. Even your body does not belong to you, and it will die someday. So there's no point in identifying or claiming anything as your own, because nothing—not your body, not your idea of who you think you are, nor your next meal—is going to last.

Many patterns of behavior and self-image come from early childhood. Many others come from the various identities we have been given by others and those we've given to ourselves. But having an identity at one time doesn't mean it should last forever or even last at all. Eating everything on your plate may have been an identity you enjoyed as a child. But if that identity no longer serves you well and is the cause of suffering, learn how to let it go.

You can explore the feelings behind eating everything on your plate. These feelings may include the desire to please, the desire to be loved, or the desire to avoid punishment. Your willingness to become intimate with these feelings is the seed of emotional nourishment. This intimacy gives you the chance to make peace with yourself by learning to open up to these feelings and enjoy the nourishment they offer. From that perspective, you can then make a decision about eating everything on your plate, depending on whether this serves you well or not. There's no need to focus on how rotten your parents were for forcing you to eat everything on your plate. That story just fuels the attachment. If someone shoots an arrow into your heart, it's useless to yell at the person. It's better to turn your attention to the wound and try to get the arrow out. That attention to the wound is at the center of letting go as well as the source of healing it.

# Tranquility

When mindfulness sheds light on tumultuous emotions, recognizes them, understands them, and transforms them, we experience tranquility. A number of excerpts in this chapter are about the experience of emotions like stress and anger. In order to give our undivided attention to these emotions, we first step back and reflect what is going on in our minds without getting caught up in the process. Then we apply awareness to see the full contours and depth of the emotion—what is beneath it, how it grows, what enhances it, whether we are reacting to someone outside of ourselves, and if so, what was the intent.

For Jerry Braza, in "Managing Stress," the act of witnessing the way our thinking turns events into stressful situations can help reduce stress. By observing the process we may avoid being carried away by it. We see the thought process that creates stress unfold in "Cat Food Lessons" by Jon Kabat-Zinn. Kabat-Zinn takes us step by step through his thoughts and feelings when something makes him angry—in this case, finding cat food in the sink. He discovers the hurt beneath the anger, looks at the intention of those who left that cat food there, and sees that the intention was not to create the hurt. A full awareness of his anger and acceptance of it allows him to untangle the complex emotions, to understand them, and to see the situation with greater clarity.

We all have different ways of dealing with stress and anger, but two of the common ways we deal with these feelings tend to backfire. We may act out our frustration by treating others with anger or hostility, or we may deny that we feel upset or angry and bury or stifle these feelings. Both cause us to lose ourselves, get stuck, and stop growing. In "Working with Anger and Aversion" by Sharon Salzberg, we see the cost of expressing anger without awareness when we strike out at others and create a "cycle of harming." Mindfulness suggests a different approach to working with anger without denying it and without losing ourselves in it.

In "Poison as Medicine" Pema Chodron suggests practicing awareness of three "poisons"—craving, aversion, and ignorance—to find what is underneath them. By bringing mindfulness to these feelings, Chodron suggests that we can use them to foster growth and healing.

Charlotte Joko Beck observes in "Responding to Pressure" that we each develop a pattern of dealing with pressures that she terms our *chief feature*. Our chief feature is an escape strategy—an attempt to hide our turmoil from ourselves. By paying attention to our chief feature, she points out, it may fade, as we come to understand the fear that created it.

# Managing Stress

from *Moment by Moment:*
*The Art and Practice of Mindfulness*
by Jerry Braza

There is a story of a farmer and his son who worked their small farm with the help of one horse. One day the horse ran away, and all the neighbors sympathetically said, "Such bad luck!" The farmer replied, "Bad luck, good luck." A short time later the lost horse returned to his stable and brought with him four wild mares. "What wonderful luck!" the neighbors now said. "Good luck, bad luck, who knows?" replied the farmer. Several weeks later the son, in training one of the wild horses, fell and broke his leg. "Bad luck, good luck," voiced his dad. Shortly thereafter, the military arrived to recruit all able young men for the service. Since the farmer's son had broken his leg, he was of no use to the military. "Bad luck or good luck?" It depends on your interpretation of the experience!

Stress is a normal psycho/physiological response to events in our life. This response is innate and is often a means of self-preservation. Conversely, distress is often the result of our interpretation of the events in our life. Epictetus, a first-century Roman philosopher, makes this clear with his statement, "Man is not disturbed by events, but by the view he takes of them." Thus, any event in our life can be labeled as stress or distress based upon our interpretation or, even more significantly, our judgment of the particular event.

The psychologist Ken Wilber has written, "If we can watch or witness our distress, we prove ourselves thereby to be 'distress-less,' free of the witnessed turmoil." Exploring that process may provide an understanding of how both mindfulness and becoming acquainted with the "witness" within you can help reduce the potential negative psychological and physical impact of events in your life.

Distress begins with a simple thought, but years later it may become a piece of unfinished business that reduces our potential for experiencing peace, joy, and happiness. The anatomy of distress essentially unfolds as follows:

1. Awareness/consciousness occurs when you see, hear, smell, taste, experience, and/or think in response to a recollection or a direct contact with some object, person, activity, and/or environment.
   Example: as you enjoy your gardening, you become aware—or conscious of—a project at work.
2. Feelings then arise that are pleasant, unpleasant, and/or neutral.
   Example: the thought of the project is unpleasant.
3. Perceptions and reasoning begins to occur. Most often, an evaluation or judgment is made.
   Example: this project is unpleasant, difficult, and you think you should be putting in extra time now, instead of gardening.
4. Distorted and exaggerated thinking often follows the judgment or evaluation. This kind of thinking most often has roots in wants, desires, our concept or perception of self, and the views and opinions (models) we often attach to one way of thinking, being, or doing.
   Example: You think, "What's wrong with me? Why is this project so hard for me and not for Joe? I shouldn't be enjoying gardening when I have more important things to do."
5. Distorted and/or exaggerated thinking continues. Now you become focused or "caught" on the problem, and this often creates distress because you continue to attach various judgmental thoughts, feelings, and bodily sensations to the experience. This is usually enhanced by the number of "shoulds" and "ought-tos" you attach to the experience!
   Example: Your preoccupation with the problem continues all weekend. You worry constantly, have trouble sleeping, and feel bad. Based on this exaggerated thinking, you have been negatively affected both mentally and physically.

Exploring this model can help us to understand how a simple thought can create suffering and distress. Learning to become mindful or simply to witness the scenario as it unfolds can be a powerful way of changing potentially distressful situations. For example, by becoming mindful at the very moment in which unpleasant thoughts arise (the project at work, for example), you can simply note and/or witness the thought ("Hmm . . . a work thought") before exaggerated thinking or judgments become the focal point of your awareness. By applying the mindfulness practice to any stressful situation, you learn to witness rather than react.

Several years ago, my wife and I had planned a ten-day vacation on the Garden Island of Kauai, Hawaii. For months we reviewed the brochures, talked with travel agents and friends who had vacationed there before. Daily we talked about our trip—time to walk on the beach, rounds of golf, snorkeling, and the whale watching trips. Soon the big day arrived and we flew to sunny Hawaii. Upon arrival we were greeted by torrential rains, which we thought would be temporary. Day after day the rain continued and our outlook dimmed. All the things we had planned to do for months were canceled day by day as the storm continued. The model that we created in our minds about our trip to Hawaii was not to be. In our preoccupation with what we wanted to experience, we missed really experiencing the island in the rain and, also, I suspect, many wonderful relaxing moments. We discovered that our models and expectations for the experience created unnecessary stress for both of us. Learning to truly witness and not become attached to wants, desires, views, and opinions allows us to be free to make choices and create new and exciting experiences.

You may be familiar with accounts of individuals who have had a near-death or out-of-body experience. These individuals often witness their trauma and the accompanying resuscitation attempts from unusual and unique vantage points, without feeling or attachment to the event. You need not have a near-death or out-of-body experience to also become a witness to events in your life!

# Cat Food Lessons

from *Wherever You Go, There You Are*

by Jon Kabat-Zinn

I hate finding caked cat dishes in the kitchen sink along with ours. I'm not sure why this pushes my buttons so strongly, but it does. Perhaps it comes from not having had a pet when I was growing up. Or maybe I think it's a public health threat (you know, viruses and the like). When I choose to clean the cats' bowls, I first clean the whole sink of our dishes, then I wash theirs. Anyway, I don't like it when I find dirty cat dishes in the sink, and I react right away when I do.

First I get angry. Then the anger gets more personal and I find myself directing it at whoever I think is the culprit, which is usually my wife, Myla. I feel hurt because she doesn't respect my feelings. I tell her on countless occasions that I don't like it, that it disgusts me. I've asked her as politely as I know not to do it, but she often does it anyway. She feels I'm being silly and compulsive, and when she's pressed for time, she just leaves the caked cat dishes soaking in the sink.

My discovery of cat food in the sink can quickly escalate to a heated dispute, mostly because I am feeling angry and hurt and above all jus-tified in "my" anger, "my" hurt, because I know "I" am right. Cat food shouldn't be in the sink! But when it is, the selfing on my part can get rather strong.

Recently, I've noticed that I am not getting so bent out of shape about this. I didn't specifically try to change how I'm dealing with it. I still feel the same about the cat food, but somehow, I'm seeing the whole thing differently too, with greater awareness and with much more of a sense of humor. For one, when it happens now—and it still does with annoying frequency—I find that I am aware of my reaction the moment it happens and I look at it. "This is it," I remind myself!

I observe the anger as it starts rising in me. It turns out that it is preceded by a mild feeling of revulsion. Then I notice the stirrings of a feeling of betrayal which is not so mild. Someone in my family didn't respect *my* request, and *I* am taking it very personally. After all, my feelings count in the family, don't they?

I have taken to experimenting with my reactions at the kitchen sink by watching them very closely without acting on them. I can report that the initial feeling of revulsion is not all that bad, and if I stay with it, breathe with it, and permit myself to just feel it, it actually goes away within a second or two. I have also noticed that it is the sense of betrayal, of being thwarted in my wishes, that makes me mad much more than the cat food itself. So, I discover, it's not really the cat food by itself that is the source of my anger. It's that I'm not feeling listened to and respected. Very different from the cat food. Aha!

Then I remember that my wife and kids see this whole thing very differently. They think I am making a big deal out of nothing, and that while they will try to respect my wishes when it feels reasonable to them, at other times it doesn't and they just do it anyway, maybe even without thinking about me at all.

So I've stopped taking it personally. When I really don't want cat food in the sink, I roll up my sleeves and I clean the dishes in that moment. Otherwise, I just leave them there and go away. We no longer have fights about it. In fact, I find myself smiling now when I do come across the offending objects in the sink. After all, they have taught me a lot.

Try: Watching your reactions in situations that annoy you or make you angry. Notice how even speaking of something "making" you angry surrenders your power to others. Such occasions are good opportunities to experiment with mindfulness as a pot into which you can put all your feelings and just be with them, letting them slowly cook, reminding yourself that you don't have to do anything with them right away, that they will become more cooked, more easily digested and understood simply by holding them in the pot of mindfulness.

Observe the ways in which your feelings are creations of your mind's view of things, and that maybe that view is not complete. Can you allow this state of affairs to be okay and neither make yourself right or wrong? Can you be patient enough and courageous enough to explore putting stronger and stronger emotions into the pot and just holding them and letting them cook, rather than projecting them outward and forcing the world to be as you want it to be now? Can you see how this practice might lead to knowing yourself in new ways, and freeing yourself from old, worn-out, limiting views?

# Working with Anger and Aversion

from *Lovingkindness: The Revolutionary Art of Happiness*

by Sharon Salzberg

When I first practiced meditation with Sayadaw U Pandita, in 1984, I went through a period of disturbing memories about all the terrible things I had ever done. Memories of spurning childhood friends, of telling lies from seemingly good motives, of holding on to things when I was perfectly capable of giving them up, all came up to haunt me. I did not even want to tell the Sayadaw that I was experiencing this, but I did. I said, "You know, I just keep thinking of event after event after event— all of these bad things I've done. I feel terrible. I feel horrible. I feel awful."

U Pandita looked at me and asked, "Well, are you finally seeing the truth about yourself?" I was shocked at his response. Even though I was enveloped in self-judgment and criticism, something in his comment made me want to challenge it. I thought to myself, "No, I'm not seeing the truth about myself." And then he simply said, "Stop thinking about it." Only later would I understand the wisdom of his advice. Who among us has not done things to hurt people or to harm other creatures, or the earth itself? Through actions born of the mind state of aversion, we harm others and we harm ourselves. We experience aversion through a host of afflictions—anger, fear, guilt, impatience, grief, disappointment, dejection, anxiety, despair. Because hatred and aversion are the opposite of the state of love, they are considered the "far enemy" of metta.

The near enemy of metta, desire, is a subtler hindrance because it brings us temporary satisfaction. These states of aversion, by contrast, tear us apart; we burn when we are caught in them. The Buddha described the states of aversion as being of great consequence but easily overcome. They are of great consequence because they easily provoke strong action, leading us to perform unskillful deeds that hurt both ourselves and others. But even though such states are dangerous, nonetheless the pain of them is obvious, tangible, and easily felt. From beginning to end they bring great pain, so we are naturally moved to let them go.

The force of aversion manifests through us in two primary ways. One is outflowing, such as anger or rage. Such states have a lot of energy; they are powerful and expressive. We also experience aversion in a held-in way, as in grief, fear, disappointment, and despair. Here aversion's energy is frozen and paralyzing. Whether we are directing aversion toward ourselves or others, whether we are containing the aversion within our minds or expressing it toward others, these are the same mind states appearing in different forms.

One of the ways in which we direct aversion toward ourselves is in the form of guilt. As I experienced with Sayadaw U Pandita, as we go deeper in practice, we often begin spontaneously to review everything harmful we have ever done. These things just start coming up. People recall having disappointed a friend twenty-six years previously by not going to her sweet sixteen party, or the bitter retorts made to a partner no longer a part of their life. People suffer from having committed insurance fraud that remained undetected, or from the subtle, ongoing fear in a current friendship because of a lie told. It is very important to be able to acknowledge such things, to experience the pain, and then, as Sayadaw advised me, to just let them go—"stop thinking about it." Otherwise, we actually enhance a mistaken sense of self.

Buddhist psychology makes an interesting distinction between guilt and remorse. The feeling of guilt, or hatred directed toward oneself, lacerates. When we experience a strong feeling of guilt in the mind, we have little or no energy available for transformation or transcendence. We are defeated by the guilt itself, because it depletes us. We also feel very alone. Our thoughts focus on our worthlessness: "I'm the worst person in the world. Only I do these terrible things." However, such an attitude is actually very "self"-promoting. We become obsessed with "self" in the egotistical sense.

Remorse, by contrast, is a state of recognition. We realize that we have at some point done something or said something unskillful that caused pain, and we feel the pain of that recognition. But, crucially, remorse frees us to let go of the past. It leaves us with some energy to move on, resolved not to repeat our mistakes.

And guilt can be deceptive. We may feel that guilt can be a noble force to motivate us to so serve others or perform wholesome actions. But guilt does not actually work in that way. When one is motivated by guilt or grief, one's own pain is center stage, just as when one is motivated by anger, one's outrage is center stage. When such feelings take the central role, we may lose consideration of what somebody else may actually need. There is not enough freedom from self-centeredness in our consciousness to see clearly, to be connected fully. Our own feelings overwhelm consciousness. We end up serving ourselves. How far this is from the invocation of Rabindranath Tagore: "Oh Lord, make me a better instrument through which you can blow."

Cultivating this mistaken concept of a permanent self also leads to aversion in the form of self-hatred or judgment. When we see the self as a fixed entity, we develop a strong habit of mind that drives our lives. If through our practice we can see the impersonal nature of the forces that arise and pass away, we experience a very different reality. For example, we can see anger, guilt, or grief arising in the mind as forces that come and go. Aversion is like a rainstorm, arising and passing away. It is not I, not me, not mine. It is not you or yours, either. In this recognition of emptiness, we look at other beings and see ourselves. Here is the birth of metta.

Self-hatred impedes this flowering of our practice. When the Dalai Lama visited Insight Meditation Society in 1979, somebody asked him, "I am a beginning meditation student and I feel quite worthless as a person. What can you say about that?" The Dalai Lama replied, "You should never think like that; that is completely wrong thinking. You have the power of thought, and therefore the power of mind, and that is all you need." He was recognizing that we all have the potential for enlightenment, and therefore we should not denigrate that capacity by saying we are worthless.

We need to recollect this potential for awakening in order to see ourselves clearly. When we fall into aversion, we lose this perspective. I once approached my very first meditation teacher, S. N. Goenka, in an accusatory fashion and demanded to know, "Isn't there an easier way?" I was fed up and hated all my aches and pains. I think I actually thought he did know an easier way and was purposely withholding it from me so that I could suffer. It is quite amusing to look back on it, because he was a very compassionate person. After I asked that question, he just looked at me for a while. I fell into his eyes, which were radiant with a vastness of perspective, which never overlooked my capacity for freedom. From the point of view of a lifetime of spiritual endeavor, my sleepiness and knee pain did not seem so momentous and terrible. Whenever we forget the larger perspective, we become lost in the moment's little drama. Lost in aversion, we forget our capacity to love.

Once I received quite an angry letter from someone. It was one of those letters you would really rather not get, listing a lot of situations and circumstances that had happened. It basically said, "That was your fault, and that was your fault, and that was your fault, and that was your fault, too." It was not very pleasant. Throughout the rest of the day, I found myself composing responses in my mind to this letter. Mostly they ran along the lines of, "Well, actually, that's not my fault. It's your fault. And that was your fault, and that was your fault, and that was your fault, and that was your fault, too." I spent much of that day spinning it all out.

This kind of self-righteous anger solidifies into an almost choking sense of "I" and "other." Anger is such a grievous state because it means the death of the possibility of love or connection in that moment, in that situation. But what do we do when we feel anger or aversion?

There is a confusion in contemporary society about how to relate to feelings of aversion. For example, it is difficult to understand the difference between *feeling* anger and *venting* anger. When we undertake a spiritual practice, it is important that we open to all that arises, that we recognize, acknowledge, and accept everything we feel. We have a long conditioning of self-deception, of keeping certain things outside the sphere of our awareness, of repressing them. Overcoming our denial and repression and opening to states of aversion can be very healing. But in the process, we may pay the price of becoming lost in anger if, through misunderstanding, we indulge it.

Most contemporary psychological research shows that when one expresses anger quite often in one's life, it leads to the easy expression of anger. Expressing anger becomes a habit. Many people assume that we have a certain amount of anger inside, and that if we do not want to keep it inside, we have to put it outside; somehow if it is outside, it is not going to be inside anymore. Anger seems like a solid thing. But, in fact, we discover, if we observe carefully, that anger has no solidity. In reality it is merely a conditioned response that arises and passes away. It is crucial for us to see that when we identify with these passing states as being solid and who we truly are, we let them rule us, and we are compelled to act in ways that cause harm to ourselves and others. Our opening needs to rest on a basis of *nonidentification*. Recognizing aversion or anger in the mind as transitory is very different from identifying with them as being who we really are, and then acting on them.

Anger is a very complex emotion, with a lot of different components. There are strands of disappointment, fear, sadness, all woven together. If the emotions and thoughts are taken as a whole, anger appears as one solid thing. But if we break it down and see its various aspects, we can see the ultimate nature of this experience. We can see that anger is impermanent, and it arises and passes away like a wave that comes and goes. We can see that anger is unsatisfactory; it does not bring us lasting joy. We can see that anger is empty of a "self" determining it; it does not arise according to our will, or whim, or wish. It arises when conditions are right for it to arise. We can see that it is not ours; we do not own it, we do not possess it. We cannot control anger's arising. We can only learn to relate to it in a skillful way.

If we look at the force of anger, we can, in fact, discover many positive aspects in it. Anger is not a passive, complacent state. It has incredible energy. Anger can impel us to let go of ways we may be inappropriately defined by the needs of others; it can teach us to say no. In this way it also serves our integrity, because anger can motivate us to turn from the demands of the outer world to the nascent voice of our inner world. It is a way to set boundaries and to challenge injustice at every level. Anger will not take things for granted or simply accept them mindlessly.

Anger also has the ability to cut through surface appearances; it does not just stay on a superficial level. It is very critical; it is very demanding. Anger has the power to pierce through the obvious to things that are more hidden. This is why anger may be transmuted to wisdom. By nature, anger has characteristics in common with wisdom.

Nevertheless, the unskillful aspects of anger are immense, and they far outweigh the positive aspects. The Buddha described it in this way: "Anger, with its poisoned source and fevered climax, murderously sweet, that you must slay to weep no more." It is sweet indeed! But the satisfaction we get from expressing anger is very short-lived, while the pain endures for a long time and debilitates us.

According to Buddhist psychology, the characteristic of anger is savageness. The function of anger is to burn up its own support, like a forest fire. It leaves us with nothing; it leaves us devastated. Just like a forest fire that ranges free and wild, anger can leave us in a place very far from where we intended to go. The deluding quality of anger is responsible for our losing ourselves in this way. When we are lost in anger, we do not see many options before us, and so we strike out recklessly.

Anger and aversion express themselves in acts of hostility and persecution. The mind becomes very narrow. It isolates someone or something, fixates on it, develops tunnel vision, sees no way out, fixes that experience, that person, or that object as being forever unchanging. Such aversion supports an endless cycle of harm and revenge. We see this reality politically: with racial struggle, with class struggle, with national struggle, with religious hatreds. Anger can bind people to each other as strongly as desire, so that they drag each other along, connected through various kinds of revenge and counterrevenge, never being able to let go, never being able to be still. The playwright and statesman Vaclav Havel has noted insightfully that hatred has much in common with desire, that it is "the fixation on others, the dependence on them, and in fact the delegation of a piece of one's own identity to them. . . . The hater longs for the object of his hatred."

So it never ends, as long as people continue to relate in the same way. We see an oppressed people being hurt and then often taking power and behaving in exactly the same way toward some other people. Someone sends a letter accusing me, and I accuse them back.

How can we let go in such a situation? How can we change it? We can focus our attention more on the suffering of the situation, both our own and the *suffering* of others, rather than on our anger. We can ask ourselves whom we are really angry at. Mostly what we are angry at is the anger in the other person. It is almost as if the other person were an instrument for the anger that moves through them and motivates them to act in unskillful ways. We do not become angry at somebody's mouth when they are shouting at us; we are angry at the anger that is motivating them to shout. If we add anger to anger, we only serve to increase it.

In a well-known phrase, the Buddha said, "Hatred can never cease by hatred. Hatred can only cease by love. This is an eternal law." We can begin to transcend the cycle of aversion when we can stop seeing ourselves personally as agents of revenge. Ultimately, all beings are the owners of their own karma. If someone has caused harm, they will suffer. If we have caused harm, we will suffer. As the Buddha said in the *Dhammapada*:

> *We are what we think.*
> *All that we are arises with our thoughts.*
> *With our thoughts we make the world.*
> *Speak or act with an impure mind*
> *And trouble will follow you*
> *As the wheel follows the ox that draws the cart. . . .*
> *Speak or act with a pure mind*
> *And happiness will follow you as your shadow, unshakable.*
> *Happiness and unhappiness depend upon our actions.*

That does not mean that we sit back with glee, thinking, "You'll get yours in this life or the next." Rather, we understand that we do not have to be agents of revenge, that if people have caused suffering, they will suffer. This is an impersonal law, affecting us as well.

On the eve of his enlightenment, the Buddha, then known as the Bodhisattva, sat under the Bodhi Tree, determined not to move until he attained enlightenment. Mara, a mythic figure in the Buddhist cosmology, the "killer of virtue" and the "killer of life," recognizing that his kingdom of delusion was greatly jeopardized by the Bodhisattva's aspiration to awaken, came with many different challenges. Attempting to get the Bodhisattva to give up his resolve, he challenged him through lust, anger, and fear. He showered him with hailstorms, mud storms, and other travails. No matter what happened, the Bodhisattva sat serenely, unmoved and unswayed in his determination.

The final challenge of Mara was self-doubt. He said to the Bodhisattva, "By what right are you even sitting there with that goal? What makes you think you have the right even to aspire to full enlightenment, to complete awakening?" In response to that challenge, the Bodhisattva reached over and touched the earth. He called upon the earth itself to bear witness to all of the lifetimes in which he had practiced generosity, patience, and morality. Lifetime after lifetime he had built a wave of moral force that had given him the right to that aspiration.

When I think of the law of karma, I sometimes think of this story. The earth is bearing witness, and if we have caused suffering, we will suffer; if others have caused suffering, they will suffer. Understanding this truth, we can let go. We can be free.

It so happened that on the very evening of the day I received that letter I reacted to so strongly, a friend brought a Tibetan lama to visit us at Insight Meditation Society. This lama had lived in a cave in the Himalayas for about fifteen years without ever leaving it. He was a master of the Tibetan practice of tumo, raising the body heat through the power of mind.

This lama had been approached in his cave and asked if he would consider going to America to be studied. He was told about how scientists, as they try to understand meditation, like to have effects that are measurable. Clearly, raising one's body heat through concentrating the mind is a very measurable thing. Because the Dalai Lama himself had made this request, the monk agreed to go. He came out of his cave and went straight to Boston. He was taken from the airport directly to the hospital, where he spent many days meditating while researchers kept taking his temperature.

At some point, our friend who had brought the lama there suggested that he take a break to come out to Insight Meditation Society, which is not too far from Boston. He came. When he walked through the door, the first thing he said was, "This place seems so different from the rest of America. What do you do here?" So we told him, and we ended up talking and spending the evening together.

This master of tumo had with him a young, articulate interpreter. The interpreter told us that this monk was considered quite extraordinary within the Tibetan tradition. He had become a monk quite late in life for that tradition, and he had gone very far in his meditation practice very fast, despite the fact that he had "skipped over" many aspects of spiritual training that the Tibetans consider necessary for such progress. He had not done the preliminary study or any of the preliminary meditation practices, which are considered to be absolutely essential in building a foundation before mastering more difficult and subtle practices. So the Tibetans considered him quite an anomalous puzzle.

We asked the lama, "Do you have any idea why you should have made such extraordinary progress in your practice, even though you did not fulfill these usual preliminaries?"

"Yes," he answered, "I do have an idea. When I was a layperson in Tibet, for many years I was a guerrilla fighter. Often I captured people and tortured and killed them. Then at some point in my life, I was captured myself by the Chinese and put in prison. I was tortured, and I underwent tremendous suffering. I made a commitment at that time not to hate the Chinese people."

The lama explained that he saw his situation in quite classical Buddhist terms. What he was experiencing at the hands of the Chinese, he understood to be the karmic fruit of his own previous actions. He pointed out that even if he had not seen it in those terms, he understood that nobody other than himself could make him suffer mentally. So he made a decision not to add the fires of hatred and bitterness to the terrible torment he was undergoing physically. He told us that he thought it was this decision that allowed him to make such extraordinary progress in his practice.

As this remarkable being was speaking, I was sitting there having images in my mind of the letter that I had been composing all day, saying, "That was your fault, and that was your fault, and that was your fault, too." I realized that I did not have to write it that way. Thanks to the propitious, timely example of the lama, I understood what is genuinely possible for human beings with a human heart. I understood, as the Buddha said, that "hatred will never cease by hatred." Never. "Hatred can only cease by love."

When our minds are full of anger and hatred toward others, in fact we are the ones who are actually suffering, caught in this mind state. But it is not so easy to access that place inside of us which can forgive, which can love. In some ways to be able to forgive, to let go, is a type of dying. It is the ability to say, "I am not that person anymore, and you are not that person anymore." Forgiveness allows us to recapture some part of ourselves that we left behind in bondage to a past event. Some part of our identity may also need to die in that letting go, so that we can reclaim the energy bound up in the past.

All of these teachings are available to us if we can be aware of what we are feeling in the deepest possible way, so that nothing is blocked from our consciousness. Then we can examine: What is our struggle? Why are we struggling? It is important to understand that no one thing makes us feel a certain way. Nothing stands alone in this conditioned world. We live in an interdependent reality, where we have the situation of the present moment and everything we are bringing to it as well.

Somebody could get up and do something in the middle of a room.

Some people would become excited. Other people would be afraid. Some people would become angry. Other people would be amused. It is not that a given action, whatever it is, dictates a certain response. There is the situation, and there is everything we bring to it.

So we must take responsibility for our own mind. We live, hopefully, not just to drift along in the wake of different reactions, going up and down all of the time. Having a sense of purpose, such as the development of a loving heart, is the key to living a liberating practice.

If we can learn to see and understand all of these painful mind states of anger, fear, grief, disappointment, and guilt as states of aversion, we can learn to be free of them. Being free does not mean that aversion will never come up in our experience. Being free means that we can purify it. We can see it clearly, understand it, and learn not to be ruled by it. And having seen it clearly, which is the function of wisdom, we can also hold it in the vast, transforming field of acceptance.

# Poison as Medicine

from *Start Where You Are*

by Pema Chodron

With the slogan "Three objects, three poisons, and three seeds of virtue" we begin to enter into the teachings on relative bodhichitta, the teachings on how to awaken compassion. We have so far been attempting to establish that the ground of all of our experience is very spacious, not as solid as we tend to make it. We don't have to make such a big deal about ourselves, our enemies, our lovers, and the whole show. This emphasis on gentleness is the pith instruction on how to reconnect with openness and freshness in our lives, how to liberate ourselves from the small world of ego. We'll keep coming back to this sense of freshness and open space and not making such a big deal, because we are now about to get into the really messy stuff.

In the Buddhist teachings, the messy stuff is called *klesha*, which means poison. Boiling it all down to the simplest possible formula, there are three main poisons: passion, aggression, and ignorance. We could talk about these in different ways—for example, craving, aversion, and couldn't care less. Addictions of all kinds come under the category of craving, which is wanting, wanting, wanting—feeling that we have to have some kind of resolution. Aversion encompasses violence, rage, hatred, and negativity of all kinds, as well as garden-variety irritation. And ignorance? Nowadays, it's usually called denial.

The pith instruction of all the Buddhist teachings and most explicitly of the lojong teachings is, whatever you do, don't try to make these unwanted feelings go away. That's an unusual thought; it's not our habitual tendency to let these feelings hang around. Our habitual tendency is definitely to try to make those things go away.

People and situations in our lives are always triggering our passion, aggression, and ignorance. A good old innocent cup of coffee triggers some people's craving; they are addicted to it; it represents comfort and all the good things in life. If they can't get it, their life is a wreck. Other people have an elaborate story line about why it's bad for you, and they have aversion and a support group. Plenty of other people couldn't care less about a cup of coffee; it doesn't mean much at all to them.

And then there's good old Mortimer, that person who is sitting next to you in the meditation hall, or perhaps someone who works in your office. Some people are lusting when they see Mortimer. He looks wonderful to them. A lot of their discursive thought is taken up with what they'd like to do with Mortimer. A certain number of people hate him. They haven't even talked to him yet, but the minute they saw him, they felt loathing. Some of us haven't noticed him, and we may never notice him. In fact, a few years from now he'll tell us he was here, and we'll be surprised.

So there are three things, which in the slogan are called three objects. One object is what we find pleasant, another is what we find unpleasant, and a third is what we're neutral about. If it's pleasant, it triggers craving; if it's unpleasant, it triggers aversion; if it's neutral, it triggers ignorance. Craving, aversion, and ignorance are the three poisons.

Our experience would write the formula as "Three objects, three poisons, and lots of misery" or "Three objects, three poisons, and three seeds of confusion, bewilderment, and pain," because the more the poisons arise and the bigger they get in our life, the more they drive us crazy. They keep us from seeing the world as it is; they make us blind, deaf, and dumb. The world doesn't speak for itself because we're so caught up in our story line that instead of feeling that there's a lot of space in which we could lead our life as a child of illusion, we're robbing ourselves, robbing ourselves from letting the world speak for itself. You just keep speaking to yourself, so nothing speaks to you.

The three poisons are always trapping you in one way or another, imprisoning you and making your world really small. When you feel craving, you could be sitting on the edge of the Grand Canyon, but all you can see is this piece of chocolate cake that you're craving. With aversion, you're sitting on the edge of the Grand Canyon, and all you can hear is the angry words you said to someone ten years ago. With ignorance, you're sitting on the edge of the Grand Canyon with a paper bag over your head. Each of the three poisons has the power to capture you so completely that you don't even perceive what's in front of you.

This "three objects, three poisons, and three seeds of virtue" is really a peculiar idea. It turns the conventional formula on its head in an unpredictable, nonhabitual way. It points to how the three poisons can be three seeds of becoming a child of illusion, how to step out of this limited world of ego fixation, how to step out of the world of tunnel vision. And the slogan is just an introduction to how this notion works. Tonglen practice will give you a very explicit method for working with this kind of lojong logic or, you could say, big-heart logic.

There's nothing really wrong with passion or aggression or ignorance, except that we take it so personally and therefore waste all that juicy stuff. The peacock eats poison and that's what makes the colors of its tail so brilliant. That's the traditional image for this practice, that the poison becomes the source of great beauty and joy; poison becomes medicine.

Whatever you do, don't try to make the poisons go away, because if you're trying to make them go away, you're losing your wealth, along with your neurosis. All this messy stuff is your richness, but saying this once is not going to convince you. If nothing else, however, it could cause you to wonder about these teachings and begin to be curious whether they could possibly be true, which might inspire you to try them for yourself.

The main point is that when Mortimer walks by and triggers your craving or your aversion or your ignorance or your jealousy or your arrogance or your feeling of worthlessness—when Mortimer walks by and a feeling arises—that could be like a little bell going off in your head or a lightbulb going on: here's an opportunity to awaken your heart. Here's an opportunity to ripen bodhichitta, to reconnect with the sense of the soft spot, because as a result of these poisons the shields usually come up. We react to the poisons by armoring our hearts.

When the poisons arise, we counter them with two main tactics. Step one: Mortimer walks by. Step two: klesha arises. (It's hard to separate the first two steps.) Step three: we either act out or repress, which is to say we either physically or mentally attack Mortimer or talk to ourself about what a jerk he is or how we're going to get even with him, or else we repress those feelings.

Acting out and repressing are the main ways that we shield our hearts, the main ways that we never really connect with our vulnerability, our compassion, our sense of the open, fresh dimension of our being. By acting out or repressing we invite suffering, bewilderment, or confusion to intensify.

Drive all blames into Mortimer. Someone once heard the slogan "Drive all blames into one" and thought it was "Drive all blames into Juan." Whether you call him or her Juan or Juanita or Mortimer, the usual tactic is either to act out or repress. If Mortimer or Juan or Juanita walks by and craving arises, you try to get together by flirting or making advances. If aversion arises, you try to get revenge. You don't stay with the raw feelings. You don't hold your seat. You take it a step further and act out.

Repressing could actually come under the category of ignorance. When you see Juan or Juanita or Mortimer, you just shut down. Maybe you don't even want to touch what they remind you of, so you just shut down. There's another common form of repression, which has to do with guilt: Juan walks by; aversion arises; you act out, and then you feel guilty about it. You think you're a bad person to be hating Juan, and so you repress it.

What we're working with in our basic shamatha-vipashyana practice—and explicitly with the tonglen practice—is the middle ground between acting out and repressing. We're discovering how to hold our seat and feel completely what's underneath all that story line of wanting, not wanting, and so forth.

In terms of "Three objects, three poisons, and three seeds of virtue," when these poisons arise, the instruction is to drop the story line, which means—instead of acting out or repressing—use the situation as an opportunity to feel your heart, to feel the wound. Use it as an opportunity to touch that soft spot. Underneath all that craving or aversion or jealousy or feeling wretched about yourself, underneath all that hopelessness and despair and depression, there's something extremely soft, which is called bodhichitta.

When these things arise, train gradually and very gently without making it into a big deal. Begin to get the hang of feeling what's underneath the story line. Feel the wounded heart that's underneath the addiction, self-loathing, or anger. If someone comes along and shoots an arrow into your heart, it's fruitless to stand there and yell at the person. It would be much better to turn your attention to the fact that there's an arrow in your heart and to relate to that wound.

When we do that, the three poisons become three seeds of how to make friends with ourselves. They give us the chance to work on patience and kindness, the chance not to give up on ourselves and not to act out or repress. They give us the chance to change our habits completely. This is what helps both ourselves and others. This is instruction on how to turn unwanted circumstances into the path of enlightenment. By following it, we can transform all that messy stuff that we usually push away into the path of awakening: reconnecting, with our soft heart, our clarity, and our ability to open further.

# Responding to Pressure

## from *Nothing Special: Living Zen*
## by Charlotte Joko Beck

Let's look at how we handle pressure or stress. What is pressure for one person may not be pressure for someone else. For a person who is shy, pressure might be walking into a crowded party. For another, pressure might be being alone, or meeting deadlines. For another, pressure might mean having a slow, dull life without any deadlines. Pressure could be a new baby, a new lover, a new friend. It might be success. Some people do well with failure but can't handle success. Pressure is what makes us tighten up, what arouses our anxiety.

We have different strategies for responding to pressure. Gurdjieff, an interpreter of Sufi mysticism, called our strategy our "chief feature." We need to learn what our chief feature is—the primary way we handle pressure. When the pressure's on, one person tends to withdraw; another struggles harder to be perfect, or to be even more of a star. Some respond to pressure by working harder, others by working less. Some evade, others try to dominate. Some get busy and talk a lot; others become quieter than usual.

We discover our chief feature by watching ourselves under pressure. Each morning when we get up, there is probably something in the day ahead that will cause pressure for us. When things are going badly, there's just nothing but pressure in our lives. At other times there's very little pressure, and we think things are going well. But life always pressures us to some degree.

Our typical pattern for responding to pressure is created early in our lives. When we meet difficulties as children, the smooth fabric of life begins to pucker. It's as if that puckering forms a little sack that we pull together to hide our fear. The way we hide our fear—the little sack that is our coping strategy—is our chief feature. Until we handle the "chief feature" and experience our fear, we can't be that seamless whole, the "formless field of benefaction." Instead we are puckered, full of bumps.

Over a lifetime of practice one's chief feature shifts almost completely. For instance, I used to be so shy that if I had to enter a room with ten or fifteen people—say, a small cocktail party—it would take me fifteen minutes of pacing outside before I could get up my courage to enter the room. Now, however, though I don't prefer big parties, I'm comfortable with them. There's a big difference between being so scared one can hardly walk into a room and being comfortable. I don't mean to say that one's basic personality changes. I will never be "the life of the party," even if I live to be one hundred and ten. I like to watch others at parties, and talk to a few people; that's my way.

We often make the mistake of supposing that we can simply retrain ourselves through effort and self-analysis. We may think of Zen practice as studying ourselves so that we can learn to think differently, in the sense that we might study chess or cooking or French. But that's not it. Zen practice isn't like learning ancient history or math or gourmet cooking. These kinds of learning have their places, of course, but when it comes to our chief feature—the way we tend to cope with pressure—it is our misuse of our individual minds that has created the emotional contraction. We can't use it to correct itself; we can't use our little mind to correct the little mind. It's a formidable problem: the very thing we're investigating is also our means or tool for investigating it. The distortion in how we think distorts our efforts to correct the distortion.

We don't know how to attack the problem. We know that something's not right with us because we're not at peace; we tend to try all sorts of false solutions. One such "solution" is training ourselves to do positive thinking. That's simply a maneuver of the little mind. In programming ourselves for positive thinking, we haven't really understood ourselves at all, and so we continue to get into difficulties. If we criticize our minds and say to ourselves, "You don't think very well, so I'll force you not to think" or "You've thought all those destructive thoughts; now you must think nice thoughts, positive thoughts," we're still using our minds to treat our minds. This point is particularly hard for intellectuals to absorb, since they have spent a lifetime using their minds to solve problems and naturally approach Zen practice in the same way. (No one knows this better than I do!) The strategy has never worked, and it never will.

There's only one way to escape this closed loop and to see ourselves clearly: we have to step outside of the little mind and observe it. That which observes is not thinking, because the observer can observe thinking. We have to observe the mind and notice what it's doing. We have to notice how the mind produces these swarms of self-centered thoughts, thus creating tension in the body. The process of stepping back is not complicated, but if we're not used to it, it seems new and strange, and perhaps scary. With persistence, it becomes easier.

Suppose we lose our job. Floods of thoughts come up, creating various emotions. Our chief feature springs in, covering our fear so that we don't deal with it directly. If we lose our job, the only thing to do is to go about finding another one, assuming we need the money. But that's often not what we do. Or, if we do look for another job, we may not do it effectively because we're so busy being upset by the activity of our chief feature.

Suppose we've been criticized by somebody in our daily life. Suddenly we feel pressure. How do we handle it? Our chief feature jumps right in. We use any mental trick we can find: worrying, justifying, blaming. We may try to evade the problem by thinking about something useless or irrelevant. We may take some sort of drug to shut it out.

The more we observe our thoughts and actions, the more our chief feature will tend to fade. The more it fades, the more we are willing to experience the fear that created it in the first place. For many years, practice is about strengthening the observer. Eventually, we're willing to do what comes up next, without resistance, and the observer fades. We don't need the observer anymore; we can be life itself. When that process is complete, one is fully realized, a buddha—though I haven't met anyone for whom the process is complete.

Sitting is like our daily lives: what comes up as we sit will be the thinking that we want to cling to, our chief feature. If we like to evade life, we'll find some way in sitting to evade our sitting. If we like to worry, we'll worry. If we like to fantasize, we'll fantasize. Whatever we do in our sitting is like a microcosm of the rest of our lives. Our sitting shows us what we're doing with our lives, and our lives show us what we do when we sit.

Transformation doesn't begin with saying to ourselves, "I should be different." Transformation begins with the realization expressed in the verse of the *Kesa*: "Vast is the field of liberation." Our very lives themselves are a vast field of liberation, a formless field of benefaction. When we wear the teachings of life, observing our thoughts, experiencing the sensory input we receive in each second, then we are engaged in saving ourselves and all sentient beings, just by being who we are.

STUDENT: My "chief feature" seems to change according to the situation. Under pressure I am usually controlling, domineering, and angry. In another situation, however, I might become withdrawn and quiet.

JOKO: Still, for any person, different behaviors in responding to pressure come from the same basic approach to handling fear, though they may look different. There is an underlying pattern that's being expressed.

STUDENT: When I feel pressured—especially when I feel criticized—I work hard and try to do well; I try not to just react, but to sit with the anxiety and fear. In the last year, however, I've come to realize that when I feel criticized, underlying my efforts to perform well is rage. I really want to attack; I'm a killer shark.

JOKO: The rage has been there the whole time; being a nice person and a fine performer is your cover. There's a killer shark in everybody. And the killer shark is unexperienced fear. Your way of covering it up is to look so nice and do so much and be so wonderful that nobody can possibly see who you really are—which is someone who is scared to death. As we uncover these layers of rage, it's important not to act out; we shouldn't inflict our rage on others. In genuine practice, our rage is simply a stage that passes. But for a time, we are more uncomfortable than when we started. That's inevitable; we're becoming more honest, and our false surface style is beginning to dissolve. The process doesn't go on forever, but it certainly can be most uncomfortable while it lasts. Occasionally we may explode, but that's better than evading or covering our reaction.

STUDENT: Often I can see other people's patterns much more quickly than my own. When I care about them, I'm tempted to set them straight. I feel like I'm seeing a friend drowning and not throwing a lifesaver. When I do intervene, however, it often feels like I'm butting into their lives when it is not my business at all.

JOKO: That's an important point. What does it mean to be a formless field of benefaction? We all see people doing things that obviously harm them. What should we do?

STUDENT: Isn't it enough to be aware and be present to them?

JOKO: Yes, that is generally the best response. Occasionally people will ask us for help. If they are sincere in asking, it's fine to respond. But we can be too quick to jump in and give advice. Many of us are fixers. An old Zen rule of thumb is not to answer until one has been asked three times. If people really want your opinion, they'll insist on having it. But we are quick to give our opinion when nobody wants it. I know; I've done it.

The observer has no emotions. It's like a mirror. Everything just passes in front of it. The mirror makes no judgment. Whenever we judge, we've added another thought that needs to be labeled. The observer is not critical. Judging is not something the observer does. The observer simply watches or reflects, like a mirror. If garbage passes in front of it, it reflects garbage. If roses pass in front of it, it reflects roses. The mirror remains a mirror, an empty mirror. The observer doesn't even accept; it just observes.

STUDENT: Isn't the observer really part of the little mind?

JOKO: No. The observer is a function of awareness that only arises when we have an object come up in our experience in the phenomenal world. If there's no object coming up (for example, in deep sleep), the observer is not there. The observer finally dies when we are just awareness and no longer need the observer.

We can never find the observer, no matter how long we look for it. Still, though we can never locate it, it is obvious that we can observe. We could say that the observer is a different dimension of mind but not an aspect of the little mind, which is on the ordinary linear level. Who we are is awareness. Nobody has ever observed awareness; yet that's who we are—a "formless field of benefaction."

STUDENT: It seems that an unpleasant sensation can anchor me in the present and focus my attention here and now.

JOKO: There's an old saying to the effect that human extremity is God's opportunity. When things are pleasant, we try to hold on to the pleasantness. In trying to cling to pleasure, we destroy it. When we are sitting and are truly still, however, the discomfort and pain draw us back to the present. Sitting makes more obvious our desire to escape or evade. When we are sitting well, there's no place to go. We tend not to learn that unless we're uncomfortable. The more unconscious we are of our discomfort and our efforts to escape, the more mayhem is created within phenomenal life—from war between nations down to personal arguments between individuals, to arguments within ourselves; all such problems arise because we separate ourselves from our experience. The discomfort and pain are not the cause of our problems; the cause is that we don't know what to do about them.

STUDENT: Even pleasure has an element of discomfort to it. For example, it's a pleasure to have some peace and quiet, but then I have an uncomfortable feeling that the noise and racket might start up again.

JOKO: Pleasure and pain are simply opposite poles. Joy is being willing for things to be as they are. With joy, there's no polarity. If the noise starts, it starts. If it stops, it stops. Both are joy. Because we want to cling to pleasure and push away pain, however, we develop an escape strategy. When something unpleasant happens to us as children, we develop a system—a chief feature for coping with unpleasantness—and live our life out of that instead of seeing it as it is.

# Harmony

Harmony is a state of being in which we are fully engaged in what we are doing at the moment. This is possible with an open, attentive, accepting, and flexible mind. Without irrelevant concerns we are free to perform at the height of our abilities, both with physical skill and with the mental freedom to make connections that flow from our creativity and intuition. Many people have tasted this state of awareness without ever having meditated. It is an experience that Mihaly Csikszentmihalyi describes in "Enjoyment and the Quality of Life."

Csikszentmihalyi characterizes the experience of harmony as an experience of pleasure that enhances our enjoyment of life. While it is not a material pleasure, it is the result of going beyond—beyond our abilities and with full attention to the task at hand, where there is no room for irrelevant information about our problems or ourselves. Our energy flows smoothly, we are relaxed and energetic.

One facet of harmony is a feeling of connectedness. In "Harmony" Jon Kabat-Zinn observes a flock of wild geese flying in unison and realizes that "they are communicating. Each one somehow knows where it is, has a place in this complex and constantly changing pattern, belongs." Kabat-Zinn feels not only the connectedness of the birds, but his participation in that moment in the world and for that moment his experience of flowing time is suspended. At such a moment there are no distractions or thoughts of other experiences and feelings to come between the observer and the observed.

In an excerpt from the classic *Zen and the Art of Motorcycle Maintenance*, Robert M. Pirsig describes harmony as "mental quietness" and "an inner peace of mind," "an identification with one's circumstances" that allows him to attend to the quality of his work. The model he uses is the mechanic who works on a motorcycle with total involvement and no sense of a boundary between himself and the motorcycle.

This sense of oneness with the experience is the subject of "The No-Boundary Moment" by Ken Wilber. He describes the experience as a "timeless moment," or a "peak moment" such as when "time disappears," when we are "lost in a sunset: transfixed by the play of moonlight on a crystal dark pond . . ." The reason for time disappearing, he tells us, is that we are totally absorbed in the present moment.

"The Knitting Sutra" speaks to the experience of being in harmony with an activity. Many of us have had this experience when we are doing something we love: fully involved in the task, losing all sense of time, and feeling moved by a natural flow of energy. It is no wonder that harmony is such a cherished value and that people long for it.

# Enjoyment and the Quality of Life
## from *Flow*
### by Mihaly Csikszentmihalyi

There are two main strategies we can adopt to improve the quality of life. The first is to try making external conditions match our goals. The second is to change how we experience external conditions to make them fit our goals better. For instance, feeling secure is an important component of happiness. The sense of security can be improved by buying a gun, installing strong locks on the front door, moving to a safer neighborhood, exerting political pressure on city hall for more police protection, or helping the community to become more conscious of the importance of civil order. All these different responses are aimed at bringing conditions in the environment more in line with our goals. The other method by which we can feel more secure involves modifying what we mean by security. If one does not expect perfect safety, recognizes that risks are inevitable, and succeeds in enjoying a less than ideally predictable world, the threat of insecurity will not have as great a chance of marring happiness.

Neither of these strategies is effective when used alone. Changing external conditions might seem to work at first, but if a person is not in control of his consciousness, the old fears or desires will soon return, reviving previous anxieties. One cannot create a complete sense of inner security even by buying one's own Caribbean island and surrounding it with armed bodyguards and attack dogs.

The myth of King Midas well illustrates the point that controlling external conditions does not necessarily improve existence. Like most people, King Midas supposed that if he were to become immensely rich, his happiness would be assured. So he made a pact with the gods, who after much haggling granted his wish that everything he touched would turn into gold. King Midas thought he had made an absolutely first-rate deal. Nothing was to prevent him now from becoming the richest, and therefore the happiest, man in the world. But we know how the story ends: Midas soon came to regret his bargain because the food in his mouth and the wine on his palate turned to gold before he could swallow them, and so he died surrounded by golden plates and golden cups.

The old fable continues to echo down the centuries. The waiting rooms of psychiatrists are filled with rich and successful patients who, in their forties or fifties, suddenly wake up to the fact that a plush sub-urban home, expensive cars, and even an Ivy League education are not enough to bring peace of mind. Yet people keep hoping that changing the external conditions of their lives will provide a solution. If only they could earn more money, be in better physical shape, or have a more understanding partner, they would really have it made. Even though we recognize that material success may not bring happiness, we engage in an endless struggle to reach external goals, expecting that they will im-prove life.

Wealth, status, and power have become in our culture all too pow-erful symbols of happiness. When we see people who are rich, famous, or good-looking, we tend to assume that their lives are rewarding, even though all the evidence might point to their being miserable. And we assume that if only we could acquire some of those same symbols, we would be much happier.

If we do actually succeed in becoming richer, or more powerful, we believe, at least for a time, that life as a whole has improved. But symbols can be deceptive: they have a tendency to distract from the reality they are supposed to represent. And the reality is that the quality of life does not depend directly on what others think of us or on what we own. The bottom line is, rather, how we feel about ourselves and about what hap-pens to us. To improve life one must improve the quality of experience.

This is not to say that money, physical fitness, or fame are irrelevant to happiness. They can be genuine blessings, but only if they help to make us feel better. Otherwise they are at best neutral, at worst obstacles to a rewarding life. Research on happiness and life satisfaction suggests that in general there is a mild correlation between wealth and well-being.

People in economically more affluent countries (including the United States) tend to rate themselves as being on the whole more happy than people in less affluent countries. Ed Diener, a researcher from the University of Illinois, found that very wealthy persons report being happy on the average 77 percent of the time, while persons of average wealth say they are happy only 62 percent of the time. This difference, while statistically significant, is not very large, especially considering that the "very wealthy" group was selected from a list of the four hundred richest Americans. It is also interesting to note that not one respondent in Diener's study believed that money by itself guaranteed happiness. The majority agreed with the statement, "Money can increase or decrease happiness, depending on how it is used." In an earlier study, Norman Bradburn found that the highest-income group reported being happy about 25 percent more often than the lowest. Again, the difference was present, but it was not very large. In a comprehensive survey entitled *The Quality of American Life* published a decade ago, the authors report that a person's financial situation is one of the least important factors affecting overall satisfaction with life.

Given these observations, instead of worrying about how to make a million dollars or how to win friends and influence people, it seems more beneficial to find out how everyday life can be made more harmonious and more satisfying, and thus achieve by a direct route what cannot be reached through the pursuit of symbolic goals.

## PLEASURE AND ENJOYMENT

When considering the kind of experience that makes life better, most people first think that happiness consists in experiencing pleasure: good food, good sex, all the comforts that money can buy. We imagine the satisfaction of traveling to exotic places or being surrounded by interesting company and expensive gadgets. If we cannot afford those goals that slick commercials and colorful ads keep reminding us to pursue, then we are happy to settle for a quiet evening in front of the television set with a glass of liquor close by.

Pleasure is a feeling of contentment that one achieves whenever information in consciousness says that expectations set by biological programs or by social conditioning have been met. The taste of food when we are hungry is pleasant because it reduces a physiological imbalance. Resting in the evening while passively absorbing information from the media, with alcohol or drugs to dull the mind overexcited by the demands of work, is pleasantly relaxing. Traveling to Acapulco is pleasant because the stimulating novelty restores our palate jaded by the repetitive routines of everyday life, and because we know that this is how the "beautiful people" also spend their time.

Pleasure is an important component of the quality of life, but by itself it does not bring happiness. Sleep, rest, food, and sex provide restorative homeostatic experiences that return consciousness to order after the needs of the body intrude and cause psychic entropy to occur. But they do not produce psychological growth. They do not add complexity to the self. Pleasure helps to maintain order, but by itself cannot create new order in consciousness.

When people ponder further about what makes their lives rewarding, they tend to move beyond pleasant memories and begin to remember other events, other experiences that overlap with pleasurable ones but fall into a category that deserves a separate name: enjoyment. Enjoyable events occur when a person has not only met some prior expectation or satisfied a need or a desire but also gone beyond what he or she has been programmed to do and achieved something unexpected, perhaps something even unimagined before.

Enjoyment is characterized by this forward movement: by a sense of novelty, of accomplishment. Playing a close game of tennis that stretches one's ability is enjoyable, as is reading a book that reveals things in a new light, as is having a conversation that leads us to express ideas we didn't know we had. Closing a contested business deal, or any piece of work well done, is enjoyable. None of these experiences may be particularly pleasurable at the time they are taking place, but afterward we think back on them and say, "That really was fun" and wish they would happen again. After an enjoyable event we know that we have changed, that our self has grown: in some respect, we have become more complex as a result of it.

Experiences that give pleasure can also give enjoyment, but the two sensations are quite different. For instance, everybody takes pleasure in eating. To enjoy food, however, is more difficult. A gourmet enjoys eating, as does anyone who pays enough attention to a meal so as to discriminate the various sensations provided by it. As this example suggests, we can experience pleasure without any investment of psychic energy, whereas enjoyment happens only as a result of unusual investments of attention. A person can feel pleasure without any effort, if the appropriate centers in his brain are electrically stimulated, or as a result of the chemical stimulation of drugs. But it is impossible to enjoy a tennis game, a book, or a conversation unless attention is fully concentrated on the activity.

It is for this reason that pleasure is so evanescent, and that the self does not grow as a consequence of pleasurable experiences. Complexity requires investing psychic energy in goals that are new, that are relatively challenging. It is easy to see this process in children: During the first few years of life every child is a little "learning machine" trying out new movements, new words daily. The rapt concentration on the child's face as she learns each new skill is a good indication of what enjoyment is about. And each instance of enjoyable learning adds to the complexity of the child's developing self.

Unfortunately, this natural connection between growth and enjoyment tends to disappear with time. Perhaps because "learning" becomes an external imposition when schooling starts, the excitement of mastering new skills gradually wears out. It becomes all too easy to settle down within the narrow boundaries of the self developed in adolescence. But if one gets to be too complacent, feeling that psychic energy invested in new directions is wasted unless there is a good chance of reaping extrinsic rewards for it, one may end up no longer enjoying life, and pleasure becomes the only source of positive experience.

## THE MERGING OF ACTION AND AWARENESS

When all a person's relevant skills are needed to cope with the challenges of a situation, that person's attention is completely absorbed by the activity. There is no excess psychic energy left over to process any information but what the activity offers. All the attention is concentrated on the relevant stimuli.

As a result, one of the most universal and distinctive features of optimal experience takes place: people become so involved in what they are doing that the activity becomes spontaneous, almost automatic; they stop being aware of themselves as separate from the actions they are performing.

A dancer describes how it feels when a performance is going well:

"Your concentration is very complete. Your mind isn't wandering, you are not thinking of something else; you are totally involved in what you are doing. . . . Your energy is flowing very smoothly. You feel relaxed, comfortable, and energetic."

A rock climber explains how it feels when he is scaling a mountain: "You are so involved in what you are doing [that] you aren't thinking of yourself as separate from the immediate activity. . . . You don't see yourself as separate from what you are doing."

A mother who enjoys the time spent with her small daughter: "Her reading is the one thing that she's really into, and we read together. She reads to me, and I read to her, and that's a time when I sort of lose touch with the rest of the world, I'm totally absorbed in what I'm doing."

A chess player tells of playing in a tournament: ". . . the concentration is like breathing—you never think of it. The roof could fall in and, if it missed you, you would be unaware of it."

It is for this reason that we called the optimal experience "flow." The short and simple word describes well the sense of seemingly effortless movement. The following words from a poet and rock climber apply to all the thousands of interviews collected by us and by others over the years: "The mystique of rock climbing is climbing; you get to the top of a rock glad it's over but really wish it would go on forever. The justification of climbing is climbing, like the justification of poetry is writing; you don't conquer anything except things in yourself. . . . The act of writing justifies poetry. Climbing is the same: recognizing that you are a flow. The purpose of the flow is to keep on flowing, not looking for a peak or utopia but staying in the flow. It is not a moving up but a continuous flowing; you move up to keep the flow going. There is no possible reason for climbing except the climbing itself—it is a self-communication."

Although the flow experience appears to be effortless, it is far from being so. It often requires strenuous physical exertion, or highly disciplined mental activity. It does not happen without the application of skilled performance. Any lapse in concentration will erase it. And yet while it lasts consciousness works smoothly, action follows action seamlessly. In normal life, we keep interrupting what we do with doubts and questions. "Why am I doing this? Should I perhaps be doing something else?" Repeatedly we question the necessity of our actions, and evaluate critically the reasons for carrying them out. But in flow there is no need to reflect, because the action carries us forward as if by magic.

## CONCENTRATION ON THE TASK AT HAND

One of the most frequently mentioned dimensions of the flow experience is that, while it lasts, one is able to forget all the unpleasant aspects of life. This feature of flow is an important by-product of the fact that enjoyable activities require a complete focusing of attention on the task at hand—thus leaving no room in the mind for irrelevant information.

In normal everyday existence, we are the prey of thoughts and worries intruding unwanted in consciousness. Because most jobs, and home life in general, lack the pressing demands of flow experiences, concentration is rarely so intense that preoccupations and anxieties can be automatically ruled out. Consequently the ordinary state of mind involves unexpected and frequent episodes of entropy interfering with the smooth run of psychic energy. This is one reason why flow improves the quality of experience: the clearly structured demands of the activity impose order, and exclude the interference of disorder in consciousness.

A professor of physics who was an avid rock climber described his state of mind while climbing as follows: "It is as if my memory input has been cut off. All I can remember is the last thirty seconds, and all I can think ahead is the next five minutes." In fact, any activity that requires concentration has a similarly narrow window of time.

But it is not only the temporal focus that counts. What is even more significant is that only a very select range of information can be allowed into awareness. Therefore all the troubling thoughts that ordinarily keep passing through the mind are temporarily kept in abeyance. As a young basketball player explains: "The court—that's all that matters. . . . Sometimes out on the court I think of a problem, like fighting with my steady girl, and I think that's nothing compared to the game. You can think about a problem all day but as soon as you get in the game, the hell with it!" And another: "Kids my age, they think a lot . . . but when you are playing basketball, that's all there is on your mind—just basketball. . . . Everything seems to follow right along."

## THE LOSS OF SELF-CONSCIOUSNESS

We have seen earlier that when an activity is thoroughly engrossing, there is not enough attention left over to allow a person to consider either the past or the future, or any other temporarily irrelevant stimuli. One item that disappears from awareness deserves special mention, because in normal life we spend so much time thinking about it: our own self. Here is a climber describing this aspect of the experience: "It's a Zen feeling, like meditation or concentration. One thing you're after is the one-pointedness of mind. You can get your ego mixed up with climbing in all sorts of ways and it isn't necessarily enlightening. But when things become automatic, it's like an egoless thing, in a way.

"Somehow the right thing is done without you ever thinking about it or doing anything at all. . . . It just happens. And yet you're more concentrated." Or, in the words of a famous long-distance ocean cruiser: "So one forgets oneself, one forgets everything, seeing only the play of the boat with the sea, the play of the sea around the boat, leaving aside everything not essential to that game. . . ."

The loss of the sense of a self separate from the world around it is sometimes accompanied by a feeling of union with the environment, whether it is the mountain, a team, or, in the case of this member of a Japanese motorcycle gang, the "run" of hundreds of cycles roaring down the streets of Kyoto: "I understand something when all of our feelings get tuned up. When running, we are not in complete harmony at the start. But if the run begins to go well, all of us, all of us feel for the others. How can I say this? . . . When our minds become one. At such a time, it's a real pleasure. . . . When all of us become one, I understand something. . . . All of a sudden I realize, 'Oh, we're one' and think, 'If we speed as fast as we can, it will become a real run. . . .' When we realize that we become one flesh, it's supreme. When we get high on speed. At such a moment, it's really super."

This "becoming one flesh" so vividly described by the Japanese teenager is a very real feature of the flow experience. Persons report feeling it as concretely as they feel relief from hunger or from pain. It is a greatly rewarding experience, but as we shall see later on, one that presents its own dangers.

Preoccupation with the self consumes psychic energy because in everyday life we often feel threatened. Whenever we are threatened we need to bring the image we have of ourselves back into awareness, so we can find out whether or not the threat is serious, and how we should meet it. For instance, if walking down the street I notice some people turning back and looking at me with grins on their faces, the normal thing to do is immediately to start worrying: "Is there something wrong! Do I look funny? Is it the way I walk, or is my face smudged?" Hundreds of times every day we are reminded of the vulnerability of our self. And every time this happens psychic energy is lost trying to restore order to consciousness.

But in flow there is no room for self-scrutiny. Because enjoyable activities have clear goals, stable rules, and challenges well matched to skills, there is little opportunity for the self to be threatened. When a climber is making a difficult ascent, he is totally taken up in the mountaineering role. He is 100 percent a climber, or he would not survive. There is no way for anything or anybody to bring into question any other aspect of his self. Whether his face is smudged makes absolutely no difference. The only possible threat is the one that comes from the mountain—but a good climber is well trained to face that threat, and does not need to bring the self into play in the process.

The absence of the self from consciousness does not mean that a person in flow has given up the control of his psychic energy, or that she is unaware of what happens in her body or in her mind. In fact the opposite is usually true. When people first learn about the flow experience they sometimes assume that lack of self-consciousness has something to do with a passive obliteration of the self, a "going with the flow" Southern California–style. But in fact the optimal experience involves a very active role for the self. A violinist must be extremely aware of every movement of her fingers, as well as of the sound entering her ears, and of the total form of the piece she is playing, both analytically, note by note, and holistically, in terms of its overall design. A good runner is usually aware of every relevant muscle in his body, of the rhythm of his breathing, as well as of the performance of his competitors within the overall strategy of the race. A chess player could not enjoy the game if he were unable to retrieve from his memory, at will, previous positions, past combinations.

So loss of self-consciousness does not involve a loss of self, and certainly not a loss of consciousness, but rather, only a loss of consciousness of the self. What slips below the threshold of awareness is the concept of self, the information we use to represent to ourselves who we are. And being able to forget temporarily who we are seems to be very enjoyable. When not preoccupied with ourselves, we actually have a chance to expand the concept of who we are. Loss of self-consciousness can lead to self-transcendence, to a feeling that the boundaries of our being have been pushed forward.

## THE AUTOTELIC EXPERIENCE

The key element of an optimal experience is that it is an end in itself. Even if initially undertaken for other reasons, the activity that consumes us becomes intrinsically rewarding. Surgeons speak of their work: "It is so enjoyable that I would do it even if I didn't have to." Sailors say: "I am spending a lot of money and time on this boat, but it is worth it—nothing quite compares with the feeling I get when I am out sailing."

The term "autotelic" derives from two Greek words, auto meaning self, and telos meaning goal. It refers to a self-contained activity, one that is done not with the expectation of some future benefit, but simply because the doing itself is the reward. Playing the stock market in order to make money is not an autotelic experience; but playing it in order to prove one's skill in foretelling future trends is—even though the outcome in terms of dollars and cents is exactly the same. Teaching children in order to turn them into good citizens is not autotelic, whereas teaching them because one enjoys interacting with children is. What transpires in the two situations is ostensibly identical; what differs is that when the experience is autotelic, the person is paying attention to the activity for its own sake; when it is not, the attention is focused on its consequences.

Most things we do are neither purely autotelic nor purely exotelic (as we shall call activities done for external reasons only), but are a combination of the two. Surgeons usually enter into their long period of training because of exotelic expectations: to help people, to make money, to achieve prestige. If they are lucky, after a while they begin to enjoy their work, and then surgery becomes to a large extent also autotelic.

Some things we are initially forced to do against our will turn out in the course of time to be intrinsically rewarding. A friend of mine, with whom I worked in an office many years ago, had a great gift. Whenever the work got to be particularly boring, he would look up with a glazed look in his half-closed eyes, and he would start to hum a piece of music—a Bach chorale, a Mozart concerto, a Beethoven symphony. But humming is a pitifully inadequate description of what he did. He reproduced the entire piece, imitating with his voice the principal instruments involved in the particular passage: now he wailed like a violin, now he crooned like a bassoon, now he blared like a baroque trumpet. We in the office listened entranced, and resumed work refreshed. What is curious is the way my friend had developed this gift. Since the age of three, he had been taken by his father to concerts of classical music. He remembers having been unspeakably bored, and occasionally falling asleep in the seat, to be awakened by a sharp slap. He grew to hate concerts, classical music, and presumably his father—but year after year he was forced to repeat this painful experience. Then one evening, when he was about seven years old, during the overture to a Mozart opera, he had what he described as an ecstatic insight: he suddenly discerned the melodic structure of the piece, and had an overwhelming sense of a new world opening up before him. It was the three years of painful listening that had prepared him for this epiphany, years during which his musical skills had developed, however unconsciously, and made it possible for him to understand the challenge Mozart had built into the music.

Of course he was lucky; many children never reach the point of recognizing the possibilities of the activity into which they are forced, and end up disliking it forever. How many children have come to hate classical music because their parents forced them to practice an instrument! Often children—and adults—need external incentives to take the first steps in an activity that requires a difficult restructuring of attention. Most enjoyable activities are not natural; they demand an effort that initially one is reluctant to make. But once the interaction starts to provide feedback to the person's skills, it usually begins to be intrinsically rewarding.

An autotelic experience is very different from the feelings we typically have in the course of life. So much of what we ordinarily do has no value in itself, and we do it only because we have to do it, or because we expect some future benefit from it. Many people feel that the time they spend at work is essentially wasted—they are alienated from it, and the psychic energy invested in the job does nothing to strengthen their self. For quite a few people free time is also wasted. Leisure provides a relaxing respite from work, but it generally consists of passively absorbing information, without using any skills or exploring new opportunities for action. As a result life passes in a sequence of boring and anxious experiences over which a person has little control.

The autotelic experience, or flow, lifts the course of life to a different level. Alienation gives way to involvement, enjoyment replaces boredom, helplessness turns into a feeling of control, and psychic energy works to reinforce the sense of self, instead of being lost in the service of external goals. When experience is intrinsically rewarding life is justified in the present, instead of being held hostage to a hypothetical future gain.

# Harmony

from *Wherever You Go, There You Are*

by Jon Kabat-Zinn

As I pull into the parking lot of the hospital, several hundred geese pass overhead. They are flying high and I do not hear their honking. What strikes me first is that they clearly know where they are going. They are flying northwest, and there are so many of them that the formation trails out far to the east, where the early November sun is hugging the horizon. As the first of them fly over, I am moved by the nobility and beauty of their purposeful assembly to grab paper and pen right there in the car and capture the pattern as best my unskilled hand and eye are able. Rapid strokes suffice . . . they will shortly be gone.

Hundreds are in Vs, but many are in more complex arrangements. Everything is in motion. Their lines dip and ascend with grace and harmony, like a cloth waving in the air. It is clear that they are communicating. Each one somehow knows where it is, has a place in this complex and constantly changing pattern, belongs.

I feel strangely blessed by their passage. This moment is a gift. I have been permitted to see and share in something I know is important, something I am not graced with that often. Part of it is their wildness, part is the harmony, order, and beauty they embody.

My usual experience of time flowing is suspended while witnessing their passing. The pattern is what scientists call " chaotic," like cloud formations or the shapes of trees. There is order, and within it, embedded disorder, yet that too is orderly. For me now, it is simply the gift of wonder and amazement. Nature is showing me as I come to work today how things actually are in one small sphere, reminding me how little we humans know, and how little we appreciate harmony, or even see it.

And so, reading the newspaper that evening, I note that the full consequences of logging the rain forests covering the high ground in the South Philippines were not apparent until the typhoon of late 1991 struck, when the denuded earth, no longer able to hold water, let it rush unchecked to the lowlands at four times the usual volume and drowned thousands of poor inhabitants of the region. As the popular bumper sticker says, "Shit happens." The trouble is, too often we are unwilling to see our role in it. There are definite risks to disdaining the harmony of things.

Nature's harmony is around us and within us at all times. Perceiving it is an occasion for great happiness; but it is often only appreciated in retrospect or in its absence. If all is going well in the body, it tends to go unnoticed. Your lack of a headache is not front-page news for your cerebral cortex. Abilities such as walking, seeing, thinking, and peeing take care of themselves, and so blend into the landscape of automaticity and unawareness. Only pain or fear or loss wake us and bring things into focus. But by then the harmony is harder to see, and we find ourselves caught up in turbulence, itself containing, like rapids and waterfalls, order of a more difficult and subtle level within the river of life. As Joni Mitchell sings, "You don't know what you've got till it's gone."

As I get out of the car, I inwardly bow to these wayfarers for anointing the airspace of this necessarily civilized hospital parking lot with a refreshing dose of natural wildness.

Try: Drawing back the veil of unawareness to perceive harmony in this moment. Can you see it in clouds, in sky, in people, in the weather, in food, in your body, in this breath? Look, and look again, right here, right now!

# Zen and the Art of Motorcycle Maintenance
by Robert M. Pirsig

Peace of mind isn't at all superficial to technical work. It's the whole thing. That which produces it is good work and that which destroys it is bad work. The specs, the measuring instruments, the quality control, the final check-out, these are all means toward the end of satisfying the peace of mind of those responsible for the work. What really counts in the end is their peace of mind, nothing else. The reason for this is that peace of mind is a prerequisite for a perception of that Quality which is beyond romantic Quality and classic Quality and which unites the two, and which must accompany the work as it proceeds. The way to see what looks good and understand the reasons it looks good, and to be at one with this goodness as the work proceeds, is to cultivate an inner quietness, a peace of mind so that goodness can shine through.

I say inner peace of mind. It has no direct relationship to external circumstances. It can occur to a monk in meditation, to a soldier in heavy combat or to a machinist taking off that last ten-thousandth of an inch. It involves unselfconsciousness, which produces a complete identification with one's circumstances, and there are levels and levels of this identification and levels and levels of quietness quite as profound and difficult of attainment as the more familiar levels of activity. The mountains of achievement are Quality discovered in one direction only, and are relatively meaningless and often unobtainable unless taken together with the ocean trenches of self-awareness—so different from self-consciousness—which result from inner peace of mind.

This inner peace of mind occurs on three levels of understanding. Physical quietness seems the easiest to achieve, although there are levels and levels of this too, as attested by the ability of Hindu mystics to live buried alive for many days. Mental quietness, in which one has no wandering thoughts at all, seems more difficult, but can be achieved. But value quietness, in which one has no wandering desires at all but simply performs the acts of his life without desire, that seems the hardest.

I've sometimes thought that inner peace of mind, this quietness is similar to if not idential with the sort of calm you sometimes get when going fishing, which accounts for much of the popularity of this sport. Just sitting with the line in the water, not moving, not really thinking about anything, not really caring about anything either, seems to draw out the inner tensions and frustrations that have prevented you from solving problems you couldn't solve before and introduced ugliness and clumsiness into your actions and thoughts.

You don't have to go fishing, of course, to fix your motorcycle. A cup of coffee, a walk around the block, sometimes just putting off the job for five minutes of silence is enough.

When you do you can almost feel yourself grow toward that inner peace of mind that reveals it all. That which turns its back on this inner calm and the Quality it reveals is bad maintenance. That which turns toward it is good. The forms of turning away and toward are infinite but the goal is always the same.

I think that when this concept of peace of mind is introduced and made central to the act of technical work, a fusion of classic and romantic Quality can take place at a basic level within a practical working context. I've said you can actually see this fusion in skilled mechanics and machinists of a certain sort, and you can see it in the work they do. To say that they are not artists is to misunderstand the nature of art. They have patience, care and attentiveness to what they're doing, but more than this—there's a kind of inner peace of mind that isn't contrived but results from a kind of harmony with the work in which there's no leader and no follower. The material and the craftsman's thoughts change together in a progression of smooth, even changes until his mind is at rest at the exact instant the material is right.

We've all had moments of that sort when we're doing something we really want to do. It's just that somehow we've gotten into an unfortunate separation of those moments from work. The mechanic I'm talking about doesn't make this separation. One says of him that he is "interested" in what he's doing, that he's "involved" in his work. What produces this involvement is, at the cutting edge of consciousness, an absence of any sense of separateness of subject and object. "Being with it," "being a natural," "taking hold," there are a lot of idiomatic expressions for what I mean by this absence of subject-object duality, because what I mean is so well understood as folklore, common sense, the everyday understanding of the shop. But in scientific parlance the words for this absence of subject-object duality are scarce because scientific minds have shut themselves off from consciousness of this kind of understanding in the assumption of the formal dualistic scientific outlook.

Zen Buddhists talk about "just sitting," a meditative practice in which the idea of a duality of self and object does not dominate one's consciousness. What I'm talking about here in motorcycle maintenance is "just fixing," in which the idea of a duality of self and object doesn't dominate one's consciousness. When one isn't dominated by feelings of separateness from what he's working on, then one can be said to "care" about what he's doing. That is what caring really is, a feeling of identification with what one's doing. When one has this feeling then he also sees the inverse side of caring, Quality itself.

So the thing to do when working on a motorcycle, as in any other task, is to cultivate the peace of mind which does not separate one's self from one's surroundings. When that is done successfully then everything else follows naturally. Peace of mind produces right values, right values produce right thoughts. Right thoughts produce right actions and right actions produce work which will be a material reflection for others to see of the serenity at the center of it all. That was what it was about that wall in Korea. It was a material reflection of a spiritual reality.

I think that if we are going to reform the world, and make it a better place to live in, the way to do it is not with talk about relationships of a political nature, which are inevitably dualistic, full of subjects and objects and their relationship to one another; or with programs full of things for other people to do. I think that kind of approach starts in at the end and presumes the end is the beginning. Programs of a political nature are important end products of social quality that can be effective only if the underlying structure of social values is right. The social values are right only if the individual values are right. The place to improve the world is first in one's own heart and head and hands, and then work outward from there. Other people can talk about how to expand the destiny of mankind. I just want to talk about how to fix a motorcycle. I think that what I have to say has more lasting value.

# The No-Boundary Moment

from *No Boundary*

by Ken Wilber

"Need there is, methinks, to understand the sense in which the scripture speaketh of time and eternity." With those words, St. Dionysius put his finger on the whole crux of mystical insight, for the enlightened sages of all times and places agree that unity consciousness is not temporal, not of time, but eternal, timeless. It knows no beginning, no birth, and no ending, no death. Thus, until we thoroughly grasp the nature of eternity, the sense of the Real will elude us.

"Who," asks St. Augustine, "will hold the heart of man that it may stand still and see how eternity, ever still-standing, neither past nor to come, uttereth the times past and to come?" Who indeed? For grasping that which is eternal—if in fact such even exists seems so weighty, momentous, and well nigh impossible a task that we are likely to shrink before it. Modern man seems so generally bereft of even the least mystical insight that he shrugs off the notion of eternity altogether, or explains it away with a positivistic fury, or demands what it has to do with "practical reality."

Yet the mystic claims that eternity is not a philosophical opinion, nor a religious dogma, nor an unattainable ideal. Eternity rather is so simple, so obvious, so present, and so straightforward that we have only to open our eyes in a radically empirical fashion and look. As Zen Master Huang Po used to repeatedly stress, "It's right in front of you!"

Part of the reason that "contacting the eternal" seems so awesome is that we generally misunderstand the true sense of the word "eternity" itself. We commonly imagine eternity to be a very, very long time, an unending stretch of years, a million times a million forever. But the mystic does not understand eternity in that fashion at all. For eternity is not an awareness of everlasting time, but an awareness which is itself totally without time. The eternal moment is a timeless moment, a moment which knows neither past nor future, before nor after, yesterday nor tomorrow, birth nor death. To live in unity consciousness is to live in and as the timeless moment, for nothing obscures the divine fight more thoroughly than the taint of time. As Meister Eckhart put it, "Time is what keeps the light from reaching us. There is no greater obstacle to God [unity consciousness] than time. And not only time but temporalities, not only temporal things but temporal affectations; not only temporal affectations but the very taint and smell of time."

And yet, we must ask, what is a timeless moment? What instant is without date or duration? What moment is not just quick or short-lived in time, but absolutely without time?

Odd as these questions initially seem, most of us would have to admit that we have known moments, peak moments, which seemed indeed to be so far beyond time that the past and the future melted away into obscurity. Lost in a sunset; transfixed by the play of moonlight on a crystal dark pond which possesses no bottom; floated out of self and time in the enraptured embrace of a loved one—caught and held still—bound by the crack of thunder echoing through mists of rain. Who has not touched the timeless?

What do all of these experiences have in common? It seems, and the mystic agrees, that time appears suspended in all of these experiences because we are totally absorbed in the present moment. Clearly, in this present moment, if we would but examine it, there is no time. The present moment is a timeless moment, and a timeless moment is an eternal one—a moment which knows neither past nor future, before nor after, yesterday nor tomorrow. To enter deeply into this present moment is thus to plunge into eternity, to step through the looking glass and into the world of the Unborn and the Undying.

For there is no beginning to this present moment, and that which has no beginning is the Unborn. That is, search as you will, you cannot find, see, or feel a beginning to your experience of this present moment. When did this present begin? Did it ever begin? Or could it possibly be that this present floats so above time that it never entered the temporal stream at any beginning? In the same vein, there is no ending to this present moment, and that which has no ending is the Undying. Again, search as you will, you cannot find, see, or feel an ending to your experience of this present moment. You never experience an ending to the present (even if you die since you would not be there to feel anything end). This is why we heard Schroedinger say that "the present is the only thing that has no end." Granted that the outer forms of the present moment cascade by in bewildering succession, still the present itself remains indestructible, untouched by what we have been taught to interpret as "time." In this present moment there is neither past nor future—there is no time. And that which is timeless is eternal. Says Zen Master Seppo, "If you want to know what eternity means, it is no further than this very moment. If you fail to catch it in this present moment, you will not get it, however many times you are reborn in hundreds of thousands of years."

# The Knitting Sutra

from *The Knitting Sutra*

by Susan Gordon Lydon

Follow the thread, the circle, the web, the pattern that winds through a life. In my middle years I've reached the age of integration and synthesis. I followed a path to the center of my being and stayed for a time, cultivating the garden of my interior self, nourishing the heartwood at my core. When I reemerged, I was traveling a path of my own making. I had become a person—as I once heard it said of the great Sitting Bull—who owns myself.

*Sutra*, from which comes *suture*, means thread, a connective cord. Our connections to one another are sacred, as all life is sacred, as all of the earth is sacred; the circle that winds around the earth forms the hoop that is also sacred. You don't have to be Native American to know this, only a person of heart. The great unity, the oneness of things, the indivisible interconnectedness of everything that exists in the cosmos is as plain as the nose on your face, if only your eyes are open to see, your ears open to hear.

In Grateful Dead drummer Mickey Hart's book *Drumming at the Edge of Magic*, he talks about a specific moment that occurs when several people drum together, the barely perceptible shift as the drummers "entrain," as he calls it, and their disparate rhythms become one. Native Americans view the drum as the heartbeat of Mother Earth. They bring their babies into the powwow arena, a sacred circle of earth, so that the drumbeat enters their hearts from the very beginning of their lives.

The path I followed to the heart of my being involved rhythm and also a miracle of thread. In knitting one takes a length of thread and, through rhythmic repetitive motions made by clicking two needles together in such a way that they catch the thread, creates interconnecting loops, which eventually grow into a garment to clothe and warm the body. Knitting, like drumming, is a feat of homegrown magic. It is the simplest and most ordinary of activities, yet somehow it mysteriously contains within itself the potential for expanding our conscious awareness.

Buddhists say that enlightenment may be achieved through the repetition of sutra, or prayer. Pattern also is formed by repetition; its beauty deepens and grows each time it is repeated.

When I first saw the Chaucer quote, "The lyf so shorte, the crafte so long to lerne." I thought then that the aim of craft was to become proficient and to spend a lifetime creating beautiful things. It seemed like something was wrong with a plan whereby you took a lifetime to achieve mastery over difficult techniques, then died just when you had become really good. I learned while writing this book that the purpose of the craft is not so much to make beautiful things as it is to become beautiful inside while you are making those things.

The finest examples of craftsmanship that come down to us through the ages exalt the human spirit. They belong to us all. They show what we are capable of and what we deserve. Tibetan *thangkas* are pictorial representations of the various Buddhas. Strict requirements must be followed while making them, including maintaining the proper attitude of reverence. Because *thangkas* depict what is most holy in the human spirit, these paintings were made with the finest materials that could be found. Colors were obtained by crushing precious gems into powders: lapis lazuli for the blues, emeralds for the greens, rubies for the reds, and so on. And yet the very finest examples of the *thangka* painters' art manifested not in the fabulous scrolls but inside the painter's self.

That is why the end result, however pleasing to the eye, is ultimately unimportant, and, to show that a work of art may be as impermanent as life itself, Tibetan monks will sometimes ritually destroy the intricate mandalas they painstakingly construct of colored sand.

Pablo Casals, the cellist, once remarked that in music the notes not played are as important as the ones that are played. These are the grace notes, the silent beats of space between audible tones of sound.

Musicians, artists, and craftspeople belong with mystics in the ranks

of shamans and visionaries. All reach into the formless void to pull something of substance and beauty out of chaos. What they do may manifest
on the material. Picasso claimed that he was able to maintain the stamina
he needed for painting well into his eighties because when he entered
his studio he left his body at the door. There is an ecstasy in the act of
creation that matches the intensity of religious rapture; both partake of
divinity and are gifts granted by the Great Creative Spirit.

# Meditation

Meditation is a discipline by which we may develop the qualities of awareness, acceptance, and letting go and through which we come to experience tranquility and harmony. It is a practice through which we can enhance and refine our ability to observe, to listen, and to experience fully by disciplining the mind to focus on what is happening at any given moment.

"Can Anybody Meditate?" Jon Kabat-Zinn asks. If one has a commitment to paying attention, whether it is to our breath, to our mind, or to taking a walk it is possible to meditate. What several of the writers in this section caution is that we should not expect anything in particular to result from meditation. As Charlotte Joko Beck says in "What Practice Is," meditation (which writers may refer to as "practice") is about facing ourselves and not about achieving any special state like enlightenment. It is not about getting lost in thought but about seeing what our thoughts are.

"Training the Puppy," like many excerpts in this section, describes what we observe when we first begin to meditate. "Our minds," writes Jack Kornfield, are "like a crazed monkey jumping from tree to tree." Meditating, he says, is the art of awakening or the art of inner listening. Kornfield provides here step-by-step meditation instructions.

In "Meditation Training," Lama Surya Das answers the question, "Why meditate?" We meditate, he says, in order to discipline the mind to cultivate awareness, to see things as they are.

Charlotte Joko Beck describes in "Opening Pandora's Box," how meditation may release a variety of pent up emotions. She reminds us that our experience with meditation is not always peaceful. As we meditate we may uncover emotions that we have hidden behind a protective wall for fear that we cannot deal with them. The release of these emotions, she says, is part of the price we pay to transform our lives.

Robert Aitken, in "Classes of Delusion," discusses different categories of distraction that we may experience when meditating These catgories may be specific to our own personality or to stages that we go through as our meditation practice evolves.

In "Venturing into the Here and Now," famed basketball coach Phil Jackson describes how the Chicago Bulls practice meditation. While not everyone on the team is comfortable with the practice, he finds that it tends to improve communication among team members and to focus the attention of individual members on the game. Professional basketball, where aggressiveness and goal orientation are considered priorities, is a remarkable setting in which to find meditation.

There are numerous approaches to meditation. In "Mindfulness Versus Concentration," Henepola Gunaratana helps to refine our understanding of one key area of potential confusion to beginners—the distinction between mindfulness and concentration. In classical Vipassana meditation, which is also called mindfulness meditation, two qualities of mind work together—one the ability to sustain a focus on one particular object of attention; the other, our ability to observe a constantly changing field of objects and see beneath the surface to a deeper unity and unifying connectedness. Concentration and mindfulness work together to help us maintain our focus while we observe with equanimity what is happening.

Jon Kabat-Zinn discusses the dynamic and potential benefits of a meditation retreat in "An Eighteen-Year Retreat," which is how he describes the experience of parenting. Just as meditation is a brief (usually a few minutes to an hour) period of inner attention, a meditation retreat is an opportunity for extended inner attention. A meditation retreat, where distractions are limited for a longer period of time, gives a greater opportunity to settle the mind.

Daniel Goleman reports on both his personal experience with meditation and the results of clinical studies of meditators. In "Meditation: Research and Practical Application," he presents the results of studies that demonstrate the beneficial effects of meditation on people who suffer from headaches, diabetes, and pain. The effect of meditation on stress, which promotes a great deal of physical and mental suffering, is a prominent feature of this excerpt. All of these beneficial effects, he points out, are the result of simply paying attention more effectively.

The collection ends with Gary Snyder's "We Wash Our Bowls in This Water," a poem yet mindful evokation of the mystery of existence, a mystery that lies at the heart of the interconnectedness of . . . everything.

# Can Anybody Meditate?

from *Wherever You Go, There You Are*

by Jon Kabat-Zinn

I get asked this question a lot. I suspect people ask because they think that probably everybody else can meditate but they can't. They want to be reassured that they are not alone, that there are at least some other people they can identify with—those hapless souls who were born incapable of meditating. But it isn't so simple.

Thinking you are unable to meditate is a little like thinking you are unable to breathe, or to concentrate or relax. Pretty much everybody can breathe easily. And under the right circumstances, pretty much anybody can concentrate, anybody can relax.

People often confuse meditation with relaxation or some other special state that you have to get to or feel. When once or twice you try and you don't get anywhere or you didn't feel anything special then you think you are one of those people who can't do it.

But meditation is not about feeling a certain way. It's about feeling the way you feel. It's not about making the mind empty or still although stillness does deepen in meditation and can be cultivated systematically. Above all, meditation is about letting the mind be as it is and knowing something about how it is in this moment. It's not about getting somewhere else, but about allowing yourself to be where you already are. If you don't understand this, you will think you are constitutionally unable to meditate. But that's just more thinking, and in this case, incorrect thinking at that.

True, meditation does require energy, and a commitment to stick with it. But then, wouldn't it be more accurate to say, "I won't stick with it," rather than, "I can't do it"? Anybody can sit down and watch their breath or watch their mind. And you don't have to be sitting. You could do it walking, standing, lying down, standing on one leg, running, or taking a bath. But to stay at it for even five minutes requires intentionality. To make it part of your life requires some discipline. So when people say they can't meditate, what they really mean is that they won't make time for it, or that when they try, they don't like what happens. It isn't what they are looking for or hoping for. It doesn't fulfill their expectations. So maybe they should try again, this time letting go of their expectations and just watching.

# What Practice Is

from *Everyday Zen: Love and Work*

by Charlotte Joko Beck

Practice is very simple. That doesn't mean it won't turn our life around, however. I want to review what we do when we sit, or do zazen. And if you think you're beyond this, well, you can think you're beyond this.

Sitting is essentially a simplified space. Our daily life is in constant movement: lots of things going on, lots of people talking, lots of events taking place. In the middle of that, it's very difficult to sense what we are in our life. When we simplify the situation, when we take away the externals and remove ourselves from the ringing phone, the television, the people who visit us, the dog who needs a walk, we get a chance—which is absolutely the most valuable thing there is—to face ourselves. Meditation is not about some state, but about the meditator. It's not about some activity, or about fixing something, or accomplishing something. It's about ourselves. If we don't simplify the situation the chance of taking a good look at ourselves is very small because what we tend to look at isn't ourselves, but everything else. If something goes wrong, what do we look at? We look at what's going wrong, and usually at others we think have made it go wrong. We're looking out there all the time, and not at ourselves.

When I say meditation is about the meditator, I do not mean that we engage in self-analysis. That's not it either. So what do we do?

Once we have assumed our best posture (which should be balanced, easy), we just sit there, we do zazen. What do I mean by "just sit there"? It's the most demanding of all activities. Usually in meditation we don't shut our eyes. But right now I'd like you to shut your eyes and just sit there. What's going on? All sorts of things. A tiny twitch in your left shoulder; a pressure in your side . . . Notice your face for a moment. Feel it. Is it tense anywhere? Around the mouth, around the forehead? Now move down a bit. Notice your neck, just feel it. Then your shoulders, your back, chest, abdominal area, your arms, thighs. Keep feeling whatever you find. And feel your breath as it comes and goes. Don't try to control it, just feel it. Our first instinct is to try to control the breath. Just let your breath be as it is. It may be high in your chest, it may be in the middle, it may be low. It may feel tense. Just experience it as it is. Now just feel all of that. If a car goes by outside, hear it. If a plane flies over, notice that. You might hear a refrigerator going on and off. Just be that. That's all you have to do, absolutely all you have to do: experience that, and just stay with it. Now you can open your eyes.

If you can just do that for three minutes, that's miraculous. Usually after about a minute we begin to think. Our interest in just being with reality (which is what we have just done) is very low. "You mean that is all there is to zazen?" We don't like that. "We're seeking enlightenment, aren't we?" Our interest in reality is extremely low. No, we want to think. We want to worry through all of our preoccupations. We want to figure life out. And so before we know it we've forgotten all about this moment, and we've drifted off into thinking about something: our boyfriend, our girlfriend, our child, our boss, our current fear . . . off we go! There's nothing sinful about such fantasizing except that when we're lost in that, we've lost something else. When we're lost in thought, when we're dreaming, what have we lost? We've lost reality. Our life has escaped us.

This is what human beings do. And we don't just do it sometimes, we do it most of the time. Why do we do that? You know the answer, of course. We do it because we are trying to protect ourselves. We're trying to rid ourselves of our current difficulty, or at least understand it. There's nothing wrong with our self-centered thoughts except that when we identify with them, our view of reality is blocked. So what should we do when the thoughts come up? We should label the thoughts. Be specific in your labeling: not just "thinking, thinking" or "worrying, worrying," but a specific label. For example: "Having a thought she's very bossy." "Having a thought that he's very unfair to me." "Having a thought that I never do anything right." Be specific. And if the thoughts are tumbling out so fast that you can't find anything except confusion, then just label the foggy mess "confusion." But if you persist in trying to find a separate thought, sooner or later you will.

When we practice like this, we get acquainted with ourselves, how our lives work, what we are doing with them. If we find that certain thoughts come up hundreds of times, we know something about ourselves that we didn't know before. Perhaps we incessantly think about the past, or the future. Some people always think about events, some people always think about other people. Some people always think about themselves. Some people's thoughts are almost entirely judgments about other people. Until we have labeled for four or five years, we don't know ourselves very well. When we label thoughts precisely and carefully, what happens to them? They begin to quiet down. We don't have to force ourselves to get rid of them. When they quiet down, we return to the experience of the body and the breath, over and over and over. I can't emphasize enough that we don't just do this three times, we do it ten thousand times, and as we do it, our life transforms. That's a theoretical description of sitting. It's very simple; there's nothing complicated about it.

Now let's take a daily life situation. Suppose you work in an aircraft plant, and you're told that the government contract is coming to an end and probably will not be renewed. You tell yourself, "I'm going to lose my job. I'm going to lose my income. I have a family to support. This is terrible!" What happens then? Your mind starts going over and over and over your problem. "What's going to happen? What shall I do?" Your mind spins faster and faster with worry.

Now there's nothing wrong with planning ahead; we have to plan. But when we become upset, we don't just plan; we obsess. We twist the problem around in a thousand ways. If we don't know what it means to practice with our worried thoughts, what happens next? The thoughts produce an emotion and we become even more agitated. All emotional agitation is caused by the mind. And if we let this happen over a period of time, we often become physically sick or mentally depressed. If the mind will not take care of a situation with awareness, the body will. It will help us out. It's as if the body says, "If you won't take care of it, I guess I've got to." So we produce our next cold, our next rash, our next ulcer, whatever is our style. A mind that is not aware will produce illness. That's not a criticism, however. I don't know of anyone who doesn't get ill, including myself. When the desire to worry is strong, we create difficulties. With regular practice, we just do it less. Anything of which we're unaware will have its fruits in our lives, one way or another.

From the human point of view, the things that go wrong in our lives are of two kinds. One kind are events outside of ourselves, and the other are things within us, such as physical illness. Both are our practice, and we handle them in the same way. We label all the thoughts that occur around them, and we experience them in our body. The process is sitting itself.

To talk about this sounds really easy. But to do it is horrendously difficult. I don't know anyone who can do it all of the time. I know of some people who can do it much of the time. But when we practice in this way, becoming aware of everything that enters our life (whether internal or external), our life begins to transform. And we gain strength and insight and even live at times in the enlightened state, which simply means experiencing life as it is. It's not a mystery.

If you are new to practice it's important to realize that simply to sit on that cushion for fifteen minutes is a victory. Just to sit with that much composure, just to be there, is fine.

If we were afraid of being in water and didn't know how to swim, the first victory would be just to lower ourselves into the water. The next step might be getting our face wet. If we were expert swimmers the challenge might be whether we can enter our hand into the water at a certain angle as we execute our stroke. Does that mean that one swimmer is better and the other worse? No. Both of them are perfect for where they are. Practice at any stage is just being who we are at that moment. It's not a question of being good or bad, or better or worse. Sometimes after my talks people will say, "I don't understand that." And that's perfect too. Our understanding grows over the years, but at any point we are perfect in being what we are.

We begin to learn that there is only one thing in life we can rely on. What is the one thing in life we can rely on? We might say, "I rely on my mate." We may love our husbands and wives; but we can't ever completely rely on them, because another person (like ourselves) is always to some extent unreliable. There is no person on earth whom we can completely rely on, though we can certainly love others and enjoy them. What then can we rely on? If it's not a person, what is it? What can we rely on in life? I asked somebody once and she said, "Myself." Can you rely on yourself? Self-reliance is nice, but is inevitably limited.

There is one thing in life that you can always rely on: life being as it is. Let's talk more concretely. Suppose there is something I want very much: perhaps I want to marry a certain person, or get an advanced degree, or have my child be healthy and happy. But life as it is might be exactly the opposite of what I want. We don't know that we'll marry that certain person. If we do, he might die tomorrow. We may or may not get our advanced degree. Probably we will, but we can't count on that. We can't count on anything. Life is always going to be the way it is. So why can't we rely on that fact? What is so hard about that? Why are we always uneasy? Suppose your living space has just been demolished by an earthquake, and you are about to lose an arm and all your life's savings. Can you then rely on life just as it is? Can you be that?

Trust in things being as they are is the secret of life. But we don't want to hear that. I can absolutely trust that in the next year my life is going to be changed, different, yet always just the way it is. If tomorrow I have a heart attack, I can rely on that, because if I have it, I have it. I can rest in life as it is.

When we make a personal investment in our thoughts we create the "I" (as Krishnamurti would say), and then our life begins not to work. That's why we label thoughts, to take the investment out again. When we've been sitting long enough we can see our thoughts as just pure sensory input. And we can see ourselves moving through the stages preliminary to that: at first we feel our thoughts are real, and out of that we create the self-centered emotions, and out of that we create the barrier to seeing life as it is; because if we are caught in self-centered emotions we can't see people or situations clearly. A thought in itself is just pure sensory input, an energy fragment. But we fear to see thoughts as they are.

When we label a thought we step back from it, we remove our identification. There's a world of difference between saying, "She's impossible" and "Having a thought that she's impossible." If we persistently label any thought the emotional overlay begins to drop out and we are left with an impersonal energy fragment to which we need not attach. But if we think our thoughts are real we act out of them. And if we act from such thoughts our life is muddled. Again, practice is to work with this until we know it in our bones. Practice is not about achieving a realization in our heads. It has to be our flesh, our bones, ourself. Of course, we have to have life-centered thoughts: how to follow a recipe, how to put on a roof, how to plan our vacation. But we don't need the emotionally self-centered activity that we call thinking. It really isn't thinking, it's an aberration of thinking.

Zen is about an active life, an involved life. When we know our minds well and the emotions that our thinking creates, we tend to see better what our lives are about and what needs to be done, which is generally just the next task under our nose. Zen is about a life of action, not a life of passively doing nothing. But our actions must be based on reality. When our actions are based on our false thought systems (which are based on our conditioning), they are poorly based. When we have seen through the thought systems we can see what needs to be done.

What we are doing is not reprogramming ourselves, but freeing ourselves from all programs, by seeing that they are empty of reality. Reprogramming is just jumping from one pot into another. We may have what we think of as a better programming, but the point of sitting is not to be run by any program. Suppose we have a program called "I lack self-confidence." Suppose we decide to reprogram that to "I have self-confidence." Neither of them will stand up very well under the pressures of life, because they involved an "I." And this "I" is a very fragile creation—unreal, actually—and is easily befuddled. In fact there never was an "I." The point is to see that it is empty, an illusion, which is different from dissolving it. When I say that it's empty, I mean that it has no basic reality; it's just a creation of the self-centered thoughts.

Doing Zen practice is never as simple as talking about it. Even students who have a fair understanding of what they're doing at times tend to desert basic practice. Still, when we sit well, everything else takes care of itself. So whether we have been sitting five years or twenty years or are just beginning, it is important to sit with great, meticulous care.

# Training the Puppy:
# Mindfulness of Breathing

from *A Path with Heart*
by Jack Kornfield

> Concentration is never a matter of force or coercion. You simply pick
> up the puppy again and return to reconnect with the here and now.

Meditation can be thought of as the art of awakening. Through the mastering of this art we can learn new ways to approach our difficulties and bring wisdom and joy alive in our life. Through developing meditation's tools and practices, we can awaken the best of our spiritual, human capacities. The key to this art is the steadiness of our attention.

When the fullness of our attention is cultivated together with a grateful and tender heart, our spiritual life will naturally grow.

As we have seen, some healing of mind and body must take place for many of us before we can sit quietly and concentrate. Yet even to begin our healing, to begin understanding ourselves, we must have some basic level of attention. To deepen our practice further, we must choose a way to develop our attention systematically and give ourselves to it quite fully. Otherwise we will drift like a boat without a rudder. To learn to concentrate we must choose a prayer or meditation and follow this path with commitment and steadiness, a willingness to work with our practice day after day, no matter what arises. This is not easy for most people. They would like their spiritual life to show immediate and cosmic results. But what great art is ever learned quickly? Any deep training opens in direct proportion to how much we give ourselves to it.

Consider the other arts. Music, for example. How long would it take to learn to play the piano well? Suppose we take months or years of lessons once a week, practicing diligently every day. Initially, almost everyone struggles to learn which fingers go for which notes and how to read basic lines of music. After some weeks or months, we could play simple tunes, and perhaps after a year or two we could play a chosen type of music. However, to master the art so that we could play music well, alone or in a group, or join a band or an orchestra, we would have to give ourselves to this discipline over and over, time and again. If we wanted to learn computer programming, oil painting, tennis, architecture, any of the thousand arts, we would have to give ourselves to it fully and wholeheartedly over a long period of time—a training, an apprenticeship, a cultivation.

Nothing less is required in the spiritual arts. Perhaps even more is asked. Yet through this mastery we master ourselves and our lives. We learn the most human art, how to connect with our truest self.

Trungpa Rinpoche called spiritual practice manual labor. It is a labor of love in which we bring a wholehearted attention to our own situation over and over again. In all sorts of weather, we steady and deepen our prayer, meditation, and discipline, learning how to see with honesty and compassion, how to let go, how to love more deeply.

However, this is not how we begin. Suppose we begin with a period of solitude in the midst of our daily life. What happens when we actually try to meditate? The most frequent first experience—whether in prayer or chanting, meditation or visualization—is that we encounter the disconnected and scattered mind. Buddhist psychology likens the untrained mind to a crazed monkey that dashes from thought to memory, from sight to sound, from plan to regret without ceasing. If we were able to sit quietly for an hour and fully observe all the places our mind went, what a script would be revealed.

When we first undertake the art of meditation, it is indeed frustrating. Inevitably, as our mind wanders and our body feels the tension it has accumulated and the speed to which it is addicted, we often see how little inner discipline, patience, or compassion we actually have. It doesn't take much time with a spiritual task to see how scattered and unsteady our attention remains even when we try to direct and focus it. While we usually think of it as "our mind," if we look honestly, we see that the mind follows its own nature, conditions, and laws. Seeing this, we also see that we must gradually discover a wise relationship to the mind that connects it to the body and heart, and steadies and calms our inner life.

The essence of this connecting is the bringing back of our attention again and again to the practice we have chosen. Prayer, meditation, repeating sacred phrases, or visualization gives us a systematic way to focus and steady our concentration. All the traditional realms and states of consciousness described in mystical and spiritual literature worldwide are arrived at through the art of concentration. These arts of concentration, of returning to the task at hand, also bring the clarity, strength of mind, peacefulness, and profound connectedness that we seek. This steadiness and connection in turn gives rise to even deeper levels of understanding and insight.

Whether a practice calls for visualization, question, prayer, sacred words, or simple meditation on feelings or breath, it always involves the steadying and conscious return, again and again, to some focus. As we learn to do this with a deeper and fuller attention, it is like learning to steady a canoe in waters that have waves. Repeating our meditation, we relax and sink into the moment, deeply connecting with what is present. We let ourselves settle into a spiritual ground; we train ourselves to come back to this moment. This is a patient process. St. Francis de Sales said, "What we need is a cup of understanding, a barrel of love, and an ocean of patience."

For some, this task of coming back a thousand or ten thousand times in meditation may seem boring or even of questionable importance. But how many times have we gone away from the reality of our life?—perhaps a million or ten million times! If we wish to awaken, we have to find our way back here with our full being, our full attention.

St. Francis de Sales continued by saying:

Bring yourself back to the point quite gently. And even if you do nothing during the whole of your hour but bring your heart back a thousand times, though it went away every time you brought it back, your hour would be very well employed.

In this way, meditation is very much like training a puppy. You put the puppy down and say, "Stay." Does the puppy listen? It gets up and it runs away. You sit the puppy back down again. "Stay." And the puppy runs away over and over again. Sometimes the puppy jumps up, runs over, and pees in the corner or makes some other mess. Our minds are much the same as the puppy, only they create even bigger messes. In training the mind, or the puppy, we have to start over and over again.

When you undertake a spiritual discipline, frustration comes with the territory. Nothing in our culture or our schooling has taught us to steady and calm our attention. One psychologist has called us a society of attentional spastics. Finding it difficult to concentrate, many people respond by forcing their attention on their breath or mantra or prayer with tense irritation and self-judgment, or worse. Is this the way you would train a puppy? Does it really help to beat it? Concentration is never a matter of force or coercion. You simply pick up the puppy again and return to reconnect with the here and now.

Developing a deep quality of interest in your spiritual practice is one of the keys to the whole art of concentration. Steadiness is nourished by the degree of interest with which we focus our meditation. Yet, to the beginning student, many meditation subjects appear plain and uninteresting. There is a traditional story about a Zen student who complained to his master that following the breath was boring. The Zen master grabbed this student and held his head under water for quite a long time while the student struggled to come up. When he finally let the student up, the Zen master asked him whether he had found breath boring in those moments under water.

Concentration combines full interest with delicacy of attention. This attention should not be confused with being removed or detached. Awareness does not mean separating ourselves from experience; it means allowing it and sensing it fully. Awareness can vary like a zoom lens. Sometimes we are in the middle of our experience. Sometimes it is as if we sit on our own shoulder and notice what is present, and sometimes we can be aware with a great spacious distance. All of these are useful aspects of awareness. They each can help us sense and touch and see our life more clearly from moment to moment. As we learn to steady the quality of our attention, it is accompanied by a deeper and deeper sense of stillness—poised, exquisite, and subtle.

The art of subtle attention was learned by one meditation student while she and her husband lived in a remote community in the mountains of British Columbia. She had studied yoga in India, and some years later she, with the help of her husband, gave birth to a baby boy, alone, without doctor or midwife. Unfortunately, it was a long and complicated breech delivery, with the baby delivered feet first and the umbilical cord wrapped around his neck. The baby was born quite blue, and he could not start to breathe on his own. His parents gave him infant artificial respiration as best they could. Then they would pause for a moment between their breathing into his lungs to see if he would begin to breathe by himself. During these excruciating moments, they watched for the tiniest movement of his breath to see if be would live or die. Finally, he started to breathe on his own. His mother smiled at me when she told this story, and said, "It was at that time that I learned what it meant to be truly aware of the breath. And it wasn't even my own breath!"

The focusing of attention on the breath is perhaps the most universal of the many hundreds of meditation subjects used worldwide. Steadying attention on the movement of the life-breath is central to yoga, to Buddhist and Hindu practices, to Sufi, Christian, and Jewish traditions. While other meditation subjects are also beneficial, and each has its unique qualities, we will continue to elaborate on the practice of breath meditation as an illustration for developing any of these practices. Breathing meditation can quiet the mind, open the body, and develop a great power of concentration. The breath is available to us at any time of day and in any circumstance. When we have learned to use it, the breath becomes a support for awareness throughout our life.

But awareness of breathing does not come right away. At first we must sit quietly, letting our body be relaxed and alert, and simply practice finding the breath in the body. Where do we actually feel it—as a coolness in the nose, a tingling in the back of the throat, as a movement in the chest, as a rise and fall of the belly? The place of strongest feeling is the first place to establish our attention. If the breath is apparent in several places, we can feel its whole movement of the body. If the breath is too soft and difficult to find, we can place our palm on our belly and feel the expansion and contraction in our hand. We must learn to focus our attention carefully. As we feel each breath we can sense how it moves in our body. Do not try to control the breath, only notice its natural movement, as a gatekeeper notices what passes by. What are its rhythms? Is it shallow or long and deep? Does it become fast or slow? Is there a temperature to the breath? The breath can become a great teacher because it is always moving and changing. In this simple breathing, we can learn about contraction and resistance, about opening and letting go. Here we can feel what it means to live gracefully, to sense the truth of the river of energy and change that we are.

Yet even with interest and a strong desire to steady our attention, distractions will arise. Distractions are the natural movement of mind. Distractions arise because our mind and heart are not initially clear or pure. Mind is more like muddy or turbulent water. Each time an enticing image or an interesting memory floats by, it is our habit to react, to get entangled, or to get lost. When painful images or feelings arise, it is our habit to avoid them and unknowingly distract ourselves. We can feel the power of these habits of desire, of distracting ourselves, of fear and reaction. In many of us these forces are so great that after a few unfamiliar moments of calm, our mind rebels. Again and again restlessness, busyness, plans, unfelt feelings, all interrupt our focus. Working with these distractions, steadying the canoe, letting the waves pass by, and coming back again and again in a quiet and collected way, is at the heart of meditation.

After your initial trial, you will begin to recognize that certain external conditions are particularly helpful in developing concentration. Finding or creating a quiet and undistracting place for your practice is necessary. Select regular and suitable times that best fit your temperament and schedule; experiment to discover whether morning or evening meditations best support the silent aspects of your inner life. You may wish to begin with a short period of inspiring reading before sitting, or do some stretching or yoga first. Some people find it extremely helpful to sit in a regular group with others or to go off to periodic retreats. Experiment with these external factors until you discover which are most helpful for your own inner peace. Then make them a regular part of your life. Creating suitable conditions means living wisely, providing the best soil for our spiritual hearts to be nourished and to grow.

As we give ourselves to the art of concentration over the weeks and months, we discover that our concentration slowly begins to settle by itself. Initially we may have struggled to focus, trying to hold on to the subject of our meditation. Then gradually the mind and the heart become eased from distractions, and periodically we sense them as purer, more workable and malleable. We feel our breath more often and more clearly, or we recite our prayers or mantra with greater wholeness. This is like beginning to read a book. When we start, we will often be interrupted by many distractions around us. But if it is a good book, perhaps a mystery novel, by the last chapter we will be so absorbed in the plot that people can walk right by us and we will not notice them. In meditation at first, thoughts carry us away and we think them for a long time. Then, as concentration grows we remember our breath in the middle of a thought. Later we can notice thoughts just as they arise or allow them to pass in the background, so focused on the breath that we are undisturbed by their movement.

As we continue, the development of concentration brings us closer to life, like the focusing of a lens. When we look at pond water in a cup, it appears clear and still. But under the simplest microscope it shows itself to be alive with creatures and movement. In the same way, the more deeply we pay attention, the less solid our breath and body become. Every place we feel breath in our body can come alive with subtle vibrations, movement, tingles, flow. The steady power of our concentration shows each part of our life to be in change and flux, like a river, even as we feel it.

As we learn to let go into the present, the breath breathes itself, allowing the flow of sensations in the body to move and open. There can come an openness and ease. Like a skilled dancer, we allow the breath and body to float and move unhindered, yet all the while being present to enjoy the opening.

As we become more skillful we also discover that concentration has its own seasons. Sometimes we sit and settle easily. At other times the conditions of mind and body are turbulent or tense. We can learn to navigate all these waters. When conditions show the mind is tight, we learn to soften and relax, to open the attention. When the mind is sleepy or flabby, we learn to sit up and focus with more energy. The Buddha compared this with the tuning of a lute, sensing when we are out of tune and gently strengthening or loosening our energy to come into balance.

In learning concentration, we feel as if we are always starting over, always losing our focus. But where have we actually gone? It is only that a mood or a thought or doubt has swept through our mind. As soon as we recognize this, we can let go and settle back again in this next moment. We can always begin again. Gradually as our interest grows and our capacity to sense deepens, new layers of our meditation open. We will find ourselves alternating, discovering periods of deep peace like an undisturbed child and strength like a great ship on a true course, only to be distracted or lost sometime later. Concentration grows in a deepening spiral, as we return to our meditation subject again and again, each time learning more of the art of inner listening. When we are listening carefully, we can sense new aspects of our breath all the time. One Burmese meditation teacher requires his students each day to tell him something new about the breath, even if they have been meditating for years.

Here, notice if you can, is there a pause between your breaths? How does it feel when your breath just starts? What is the end of the breath like? What is that space when the breathing has stopped? What does the impulse to breathe feel like before the breath even begins? How is the breath a reflection of your moods?

At first when we feel the breath, it seems like only one small movement, but as we develop the art of concentration, we can feel a hundred things in the breath: the subtlest sensations, the variations in its length, the temperature, the swirl, the expansion, the contraction, the tingles that come along with it, the echoes of the breath in different parts of our body, and so much more.

Sticking with a spiritual training requires an ocean of patience because our habit of wanting to be somewhere else is so strong. We've distracted ourselves from the present for so many moments, for so many years, even lifetimes. Here is an accomplishment in *The Guinness Book of World Records* that I like to note at meditation retreats when people are feeling frustrated. It indicates that the record for persistence in taking and failing a driving test is held by Mrs. Miriam Hargrave of Wakefield, England. Mrs. Hargrave failed her thirty-ninth driving test in April, 1970, when she crashed, driving through a set of red lights. In August of the following year she finally passed her fortieth test. Unfortunately, she could no longer afford to buy a car because she had spent so much on driving lessons. In the same spirit, Mrs. Fanny Turner of Little Rock, Arkansas, passed her written test for a driver's license on her 104th attempt in October 1978. If we can bring such persistence to passing a driving test or mastering the art of skateboarding or any one of a hundred other endeavors, surely we can also master the art of connecting with ourselves. As human beings we can dedicate ourselves to almost anything, and this heartfelt perseverance and dedication brings spiritual practice alive.

Always remember that in training a puppy we want to end up with the puppy as our friend. In the same way, we must practice seeing our mind and body as "friend." Even its wanderings can be included in our meditation with a friendly interest and curiosity. Right away we can notice how it moves. The mind produces waves. Our breath is a wave, the sensations of our body are a wave. We don't have to fight the waves. We can simply acknowledge, "Surf's up." "Here's the wave of memories from three years old." "Here's the planning wave." Then it's time to reconnect with the wave of the breath. It takes a gentleness and a kindhearted understanding to deepen the art of concentration. We can't be present for a long period without actually softening, dropping into our bodies, coming to rest. Any other kind of concentration, achieved by force and tension, will only be short-lived. Our task is to train the puppy to become our lifelong friend.

The attitude or spirit with which we do our meditation helps us perhaps more than any other aspect. What is called for is a sense of perseverance and dedication combined with a basic friendliness. We need a willingness to directly relate again and again to what is actually here, with a lightness of heart and sense of humor. We do not want the training of our puppy to become too serious a matter.

The Christian Desert Fathers tell of a new student who was commanded by his master that for three years he must give money to everyone who insulted him. When this period of trial was over, the master said, "Now you can go to Alexandria and truly learn wisdom." When the student entered Alexandria, he met a certain wise man whose way of teaching was to sit at the city gate insulting everyone who came and went. He naturally insulted the student also, who immediately burst out laughing. "Why do you laugh when I insult you?" said the wise man. "Because," said the student, "for years I've been paying for this kind of thing, and now you give it to me for free!" "Enter the city," said the wise man. "It is all yours."

Meditation is a practice that can teach us to enter each moment with wisdom, lightness, and a sense of humor. It is an art of opening and letting go, rather than accumulation or struggle. Then, even within our frustrations and difficulties, a remarkable inner sense of support and perspective can grow. Breathing in, "Wow, this experience is interesting, isn't it? Let me take another breath. Ah, this one is difficult, even terrifying, isn't it?" Breathing out, "Ah." It is an amazing process we have entered when we can train our hearts and minds to be open and steady and awake through it all.

## ESTABLISHING A DAILY MEDITATION

First select a suitable space for your regular meditation. It can be wherever you can sit easily with minimal disturbance: a corner of your bedroom or any other quiet spot in your home. Place a meditation cushion or chair there for your use. Arrange what is around so that you are reminded of your meditative purpose, so that it feels like a sacred and peaceful space. You may wish to make a simple altar with a flower or sacred image, or place your favorite spiritual books there for a few moments of inspiring reading. Let yourself enjoy creating this space for yourself.

Then select a regular time for practice that suits your schedule and temperament. If you are a morning person, experiment with a sitting before breakfast. If evening fits your temperament or schedule better, try that first. Begin with sitting ten or twenty minutes at a time. Later you can sit longer or more frequently. Daily meditation can become like bathing or toothbrushing. It can bring a regular cleansing and calming to your heart and mind.

Find a posture on the chair or cushion in which you can easily sit erect without being rigid. Let your body be firmly planted on the earth, your hands resting easily, your heart soft, your eyes closed gently. At first feel your body and consciously soften any obvious tension. Let go of any habitual thoughts or plans. Bring your attention to feel the sensations of your breathing. Take a few deep breaths to sense where you can feel the breath most easily, as coolness or tingling in the nostrils or throat, as movement of the chest, or rise and fall of the belly. Then let your breath be natural. Feel the sensations of your natural breathing very carefully, relaxing into each breath as you feel it, noticing how the soft sensations of breathing come and go with the changing breath.

After a few breaths your mind will probably wander. When you notice this, no matter how long or short a time you have been away, simply come back to the next breath. Before you return, you can mindfully acknowledge where you have gone with a soft word in the back of your mind, such as "thinking," "wandering," "hearing," "itching." After softly and silently naming to yourself where your attention has been, gently and directly return to feel the next breath. Later on in your meditation you will be able to work with the places your mind wanders to, but for initial training, one word of acknowledgment and a simple return to the breath is best.

# Meditation Training

from *Awakening the Buddha Within*

by Lama Surya Das

Westerners who are attracted to Buddhism because of meditation often make the mistake of seeing meditation in the most narrow sense of going into a quiet room, crossing your legs, and closing your eyes. What the Buddha actually intended by this part of the path of mental discipline was an effort to train the mind through the cultivation of mindful awareness and attention to the present moment. If all the difficulties of life are the result of ignorance, deluded thinking and conflicting emotions, then the obvious solution is to get wiser, more aware, balanced and loving. We do this through the practice of meditation training or *samadhi*, which is the ancient word for mental discipline or contemplation. Meditation training includes Right Effort, Right Mindfulness, and Right Concentration.

Awareness is the common denominator of all sentient beings. Meditation is the most direct and effective way to cultivate that innate awareness; it is the essential ingredient on the path to awakening the Buddha within. We meditate in order to purify and discipline our minds. We meditate in order to become enlightened—in order to understand and directly perceive reality or truth—defined by the Buddha as "clear seeing," or "seeing things as they are." We meditate in order to wake up to what is, and thus arrive at the total immediacy and authenticity of life in this very present moment. That's the goal, and it is also the practice. Cultivating present, moment-by-moment awareness helps you come home to who you are and always have been.

Demystified and divested of religious and cultural trappings, meditation basically means the intentional cultivation of mindful awareness
and pure attention—an alert, wakeful presence of mind. This development of awareness eradicates ignorance—about ourselves and others as
well as reality. Meditation awakens and frees the mind, and opens the
heart, helping us develop inner wisdom, clarity, joy, and compassion,
thus bringing spirituality and a larger perspective into every aspect of
daily life. Meditation training helps us to concentrate as well as to see
and think more clearly. In this way we develop spiritually into wiser,
more selfless and caring men and women.

Meditation is not just something to do; it's a method of being and
seeing—an unconditional way of living moment to moment. Through
meditation we perceive and know things as they actually are. This directly
connects and brings us to truth according to its simplest definition—
things just as they are. Meditation is how Buddhas pray.

The Dharma teaches that everything, good and bad, originates within
our minds—minds that have been conditioned by years (and lifetimes)
of deluded and delusional thinking. Don't our minds buzz with anxieties,
with regrets for the past as well as plots and plans for the future? Doesn't
it sometimes seem as though our minds are awash with conflicting feelings, thoughts, and fantasies? Every second of every day, the mind and
senses are being flooded by external stimuli—sounds, smells, sights. So
much is going on—so much extraneous information is going in and out
of the mind that it seems impossible to "see straight"—to see with clarity.

The mind is capable of so much: It has given birth to all the marvels
as well as the horrors of the modern world. How we use our unique gift
of consciousness makes all the difference. Thought and intellect are good
servants—great tools, but poor masters. We so often fall prey to the
tyranny of thought and are controlled by our own motor minds and
surrounded by the static and empty echoes of our own motor mouths.
Our restless imaginings, obsessions, and incessant anxieties, uncertain-
ties, and worries run amok, leaving us not a moment's peace. At these
times, it's good to take stock and renew our heart's soulful search for
happiness and fulfillment, to begin afresh our journey and exploration
toward finding what really matters in life, and staying with it. What really
matters—to us? How to learn to love and live better. How to make a life,
not just a living. How to make life into something worth living. How to
find ourselves—our true selves—not just our persona or image. How to
use the special talents and gifts we have.

If we want to simplify and deepen our lives, we must simplify and deepen our minds. When we become more centered, clear, spacious, caring and open, there is suddenly much more room in our frenetic lives for both others and ourselves. Marshall McLuhan said, "Our mind is a magazine with a new edition every four seconds." In the Dhammapada, the Buddha said, "The mind is restless, unsteady, hard to guard, hard to control. The wise one makes it straight, like a fletcher straightens an arrow. The mind is mercurial, hard to restrain, alighting where it wishes. It is good to tame and master this mind, for a disciplined mind brings happiness."

# Opening Pandora's Box
## from *Everyday Zen: Love and Work*
### by Charlotte Joko Beck

The quality of our practice is always reflected in the quality of our life. If we are truly practicing there will be a difference over time. Now one of the illusions we may have about our practice is that practice will make things more comfortable, clearer, easier, more peaceful, and so on. Nothing could be further from the truth. This morning as I was drinking my coffee two fairy tales popped into my head, and I suppose that nothing pops in except for some reason or another. Fairy tales embody some basic, fundamental truths about people; that's why they have existed for as long as they have.

The first fairy tale that came into my mind was about the princess and the pea: long ago the test of a true princess was that, if she slept atop a pile of thirty mattresses, she could feel a pea beneath the bottom mattress. Now you might say that practice turns us into princesses; we become more sensitive. We know things about ourselves and others that we didn't know before. We become much more sensitive, but sometimes we become more edgy, too.

The other story is about Pandora's box. You remember—somebody was so curious about the contents of that mysterious box that she finally opened it—and the evil contents poured out, creating chaos. Practice is often like that for us; it opens Pandora's box.

All of us feel we are separate from life; we feel as if we have a wall around us. The wall may not be very visible; it may even be invisible— but the wall is there. As long as we feel separate from life we feel the presence of a wall. An enlightened person wouldn't have a wall. But I've never met someone who I felt was completely free of one. Still, with practice that wall keeps getting thinner and more transparent.

That wall has been keeping us out of touch. We may be anxious, we may have disturbing thoughts, but our wall keeps us unaware of that. But as we practice (and many of you know this very well) this wall begins to have holes in it. Before it was like a plank covering bubbling water; but now the plank has begun to develop holes, as practice makes us more aware and sensitive. We can't sit motionless for even thirty minutes without learning something. And when that thirty minutes goes on day after day after day after day, we learn and learn. Whether we like it or not, we learn.

Pieces of the plank may even fall away so that the water begins to bubble up through the holes and gaps. Of course what we have covered is that which we do not wish to know about ourselves. When it bubbles up (as it will if we practice) it's as though Pandora's box begins to open. Ideally in practice that box should never be thrown wide open all at once. But since the release is not completely predictable, there can be some surprises, even casualties. At times the lid comes off and everything we've never wanted to see about ourself comes boiling up—and instead of feeling better, we feel worse.

Pandora's box is all of our self-centered activities, and the corresponding emotions that they create. Even if we're practicing well there will be times (not for everybody, but for some people) when the box seems to explode—and suddenly a hurricane of emotions is whirling around. Most people don't like to sit when this is happening, but the people for whom this eruption resolves most easily are those who never give up sitting, whether they want to do it or not. In my own life the release went quite unobtrusively, probably because I was sitting so much and doing so many sesshins.

As practice at the Center matures I see most students' lives transforming. That doesn't mean that Pandora's box is not opening; the two go together, the transformation and the discomfort. For some this is a very painful time, when the box begins to open. For example, unexpected anger may surface (but please don't take it out on someone else). So the illusion we have, that practice should always be peaceful and loving, just isn't so. That the box opens is perfectly normal and necessary. It's not good or bad, it's just what has to happen if we really want our lives to settle down, and be more free of a reactive way of living. None of this process is undesirable; in fact, properly worked with, it's desirable. But how we practice with the boiling up is the crucial thing.

Practice is not easy. It will transform our life. But if we have a naïve idea that this transformation can take place without a price being paid, we fool ourselves. Don't practice unless you feel there's nothing else you can do. Instead, step up your surfing or your physics or your music. If that satisfies you, do it. Don't practice unless you feel you must. It takes enormous courage to have a real practice. You have to face everything about yourself hidden in that box, including some unpleasant things you don't even want to know about.

To do Zen practice, we have to desire a certain kind of a life. In traditional terms, it's a life in which our vows override our ordinary personal considerations: we must be determined that our lives develop a universal context and that the lives of others also develop that context. If we're at a stage in our lives (and it's not good or bad, it's just a stage) in which the only thing that matters to us is how we feel and what we want, then practice will be too difficult. Perhaps we should wait a while. As a teacher I can facilitate practice and of course encourage a person's effort, but I can't give anyone that initial determination; and it has to be there for practice to take hold.

The box that right now is opening for many of you—how will you work with it? Some things you should know about this upsetting phase of practice. One, for people on this path, it's normal, in fact, necessary. Two, it doesn't last forever. And three, more than at any other time, it's a time when we need to understand our practice, and to know what patience is. And it's particularly a time to do sesshin. If you've been sitting for twenty, thirty years, whether or not you do sesshins is not as crucial. But there are certain years when it's vitally important and you should do as many as your life situation permits. And that advice presupposes the strength to maintain such intensity of practice. It's not "bad" not to want such a dedicated practice. I want to emphasize that. Sometimes people need another ten years or so of just knocking around, letting life present its lessons, before they're ready to commit to an intense practice.

So Pandora's box, that which upsets and disturbs us, is the emergence (sometimes in a flood) of that which we have not been aware of before: our anger toward life. It has to boil out sooner or later. This is the ego, our anger that life is not the way we want it to be. "It doesn't suit me! It doesn't give me what I want! I want life to be nice to me!" It is our fury when the people or events in our lives simply don't give us what we demand.

Perhaps right now you are in the middle of opening the box. At some point I would like you to share what you have found useful in your practice at this time. A student, in some ways, can be more useful to others than a person like myself, who can hardly remember this stage. I understand the conflict pretty well, but the actual memory of how difficult it can be is fading. That's one of the great things about a sangha: it's a group of people who have a mutual framework for practice. In the sangha we can be honest, we don't have to hide or cover our struggles. The most painful thing is to think that there's something wrong with *me*, and that nobody else is having the trouble I am. That's not true, of course.

## "DO NOT BE ANGRY"

When I give a talk I'm trying to elucidate, by any means I can find, what life is about for me and what it might be for someone else, as opposed to our illusions about it. It's a very difficult thing to talk about. I never give a dharma talk that I don't hate, because it's never possible to tell the exact truth: I always tend to go a little too far this way, or a little too far that way, or I use the wrong words and somebody gets mixed up . . . but again, that's part of our training. Dharma talks are not necessarily something to understand; if they shake you up and confuse you, sometimes that's just right. For example: we can say that everybody in the universe at this particular moment is doing the best that he or she can. And then the word "best" creates trouble. It's the same difficulty we have with the sentence, "Everything, just as it is, is perfection." Perfect? Doing their best? You mean, when someone's doing something horrible they're doing their best? Just through our use of words we get awfully mixed up in our life and in our practice.

In fact our whole life is confused because we mix up our concepts (which are themselves absolutely necessary) with reality. So dharma talks tend to challenge our usual concepts. And using words in a certain way adds lots of confusion and that's just fine. Today I want to add to the confusion. I'm going to tell a little story and then head off in some other directions, and see what we make of all that. At this center we don't talk much about the precepts or the eight-fold path, for a very good reason: people misinterpret the precepts as being prohibitions, "thou shalt not's." And that's not what they are at all. Nevertheless, my talk today is about the precept "Do not be angry." I won't mention it again! But that's what the talk is about: "Do not be angry."

Suppose we are out on a lake and it's a bit foggy—not too foggy, but a bit foggy—and we're rowing along in our little boat having a good time. And then, all of a sudden, coming out of the fog, there's this other rowboat and it's heading right at us. And . . . crash! Well, for a second we're really angry—what is that fool doing? I just painted my boat! And here he comes—crash!—right into it. And then suddenly we notice that the rowboat is empty. What happens to our anger? Well, the anger collapses . . . I'll just have to paint my boat again, that's all. But if that rowboat that hit ours had another person in it, how would we react? You know what would happen! Now our encounters with life, with other people, with events, are like being bumped by an empty rowboat. But we don't experience life that way. We experience it as though there are people in that other rowboat and we're really getting clobbered by them. What am I talking about when I say that all of life is an encounter, a collision with an empty rowboat? What's that all about?

Let's leave that question for a moment. People often ask, "What do I get out of practice? What is the change? What is the transformation?" Zen practice is very hard work. It's restrictive and difficult. We're told we have to sit every day. What do we get out of this? People usually think, "I'm going to improve. I'm going to get better. If I lose my temper easily, maybe after sitting I won't lose it so easily." Or, "To be truthful, I'm not so kind; maybe through sitting I'll get to be a very kind person." And this isn't quite right. So I want to tell you a few little incidents to clarify this a bit.

I want to talk about the dishpan at our house, where I live with Elizabeth. Now, since I'm retired from work, I am home most of the day. After I rinse the sink I like to set the dishpan in there like a dish, so if there's a spare cup during the day I can conceal it in the dishpan. Since that's the way I want the dishpan, it's obviously the right way, right? But when Elizabeth does the dishes, she rinses the dishpan and turns it over so it can dry. At noon I have the house to myself. But at five o'clock I know she's coming home. So I think, "Well, am I a man or a mouse? What am I going to do about the dishpan? Am I going to put it the way

Elizabeth wants it?" So what do I do? Actually, I usually forget the whole thing and put it any old way.

And then there's another thing about Elizabeth. I live with her and she's wonderful. But there couldn't be two people who are more unlike. The joy of my life is to find the one item in the closet that I can throw out . . . it's great! Elizabeth has three of everything and doesn't want to throw anything out. So it means that when I want to find something, I can't find it because I've thrown it out; when she wants to find something, she can't find it because she's got so much stuff she can't find it.

One more example and then we'll get to the point of all this: I'll tell you what it's like if I go to the movies with my daughter: "Mom, you know your taste in movies is just impossible!" And I say, "Well, you're not remembering the one we went to that *you* wanted to see! What about that?" So, squabble, squabble, squabble . . . and we end up going to a movie which may be . . . whatever it is.

What is the point of all those stories? Basically, I could care less about the dishpan. But we do not lose all our particular, little neurotic quirks from practice. Neither my daughter nor I really cares about the movie, but these little squabbling interchanges are what life is all about. That's just the fun of it. Do you understand? We don't have to analyze it, pick it apart, or "communicate" about it. The wonder of living with anything is . . . what? It's perfect in being as it is.

Now you may say that's all very well with things on this level, which are of course fairly trivial. What about serious problems, such as grief and anguish? What I'm saying is that they're not different. If someone close to you dies, then the wonder of life is just being that grief itself, being what you are. And being with it in the way that *you're* with it, which is your way, not my way. Practice is in just being willing to be with it as it is. Even "willing"—that word is not quite right either. Most of life, as we see it in the stories I told, is hilarious, that's all you can say about it. But we do not view it as hilarious. We think that the other person should be different: "They should be the way I think they should be!" When we come to what we call "crisis points" in our life, it's not fun—I'm not saying that—but it still is as it is. It is still the perfection.

Now I want to take one more point: I think maturing practice is the ability to be with life and just be in it as it is. That doesn't mean that you don't have all your little considerations, all your stuff going on about it.

You will! That's not the point. But it is *held* differently. And all of practice is to move what I call the cut-off point, so that we can hold more and more in this way. At first we can hold only certain things that way. Maybe in six months of practice you hold this much that way. Maybe in a year this. Ten years, this. And so on. But there's always that cut-off point at which you can't hold it. And we all have that point. As long as we live we're going to have that point.

As our practice becomes more sophisticated we begin to sense our tremendous deficiencies, our tremendous cruelty. We see the things in life we're not willing to take care of, the things we can't let be, the things we hate, the things we just can't stand. And if we've been practicing a long time there's grief in that. But what we fail to see is the area which with practice grows—the area in which we can have compassion for life, just because it is as it is. Just the wonder of Elizabeth being Elizabeth. It's not that she should possibly be different; she is perfect in being as she is. And myself. And you. Everybody. That area grows, but always there's that point where we can't possibly see the perfection, and that's the point where our practice is. If you've been sitting a short time, it's here, that's fine; why should it be anyplace else? And then over a lifetime that cut-off point just moves and it never ceases to occur. There's always that point. And that's what we're doing here. Sitting as we sit, just letting what comes up in ourselves come up, be there, and die. Come up, be there, and die. But when we get to the cut-off point we're not going to remember any of that! Because it's tough when we're at this point. Practice is not easy.

The little stuff in life doesn't bother me particularly. I *enjoy* all this little stuff that goes on. It's fun! I enjoy my squabbles with my daughter. "Mom, all these years and you still can't get a seat belt on?" "Well, I *can't*." That's the fun, the fun of being with another person. But what about the cut-off point? That is where practice is. And to understand that and to work with it, and also remembering that most of the time we're very unwilling to work with it—that's also practice. We're not attempting to become some sort of saint, but to be real people, with all of our stuff going on and allowing it to go on in others. And when we can't do that, then we know a signal has been given: time to practice. I know—I went through a point last week. It wasn't easy. And yet, I went through it and now what awaits is the next point. It's going to come up. And it will be my practice.

As we get more sensitive to our life and what it truly is, we can't run away. We can try for a while, and most of us will try for as long as we can. But we really can't run indefinitely. And if we've been sitting for some years it gets harder and harder to *run*. So I want you to appreciate your sitting and appreciate your life and each other. That's all this is about. Nothing fancy. And be aware of your cut-off point. It exists in all of us. You may turn away from it and refuse to see it; but if you do, you won't grow and life around you won't grow either. But probably, you can't avoid it for more than a certain length of time.

STUDENT: Sometimes when I read about Zen, it seems that you're just a spectator.

JOKO: No, no, not a spectator at all. Zen is action itself.

STUDENT: And it seems to be connected with the cut-off point. When you're at the cut-off point the action you take doesn't seem as wise as it might be . . .

JOKO: Let's return to the rowboat. For instance, most of us in dealing with young children can see that whatever they do—even if they come up and give you a kick in the shins—that's an empty rowboat, right? You just deal with it. I think the Buddha said, "All the world are my children." The point is to keep moving that cut-off point, we must practice when we can't let "all the world be my children." And I think that's what you're saying.

STUDENT: To carry that analogy one step further: say the child is not about to kick you in the shins, but is about to set fire to the house.

JOKO: Well, stop him! Take the matches away! But still he's just doing what he's doing for whatever reason. Try to find a way to help him learn from the incident.

STUDENT: But when you simply stop him, what are you doing differently than if you felt it was a personal attack?

JOKO: Well, let's face it, with our children, quite often we do see it as a personal attack, right? But if we think for ten seconds we usually know that we just have to deal with the behavior in a way that's appropriate for the child. And we can do this unless we feel our own ego threatened by the way our child is. And that's *not* an empty rowboat. And all parents have this reaction at times. We want our children to be perfect. They should be models because otherwise people could criticize us. And yet our children are just children. We're not perfect and they're not perfect.

STUDENT: You mentioned *"Be not angry."* I wanted to ask you a question about that. You said that when anger comes up, let it happen; be there and let it go. But if you have an habituated anger response to something over a long period of time, how do you let it go?

JOKO: By experiencing the anger nonverbally, physically. You can't force it to go, but you don't necessarily have to visit it on other people.

STUDENT: I want to extend the rowboat analogy: If we saw that the rowboat was coming toward us and there was someone in it, we'd probably start screaming and yelling "Stop that and *keep that away!*" Whereas if it was an empty rowboat we'd probably just take our oar and push the rowboat aside, so it wouldn't crash into ours.

JOKO: Right, we'd take appropriate action.

STUDENT: I don't know about that, because often you yell anyway, even if it's an empty rowboat; you curse at the universe, or whatever!

JOKO: Yeah, it's something like the dishpan. You may yell, but there's a difference between that momentary response and thinking about it for the next ten miles.

STUDENT: But even though there isn't anyone out there, we manage to think that the universe is doing something to us. Even when it is an empty rowboat, we put a person there.

JOKO: Yes, right. Well, it's *always* an empty rowboat. Again, the point is, the longer we practice the less likely that is to come up. Not because we say, "I won't be angry"—the reaction just isn't there. We feel differently and we may not even know why.

STUDENT: If you do experience the anger coming up, is that a sure sign that you're at your cut-off point?

JOKO: Yes, that's why I said the title of this talk is do not be angry. But again, the point is to understand what practice means with anger; it's not some simple prohibition, which would be useless anyway.

STUDENT: Well, obviously I still have to practice some more. What happens to me when some kind of tragedy occurs is, "I don't deserve it," "My friend doesn't deserve it," "How can this happen?" I get all caught up in the injustice of it and start railing against the unfairness of it.

JOKO: OK. That's very difficult. Very, very difficult. Still, it's a practice opportunity.

STUDENT: I get confused when I hear about sudden enlightenment. If this is a process, how is there an enlightened state?

JOKO: I didn't say there *was*, for one thing! But an enlightenment experience—suddenly seeing reality just as it is—just means that for a moment one's personal considerations about life are gone. And for a second one sees the universal. The problem with most enlightenment experiences is that people hold on to them, treasure them, and then they become a hindrance. The point isn't the experience—it's going on with our life. And any value that experience has is within ourselves; we don't need to worry about it. For most of us that rowboat is full of other people all the time; it's very rare that it's empty. And so . . . our cut-off point is *here*, we just work where we are. Remember the two verses from the Fifth Patriarch—one is about endlessly polishing the mirror, and the other is seeing that from the very beginning there's no mirror to polish. Most people assume that since the second is the correct understanding, the first is useless. But no, our practice is paradoxically the first. Polishing that mirror. The cut-off point is where you polish the mirror. Absolutely necessary. Because only by doing that will we eventually see the perfection of everything, just as it is. We can't see that unless we go through really rigorous, stringent practice.

STUDENT: So it's good to experience anger.

JOKO: If you learn from it. I didn't say anything about putting that anger out on others. That's very different. We may do that sometimes.

I'm not saying we won't; still, it's not productive to do it. The experiencing of anger is very quiet. Not anything noisy at all.

STUDENT: I think part of the problem comes when you say, "Don't be angry" and then you say, "Be angry."

JOKO: Let's be careful here . . . I'm saying that if anger is what you are, experience it. After all, it is the reality of the moment. So if we pretend anger is not there and cover it with a directive like "Do not be angry," then right away there's no chance to really know anger for what it is. The other side of anger, if we experience its emptiness and go through it, is always compassion. If we really, really go through it. OK, enough.

# Classes of Delusion

## from *Taking the Path of Zen*
### by Robert Aitken

In this section I would like to describe three general classes of delusion that almost everyone encounters sooner or later in the practice. Do not suppose the term "delusion" refers to something harmful or sinful. A delusion, in this sense, is simply a distraction from the path of enlightenment and compassion.

1. *The Pursuit of Fantasy*. The first of the three kinds of delusion that plague us most often is the pursuit of fantasy. Actually, there is a question of who is pursuing whom. The fantasy pursues the student, or at least it often seems that way.

   When caught up in this delusion, you plan, scheme, tell yourself stories, or recall something in full detail from the past. The ordinary self is always at the heart of these mental activities. They have their appropriate place in our daily life, but they are out of context while we are sitting at zazen.

   It is not an easy task to break this delusion. You will not be successful if you just try to block your thoughts. You are trying to block yourself, you will end by tiring yourself out, and the fantasy will be as feisty as ever. It is important to sit with a mind that is open, as open as the air. When there is a little sound, let that sound go right through. Notice that if you are absorbed in fantasy, you are enclosed in yourself. You don't hear the little sound. If you are counting your breaths with a pure mind, you are completely open.

When you are caught up by the delusion, at that moment the delusion will occupy you completely. But when it fades a little, you will notice that you have been straying, and you will be able to switch back to breath counting or koan work.

The deliberate pursuit of fantasy is the *bête noir* of zazen. You decide, "I will just put my practice aside for a while and think about this other thing." I once knew a man who used the quiet time of zazen to work on his own business problems. Ultimately he gave up coming to meetings. Perhaps he solved all his problems. If you follow such a way, you are forming bad habits, and will someday have to break them if you are to quiet your mind. It is better not to form them in the first place. There is a time to work out your personal, social, or financial concerns, but zazen is not that time.

2. *Random Thoughts.* The second kind of delusion in zazen is random thoughts. This too may be a creative process during free time, but on your cushions it is a separation from the practice. You drift and dream, carried along by the flow of images, music, memories, and fantasies. You may not be putting energy into these fragments of mental activity and they may have no particular coherence. Often you may find that you are counting your breaths or working on your koan while these thoughts chatter idly in the background. This is dull zazen, and you need consciously to bring yourself to a sharper effort.

When you begin your practice, and perhaps for a long time afterwards, background noise in your mind will be rather a distraction. This can't be helped. Thinking is the function of your brain, and you are not trying to shut that function down. You are trying to invest in the theme of your practice. In so doing, your random thoughts will die down gradually and naturally.

As Yasutani Roshi used to point out, there are people who have done zazen for several years who think that their object is to quiet all thoughts. It is possible to achieve this condition, but hardly desirable. Our creativity would also be quieted, and where would realization come from? We would become zombies, which is certainly not our object. Our object is to become "one," to become "two," and so on through our breath counting sequence. This practice actually sharpens our ability to think clearly and encourages incisive realization.

3. *Makyō*. The third class of delusion is *makyō*, "uncanny realm." This is a deep-dream experience that may involve a dramatic vision, a feeling of bodily distortion, or less commonly a sensation of hearing or smelling something that is not there in objective fact.

Flora Courtois, in her little book, *An American Woman's Experience of Enlightenment*, vividly describes several makyō, one of which will illustrate the phenomenon:

> A scene appeared as from an incalculably remote and primitive time. I seemed to be a member of a small family of cave dwellers. There was a darkness, a gloomy darkness about our lives and surroundings. In our cave we had found a place of security and protection from what I sensed to be a hostile outside world. Gradually, however, we found within ourselves the courage as a family to venture forth together to seek a brighter, more open place. Now we found ourselves on a great, open light plain which stretched in all directions and where the horizon seemed to beckon to us with untold possibilities.*

For Ms. Courtois, this was the turning point in her practice. The others in her family and indeed most of the human race turned back to the cave, leaving her to go on alone.

Not all makyō are this rich in detail, but all of them are vivid. One student told me of a flock of white doves descending into her body. My own most significant makyo placed me in an ancient temple, also of an incalculably remote time. Its stone pillars reached up to a vastly high ceiling. I was seated on the stone floor and tall monks garbed in black robes walked around me in a circle reciting sutras. Like all deep makyō, this experience was accompanied by a strong feeling of encouragement.

In Zen, makyō are a sign that you are making progress with your practice. You have passed beyond the superficial stage of thinking this or that. You are no longer in the world of everyday delusion, and you may be encouraged to feel that if you press on earnestly in your practice, you will realize your true nature before long.

---

* Nyogen Senzaki, *Buddha and His Disciples: A Guide to Buddhism* (Tokyo: Sanyusha, 1932), p. vii. This work is out of print.

I have heard some Zen students, who really should know better, describe makyō as something ultimate. In one sense this is true, but please be careful. "God's voice" is the voice of your own psyche in its present place. It may show that you are near, but that is all.


## CONDITION

One specific delusion is preoccupation with personal condition. This is an important matter and deserves extended consideration. First of all, we should notice that many of the things that trouble us seem to have their origins in outward circumstances but are really rooted within. An example is the anger expressed by persons suffering from old age or illness.

During sesshin and at a training center at all times, there is a certain amount of tension. Meals are light; sleep is short; the zazen is hard work; and the living conditions are crowded. One feels quite sensitive, almost transparent. Pockets of feeling that are otherwise unnoticed or are covered over suddenly manifest themselves, perhaps with great virulence, and attach themselves to circumstances. You may feel that someone is deliberately trying to annoy you with wiggling or coughing. You may be deeply suspicious of the monitor and the teacher, convinced that they are unfriendly, or that they think you are hopeless. You may experience violent resentment of the training and the schedule. Or perhaps long repressed anger against relatives may suddenly come forth like a forest fire, consuming all your energy.

It is probably healthy that such feelings rise into consciousness. It may not be possible just to return to counting when you notice them. They may be too powerful, and will overcome your efforts to ignore them. You must deal with them, but how? One way is to go along with them. "My damned mother" then becomes your meditation. That is no good. A better way is to reflect, "I am angry with my mother." Noticing and acknowledging your feelings is a step toward taking responsibility for them and reflecting, "This anger comes from me." When this acceptance is wholehearted, then it is possible to return to your counting.

Likewise, if you become angry when your neighbor in the dojo is wiggling unconscionably, it will be easy for you to come back to your practice if you reflect on the true source of your anger. Your fellow student is having a hard time with physical pain or mental anguish. Why are you so unsympathetic? Besides, the monitor is undoubtedly noticing the movement too and will caution the restless one at the appropriate time. There is no need for you to worry about it.

Anger is one kind of condition. Bliss is another condition. The sensation of transparency is still another, sleepiness another, and so on. These conditions are only superficial waves of the sea of your mind. They are the context of your practice. When you are angry, have angry zazen. Just continue to count your breaths, just continue to work on your koan, in that blaze of feeling. When you are in a blissful condition, have blissful zazen. When you congratulate yourself on your blissful condition, it disappears immediately. It is simply the nature of the shadow that is your environment.

When you are sleepy, have sleepy zazen. Sleepiness is somehow related to deep zazen, for both are times when the cortex is quieter than usual. Makyō may readily appear. The time of falling asleep or waking up may be the time of realization for the mature student. Don't fight it. During periods of zazen, sit with that sleepiness. Each time you nod, bring yourself back serenely and easily.

You can sometimes break a cycle of condition by washing your face between periods of sitting, or just taking a drink of water. However, sometimes there is nothing much you can do, and perhaps a whole morning or a whole day during sesshin will pass in which a particular condition is especially vivid. But it will go by eventually. Even moderate pain goes away during sesshin as your condition deepens. It is like having a persistent dream in the night: when daylight comes, the dream is no longer there.

Thinking, too, is a condition. Sit in the context of your thoughts. Your thoughts are the environment of your zazen, as much as your room and the TV next door. Sit with those thoughts and don't let them master you. Count "one," "two," "three," and all distractions will become unimportant. You are not, fundamentally, seeking "good condition" of quiet, or avoiding "bad condition" of noise.

Commonly, the Zen teacher will encounter questions that reveal a preoccupation with *samadhi*, or quality of meditation. With careful reading of Zen literature in English, you will find teachers who recommend various samadhi devices—breathing in a certain way; centering your mind in the lower abdomen, and so on. Of course, in one respect, zazen itself is a samadhi device, but it must be understood clearly, once and for all, that samadhi is not the full purpose of our practice. It is more accurate to say that our purpose is to respond to Paul Gaugun's questions, "Where do we come from? What are we? Where do we go?" Or to say that zazen is its own purpose.

I think the proper way to respond to most questions about samadhi is to encourage the student to become one with the practice, to breathe the count or the koan, to have the count do the counting, to have the koan work on the koan. There is no special way to direct one's muscles in order to do this, except to relax them within correct posture and to permit the belly to hang out naturally. My own experience with Zen training, which extends over thirty years, is that a teacher's emphasis on samadhi is often in inverse proportion to his emphasis on realization.

## PAIN

Yamada Roshi says, "Pain in the legs is the taste of Zen." Sometimes he adds, looking around at his students with a smile, "I wonder if you know what I mean." Everybody knows. Everybody hurts during sesshin. Pain is a condition that deserves a special section in this chapter.

It hurts to stretch our legs, but if we avoid that pain, we suffer the pain of not being able to do zazen. Everybody has a different physical makeup and some people can never hope to sit on cushions. This is all right. Sit at the forward edge of your physical endurance and you will be doing true zazen, even though you are sitting in a chair.

Some people will baby themselves. Looking around the dojo, I see people who are old timers in the practice, though young in years, still sitting in seiza as a regular practice or still moving from cushions to chair and back again. In cases of old injuries that won't heal, this is understandable, but where there is physical resistance, there is spiritual resistance.

## THE SICK SOUL

One further comment on condition relates to what William James called "the sick soul," what San Juan de la Cruz called "the dark night of our soul," and what David the Psalmist called "the valley of the shadow of death." This is the experience of the spiritual desert, where there is no moisture, no sustenance. It is a supreme attack of the "blahs." Nothing seems of any value or purpose. Everything that was meaningful before now seems absurd, pointless. The student feels pessimistic and discouraged.

This condition may simply be chronic pessimism: the student is overcritical of himself or herself, overidealistic about potential attainment, and perhaps perfectionistic in matters of personal purity. Maybe all such negativity has suddenly come to a head. Teachers can then only encourage students to recognize that they are human beings with a certain capacity, just as all the Buddhas and teachers of the past were individuals with their own unique capacities. There is no reason why all cannot fulfill their capacities. But the person—or personality—is the agent of realization. In one sense, attaining realization is a matter of fully appreciating its agent. Self-hate and self-rejection are blind alleys for the Zen student.

On the other hand, the sick soul may be a condition that directly precedes realization—itself a kind of religious experience. It is an unhappy condition, however, and as David implies in the Twenty-third Psalm, it requires a lot of trust and courage to press on. The Christian and Jew put faith in God in this lonely place. Zen students feel even more alone and must plod along with trust in the zazen process. The sick soul is actually about to be transformed in great death, the step of dying to oneself that is coincident with rebirth in realization. In the desert of the sick soul, it is important to maintain the practice, to let go of the desert, let go of the sick soul. Simply continue in the same way you have pursued your Zen work up to now. As best you can, invest yourself in the practice. Forget yourself in doing breath counting, in becoming one with the koan.

## PERSONAL PROBLEMS

Preoccupation with personal problems is another kind of delusion that most Zen students have to cope with. Such preoccupation may be dealt with in three ways. First the problems may be ignored. This seems rather simplistic, perhaps, but it is true that if we feed our problems by paying attention to them, they will grow and flourish. Often the problem is just in one's head. I think it was Josh Billings who said, "I am an old man, and I've had many troubles, most of which never happened." Treat the problem as you would any distraction in your zazen. Pass it by. Unite with your practice and let the problem go away.

However, the problem may be too persistent to ignore. Perhaps you can take practical steps to resolve. it. Talk it over with a trusted friend, write the necessary letter, make the necessary phone call, or try working with a book like *Focusing*. Look the problem in the eye and its hidden cause may come forth and surprise you.

Sometimes the problem won't go away when you ignore it, or even when you take practical steps to resolve it. If it interferes seriously with your practice, professional counseling may be required. I hope the counselor can be one who sympathizes with the zazen process. Perhaps this psychological work can run in tandem with zazen. Maybe the zazen will have to stop for a while.

## SELF-DOUBT

Perfectionism may evoke the question, "Am I sincere enough to do zazen?" When asked about sincerity, Yasutani Roshi said, "Five-percent sincerity is enough to begin with. If you were completely sincere, you would be enlightened at this moment." Sincerity builds, like everything else in our practice. There is no use blaming ourselves for being human.

Sometimes you may feel that your zazen is worse than it was a few months earlier. This may be true; zazen is a zigzag path, but only when judged by samadhi terms of a quiet mind or a concentration of spirit. You can be confident that you are ripening all the while. However, it is more likely that your memory is playing tricks on you. The enthusiasm you felt at the outset of your practice has worn away and you are left with the reality of difficult training. Or you may be more sensitive to distractions, and the noisy mind you hardly noticed before is all too distracting now. This kind of concern is just another preoccupation with condition. Wipe it away and return to your practice.

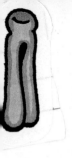

# Venturing into the Here and Now
## from *Sacred Hoops*
### by Phil Jackson

The meditation practice we teach players is called mindfulness. To become mindful, one must cultivate what Suzuki Roshi calls "beginner's mind," an "empty" state free from limiting self-centered thoughts. "If your mind is empty," he writes in *Zen Mind, Beginner's Mind*, "it is always ready for anything; it is open to everything. In the beginner's mind there are many possibilities; in the expert's mind there are few."

When I was coaching in Albany, Charley Rosen and I used to give a workshop called "Beyond Basketball" at the Omega Institute in Rhinebeck, New York. The workshop served as a laboratory where I could experiment with a number of spiritual and psychological practices I'd been itching to try in combination with basketball. Part of the program involved mindfulness meditation, and it worked so well I decided to use it with the Bulls.

We started slowly. Before tape sessions, I'd turn down the lights and lead the players through a short meditation to put them in the right frame of mind. Later I invited George Mumford, a meditation instructor, to give the players a three-day mindfulness course during training camp. Mumford is a colleague of Jon Kabat-Zinn, executive director of the Center for Mindfulness in Medicine at the University of Massachusetts Medical Center, who has had remarkable results teaching meditation to people coping with illness and chronic pain.

Here's the basic approach Mumford taught the players: Sit in a chair with your spine straight and your eyes downcast. Focus your attention on your breath as it rises and falls. When your mind wanders (which it will, repeatedly), note the source of the distraction (a noise, a thought, an emotion, a bodily sensation), then gently return the attention to the breath. This process of noting thoughts and sensations, then returning the awareness to the breath is repeated for the duration of the sitting. Though the practice may sound boring, it's remarkable how any experience, including boredom, becomes interesting when it's an object of moment-to-moment investigation.

Little by little, with regular practice, you start to discriminate raw sensory events from your reactions to them. Eventually, you begin to experience a point of stillness within. As the stillness becomes more stable, you tend to identify less with fleeting thoughts and feelings, such as fear, anger, or pain, and experience a state of inner harmony, regardless of changing circumstances. For me, meditation is a tool that allows me to stay calm and centered (well, most of the time) during the stressful highs and lows of basketball and life outside the arena. During games I often get agitated by bad calls, but years of meditation practice have taught me how to find that still point within so that I can argue passionately with the refs without being overwhelmed by anger.

How do the players take to meditation? Some of them find the exercises amusing. Bill Cartwright once quipped that he liked the sessions because they gave him extra time to take a nap. But even those players who drift off during meditation practice get the basic point: awareness is everything. Also, the experience of sitting silently together in a group tends to bring about a subtle shift in consciousness that strengthens the team bond. Sometimes we extend mindfulness to the court and conduct whole practices in silence. The deep level of concentration and nonverbal communication that arises when we do this never fails to astonish me.

More than any other player, B. J. Armstrong took meditation to heart and studied it on his own. Indeed, he attributes much of his success as a player to his understanding of not thinking, just doing. "A lot of guys second-guess themselves," he says. "They don't know whether to pass or shoot or what. But I just go for it. If I'm open, I'll shoot, and if I'm not, I'll pass. When there's a loose ball, I just go after it. The game happens so fast, the less I can think and the more I can just react to what's going on, the better it will be for me and, ultimately, the team."

# Mindfulness Versus Concentration

from *Mindfulness in Plain English*

by Venerable Henepola Gunaratana

Vipassana meditation is something of a mental balancing act. You are going to be cultivating two separate qualities of the mind—mindfulness and concentration. Ideally, these two work together as a team. They pull in tandem, so to speak. Therefore it is important to cultivate them side-by-side and in a balanced manner. If one of the factors is strengthened at the expense of another, the balance of the mind is lost and meditation becomes impossible.

Concentration and mindfulness are distinctly different functions. They each have their role to play in meditation, and the relationship between them is definite and delicate. Concentration is often called one-pointedness of mind. It consists of forcing the mind to remain on one static point. Please note the word *force*. Concentration is pretty much a forced type of activity. It can be developed by force, by sheer unremitting willpower. And once developed, it retains some of that forced flavor. Mindfulness, on the other hand, is a delicate function leading to refined sensibilities. These two are partners in the job of meditation. Mindfulness is the sensitive one. He notices things. Concentration provides the power. He keeps the attention pinned down to one item. Ideally, mindfulness is in this relationship. Mindfulness picks the objects of attention, and notices when the attention has gone astray. Concentration does the actual work of holding the attention steady on that chosen object. If either of these partners is weak, your meditation goes astray.

Concentration could be defined as that faculty of the mind which focuses single-mindedly on one object without interruption. It must be emphasized that true concentration is a wholesome one-pointedness of mind. That is, the state is free from greed, hatred, and delusion. Unwholesome one-pointedness is also possible, but it will not lead to Liberation. You can be very single-minded in a state of lust. But that gets you nowhere. Uninterrupted focus on something that you hate does not help you at all. In fact, such unwholesome concentration is fairly short-lived even when it is achieved—especially when it is used to harm others. True concentration itself is free from such contaminants. It is a state in which the mind is gathered together and thus gains power and intensity. We might use the analogy of a lens. Parallel waves of sunlight falling on a piece of paper will do no more than warm the surface. But that same amount of light, when focused through a lens, falls on a single point and the paper bursts into flames. Concentration is the lens. It produces the burning intensity necessary to see into the deeper reaches of the mind. Mindfulness selects the object that the lens will focus on and looks through the lens to see what is there.

Concentration should be regarded as a tool. Like any tool, it can be used for good or for ill. A sharp knife can be used to create a beautiful carving or to harm someone. It is all up to the one who uses the knife. Concentration is similar. Properly used, it can assist you toward Liberation. But it can also be used in the service of the ego. It can operate in the framework of achievement and competition. You can use concentration to dominate others. You can use it to be selfish. The real problem is that concentration alone will not give you a perspective on yourself. It won't throw light on the basic problems of selfishness and the nature of suffering. It can be used to dig down into deep psychological states. But even then, the forces of egotism won't be understood. Only mindfulness can do that. If mindfulness is not there to look into the lens and see what has been uncovered, then it is all for nothing. Only mindfulness understands. Only mindfulness brings wisdom. Concentration has other limitations, too.

Really deep concentration can only take place under certain specific conditions. Buddhists go to a lot of trouble to build meditation halls and monasteries. Their main purpose is to create a physical environment free of distractions in which to learn this skill. No noise, no interruptions. Just as important, however, is the creation of a distraction-free emotional environment. The development of concentration will be blocked by the presence of certain mental states which we call the five hindrances. They are greed for sensual pleasure, hatred, mental lethargy, restlessness, and mental vacillation.

A monastery is a controlled environment where this sort of emotional noise is kept to a minimum. No members of the opposite sex are allowed to live together there. Therefore, there is less opportunity for lust to arise. No possessions are allowed. Therefore, no ownership squabbles and less chance for greed and for coveting. Another hurdle for concentration should also be mentioned. In really deep concentration, you get so absorbed in the object of concentration that you forget all about trifles. Like your body, for instance, and your identity and everything around you. Here again the monastery is a useful convenience. It is nice to know that there is somebody to take care of you by watching over all the mundane matters of food and physical security. Without such assurance, one hesitates to go as deeply into concentration as one might.

Mindfulness, on the other hand, is free from all these drawbacks. Mindfulness is not dependent on any such particular circumstance, physical or otherwise. It is a pure noticing factor. Thus it is free to notice whatever comes up—lust, hatred, or noise. Mindfulness is not limited by any condition. It exists to some extent in every moment, in every circumstance that arises. Also, mindfulness has no fixed object of focus. It observes change. Thus, it has an unlimited number of objects of attention. It just looks at whatever is passing through the mind and it does not categorize. Distractions and interruptions are noticed with the same amount of attention as the formal objects of meditation. In a state of pure mindfulness your attention just flows along with whatever changes are taking place in the mind. "Shift, shift, shift. Now this, now this, and now this."

You can't develop mindfulness by force. Active teeth-gritting willpower won't do you any good at all. As a matter of fact, it will hinder progress. Mindfulness cannot be cultivated by struggle. It grows by realizing, by letting go, by just settling down in the moment and letting yourself get comfortable with whatever you are experiencing. This does not mean that mindfulness happens all by itself. Far from it. Energy is required. Effort is required. But this effort is different from force. Mindfulness is cultivated by a gentle effort. The meditator cultivates mindfulness by constantly reminding himself in a gentle way to maintain his awareness of whatever is happening right now. Persistence and a light touch are the secrets. Mindfulness is cultivated by constantly pulling oneself back to a state of awareness, gently, gently, gently.

Mindfulness can't be used in any selfish way, either. It is egoless alertness. There no "me" in a state of pure mindfulness. So there is no self to be selfish. On the contrary, it is mindfulness which gives you real perspective on yourself. It allows you to take that crucial mental step backward from your own desires and aversions so that you can then look and say, "Ah ha, so that's how I really am."

In a state of mindfulness, you see yourself exactly as you are. You see your own selfish behavior. You see your own suffering. And you see how you create that suffering. You see how you hurt others. You pierce right through the layer of lies that you normally tell yourself, and you see what is really there. Mindfulness leads to wisdom.

Mindfulness is not trying to achieve anything. It is just looking. Therefore, desire and aversion are not involved. Competition and struggle for achievement have no place in the process. Mindfulness does not aim at anything. It just sees whatever is already there.

Mindfulness is a broader and larger function than concentration. It is an all-encompassing function. Concentration is exclusive. It settles down on one item and ignores everything else. Mindfulness is inclusive. It stands back from the focus of attention and watches with a broad focus, quick to notice any change that occurs. If you have focused the mind on a stone, concentration will see only the stone. Mindfulness stands back from this process, aware of the stone, aware of concentration focusing on the stone, aware of the intensity of that focus and instantly aware of the shift of attention when concentration is distracted. It is mindfulness which notices that the distraction has occurred, and it is mindfulness which redirects the attention to the stone. Mindfulness is more difficult to cultivate than concentration because it is a deeper-reaching function. Concentration is merely focusing the mind, rather like a laser beam. It has the power to burn its way deep into the mind and illuminate what is there. But it does not understand what it sees. Mindfulness can examine the mechanics of selfishness and understand what it sees. Mindfulness can pierce the mystery of suffering and the mechanism of discomfort. Mindfulness can make you free.

There is, however, another catch-22. Mindfulness does not react to what it sees. It just sees and understands. Mindfulness is the essence of patience. Therefore, whatever you see must simply be accepted, acknowledged, and dispassionately observed. This is not easy, but it is utterly necessary. We are ignorant. We are selfish and greedy and boastful. We lust, and we lie. These are facts. Mindfulness means seeing these facts and being patient with ourselves, accepting ourselves as we are. That goes against the grain. We don't want to accept it. We want to deny it. Or change it or justify it. But acceptance is the essence of mindfulness.

If we want to grow in mindfulness we must accept what mindfulness finds. It may be boredom, irritation, or fear. It may be weakness, inadequacy, or faults. Whatever it is, that is the way we are. That is what is real.

Mindfulness simply accepts whatever is there. If you want to grow in mindfulness, patient acceptance is the only route. Mindfulness grows only one way: by continuous practice of mindfulness, by simply trying to be mindful, and that means being patient. The process cannot be forced and it cannot be rushed. It proceeds at its own pace.

Concentration and mindfulness go hand in hand in the job of meditation. Mindfulness directs the power of concentration. Mindfulness is the manager of the operation. Concentration furnishes the power by which mindfulness can penetrate into the deepest level of mind. Their cooperation results in insight and understanding. These must be cultivated together in a balanced manner. Just a bit more emphasis is given to mindfulness because mindfulness is the center of meditation. The deepest levels of concentration are not really needed to do the job of liberation. Still, a balance is essential. Too much awareness without calm to balance it will result in a wildly oversensitized state similar to abusing LSD. Too much concentration without a balancing ratio of awareness will result in the "Stone Buddha" syndrome. The meditator gets so tranquilized that he sits there like a rock. Both of these are to be avoided.

The initial stages of mental cultivation are especially delicate. Too much emphasis on mindfulness at this point will actually retard the development of concentration. When getting started in meditation, one of the first things you will notice is how incredibly active the mind really is. The Theravada tradition calls this phenomenon "monkey mind." The Tibetan tradition likens it to a waterfall of thought. If you emphasize the awareness function at this point, there will be so much to be aware of that concentration will be impossible. Don't get discouraged. This happens to everybody. And there is a simple solution. Put most of your effort into one-pointedness at the beginning. Just keep calling the attention from wandering over and over again. Tough it out. A couple of months down the track and you will have developed concentration power. Then you can start pumping your energy into mindfulness.

Do not, however, go so far with concentration that you find yourself going into a stupor.

Mindfulness still is the more important of the two components. It should be built as soon as you comfortably can do so. Mindfulness provides the needed foundation for the subsequent development of deeper concentration. Most blunders in this area of balance will correct themselves in time. Right concentration develops naturally in the wake of strong mindfulness. The more you develop the noticing factor, the quicker you will notice the distraction and the quicker you will pull out of it and return to the formal object of attention. The natural result is increased concentration. And as concentration develops, it assists the development of mindfulness. The more concentration power you have, the less chance there is of launching off on a long chain of analysis about the distraction. You simply note the distraction and return your attention to where it is supposed to be.

Thus the two factors tend to balance and support each other's growth quite naturally. Just about the only rule you need to follow at this point is to put your effort on concentration at the beginning, until the monkey mind phenomenon has cooled down a bit. After that, emphasize mindfulness. If you find yourself getting frantic, emphasize concentration. If you find yourself going into a stupor, emphasize mindfulness. Overall, mindfulness is the one to emphasize.

Mindfulness guides your development in meditation because mindfulness has the ability to be aware of itself. It is mindfulness which will give you a perspective on your practice. Mindfulness will let you know how you are doing. But don't worry too much about that. This is not a race. You are not in competition with anybody, and there is no schedule.

One of the most difficult things to learn is that mindfulness is not dependent on any emotional or mental state. We have certain images of meditation. Meditation is something done in quiet caves by tranquil people who move slowly. Those are training conditions. They are set up to foster concentration and to learn the skill of mindfulness. Once you have learned that skill, however, you can dispense with the training restrictions, and you should. You don't need to move at a snail's pace to be mindful. You don't even need to be calm. You can be mindful while solving problems in intensive calculus. You can be mindful in the middle of a football scrimmage. You can even be mindful in the midst of a raging fury. Mental and physical activities are no bar to mindfulness. If you find your mind extremely active, then simply observe the nature and degree of that activity. It is just a part of the passing show within.

# An Eighteen-Year Retreat

from *Everyday Blessings*

by Myla Kabat-Zinn and Jon Kabat-Zinn

Just as it might be useful to look at our children as little Buddhas or Zen Masters in order to help us to parent them better and to continue to grow ourselves, I (JKZ) have often felt that parenting could be looked at as an extended meditation retreat—an opportunity to do a certain kind of deep and concentrated inner work of potentially profound and continuing benefit to children and parents alike within a family.

Usually, meditation retreats last for days, weeks, or months, but in this case, the "parenting retreat" would last on the order of at least eighteen years per child. Of course, the demands of parenting from day to day are very different from those of a secluded and intensive meditation retreat, but seeing them as related ways of doing sustained inner work has energized and sustained me at times in bringing a tenacious and overarching perspective to the inner calling of parenting, and to the years of constant and ultimately selfless attention, caring, and wisdom that it asks of us.

What, then, is a meditation retreat? What is its purpose? And how might seeing parenting as a kind of retreat help us understand and deepen what is being asked of us when we engage in mindful parenting, even for those of us who don't meditate regularly or who have no personal experience of such retreats? And how might looking at parenting in this way contribute to our own growth and development?

A meditation retreat is in opportunity to do a certain kind of inner work on ourselves that is extremely difficult to do outside of the retreat setting because of all the competing obligations, distractions, and entice-ments of everyday life. On retreat, because we are off in a special place for an extended period of time, away from the demands of family and work, we have a rare and precious chance to simplify our lives and give enormous care and attention to the domain of being.

Meditation retreats are often guided by one or more skilled teachers, who serve to encourage, inspire, guide, instruct, and listen to the expe-riences of the retreatants. The basic practice consists mostly of periods of sitting and walking, all in silence, typically from early morning to late at night. Just sitting. Just walking. Usually there is a period of work as well, also silent, so that the same mind that we cultivate in sitting and walking can be brought to cleaning the bathroom, or washing pots, or weeding the garden. What the task is is not so important . . . the mind that we bring to it is exquisitely important.

Attention is directed primarily inwardly, toward a few basic aspects of life experience that are ordinarily taken completely for granted, such as the breath flowing in and out, and what there is to be perceived moment by moment in your own body and in your own mind. Other than that, you eat, also in silence, and you sleep. Usually there is no reading, no writing, and no telephone calls, So you are really on your own except for occasional interviews with the teacher. Such retreats can be extremely arduous and challenging—and deeply healing.

Over time, the mind gradually settles into the retreat. It can become deeply concentrated and one-pointed, remaining focused and relatively balanced and still over extended periods of time. Through the disciplined cultivation of attention, coupled with recognition and acceptance of what you are observing, you can come to know the landscape of your own mind and your own heart in radically new ways. A highly penetrative awareness develops, which can provide a deep look into the very nature of your being, underneath surface appearances, attachments, and personal history. Intensive and sustained attention of this kind can some-times catalyze profound insights—awakenings that are truly enlighten-ing—and can reveal you to yourself in ways you never knew or thought possible.

Intensive meditation practice is both a mirror and purification pro-cess. We may come to a larger and more accurate way of seeing, which can give rise to deep learning about ourselves, and an equally deep letting go, perhaps most important, a letting go of whatever we find we identify with in absolute and rigid ways. . . . Our attachments to things, ways of seeing, ideas.

In paying sustained attention to your own mind, you can discover that the mind actually behaves in fairly structured ways, in patterns that are recognizable, if sometimes excruciatingly repetitive and unrelenting. You might come to see, just by sitting and walking in silence, how cease-lessly the stream of thinking flows, how chaotic the thought process is (order within it is sometimes difficult to discern), and how unreliable and inaccurate most of our thoughts are. You might come to see how reactive the mind is, and how powerful its emotional storms.

You might see that the mind spends enormous amounts of time in the past, reminiscing, resenting, or blaming, and in the future, worrying, planning, hoping, dreaming. You might see that the mind tends con-stantly to judge itself and everything else, depending on whether an experience is felt to be pleasant, unpleasant, or neutral at any particular moment. You might see how strong the mind's attachments are, its in-cessant identification with things and opinions, and how so much of the time it is driven by wishful thinking and the desire to be somewhere else, to have things and relationships be different from how they actually are.

You might see how hard it is for the mind to settle into the present moment as it is, but also that, over time, the mind can actually calm down enough to see much of this ceaseless activity that it is engaged in, and come to an inner stillness and calmness and balance that is less easily disturbed by its own activity.

If you are motivated enough to stick with the practice through the hard times, if you can stay with the pain in your body that may come from long periods of sitting still, if you can stay with the yearning in the mind for talk, or for entertainment and distraction and novelty, if you can stay with the boredom, resistance, the grief, terror, and confusion that can and do arise on occasion, and if, all the while, you ruthlessly and with utter kindness and gentleness, without expectations, persist in simply observing whatever comes up in the field of your awareness, moment by moment, you may come to encounter, at certain points in your practice, great oceanlike depths of silence, well-being, and wisdom within your own mind.

For, in many ways, the mind does resemble a body of water, a veri-table ocean. On the surface, depending on the season, the weather, and the winds, the surface can be anything from completely calm and flat to hugely tumultuous and turbulent, with forty-foot waves or higher. But even at its most stormy, if one goes down deep enough, the water will be very still.

Persisting in the practice, we might come to see on such a retreat that our own mind is much the same—that calmness and deep stillness are intrinsic to its nature, that they are always present, and that even when we are caught up in huge storms of emotional turmoil, for whatever reasons, the calmness and the stillness and the capacity to be aware are still here, underneath, embedded in and an integral part of our being. They can be called upon, and used, not to extinguish the surface turbulence of the mind (just as we don't try to flatten the waves on the ocean), but to understand it and to provide a larger container for it, a context in which the very turbulence itself can be held, seen, and even used to deepen our understanding.

We may come to see that our thoughts and emotions do not have to carry us away or blind us in one way or another, as so frequently happens in life. Nor do we have to make any effort to suppress them to be free from much of the suffering they contain or engender.

Working in this way with the activity of our own mind, we might also come to see that it is a fiction that we are isolated, separate, and alone. We might see that "I," "me," and "mine" are themselves thoughts, powerful, deeply rooted and tenacious habits of mind, but thoughts all the same. Beneath the sense of ourselves as being separate and preoccupied so much of the time with concerns about our individual self and our own personal gains and losses, we might see that we are part of a flowing movement of wholeness that is larger than we are and to which we belong.

We might see that there is a deep mystery in our individual life emerging from the union of our parents and, before them, from their parents, and so on back into time; that we are an intermediary between our parents and our children, between all those who have come before, whom we will never know, and all those who will come after our children's children's children, whom we will also never know.

We may come to see that the deepest nature of the universe is that it is one, a seamless whole, and that everything that is is an aspect of everything else. We may come to see that everything is embedded in and reflected in everything else, that everything and every being is whole and part of a larger wholeness, and that interconnectedness and interdependence are the root relationships out of which meaning and the particulars of our fleeting and constantly changing individual lives arise.

And you may come to see with fresh eyes and a new understanding and appreciation that, together with the ways in which the unfolding of life is impersonal, it is all the same very personal. You may realize directly, as the veils of thinking and strong attachment thin, that right now and right here, you are who you are; that the being that is you is unique, with your own face and character and desires, with a particular history that is the legacy of having the parents that you had and growing up the way you did, and with your own unique and mysterious path or calling that can infuse your life with vision and passion. You work where you work, you live where you live, your responsibilities are your responsibilities, your children are your children, your hopes are your hopes, your fears your fears.

We might come to see that "separate" and "not separate" are themselves just thoughts, attempts to describe a deeper reality that is us. We might see the possibility of living more gracefully, knowing that the things that happen to us are happening to us, yet also knowing that it is not wise to take them entirely personally, because everything is also impersonal, and it is problematic—Buddhists would say, impossible— to point to a solid, permanent "you" who is here to take them personally. You are certainly who you are, and you are responsible for many things; but you are certainly not who you think you are because thinking itself is limited, and your true nature is limitless.

On retreat, we might also come to know that we are not our body, not our thoughts, not our emotions, not our ideas and opinions, not our fears and our insecurities and our woundedness, even though they are an intimate part of our experience and can influence our lives enormously, much as the weather influences the surface of the ocean. Their influence is particularly strong if we form strong and unconscious attachments to them, to which we cling for dear life, and through which we see everything as through dark, or light, or colored, or kaleidoscopic glasses.

We are not our ideas and opinions. If we could live our lives knowing this, and take off the glasses through which we filter our experience, what a difference it might make in the way we see, in our choices, and in the way we conduct our lives from day to day. This insight alone might cause us to see ourselves very differently, to see our parenting very differently, and indeed, to live differently.

We may also see that, like everybody else, we are only here very briefly, but that brief moment we call a lifetime is also infinitely long if we can bring awareness to our moments, since there are infinite moments in any lifetime. In living in the present, we step out of clock time into a timeless present. Such experiences may show us that we are not by nature entirely bound by time.

We might, thus, also begin to taste impermanence in a new way, since nothing we focus our attention on endures for long. Each breath comes and goes, sensations in the body come and go, thoughts come and go, emotions come and go, ideas and opinions come and go, moments come and go, days and nights come and go. We may see that, similarly, seasons and years come and go, youth comes and goes, jobs and people come and go. Even mountains and rivers and species come and go. Nothing is fixed. Nothing is permanent, although things may appear that way to us. Everything is always moving, changing, becoming, dissolving, emerging, evolving, in a complex dance, the outer dance of the world not so different from the inner dance of our own mind. We might see that our children are also part of this dance . . . that, like us, they too are only brief visitors to this beautiful and strange world, and our time with them even briefer, its duration unknown.

Might not this realization strike us deeply and teach us something of great value? Might it not suggest how precious the time we do share together with our children is, and how to hold our essentially fleeting moments with them in awareness? Might it not influence how we hug and kiss our children, and say good night to them, and watch them sleep, and wake them in the morning? Might such understanding not influence how hard a time we give them when, in seeking to find their own ways they scrape up against our ideas and opinions, the limits of our patience, and our ego investments in being right and all-knowing, forgetting in those moments what we actually know that is far larger and more life-affirming?

Perhaps taking on parenting as a kind of meditation retreat, and doing the inner work of mindful parenting day by day and moment by moment in the same spirit of concentrated and sustained effort of attention and presence as on a retreat, might help us to realize the enormous power in seeing and remembering the larger context of wholeness, so that we are not lost in the surface waves of our own minds and our sometimes narrowly conceived and citing to lives. Perhaps we would hold our moments differently. Perhaps they would not slip by so unnoticed, so unused, so filled up by us with busyness or diversions. Perhaps we would appreciate more what is given to us, from our own body and life, to our relationships, to our children and our parents, and our children's children, to the world in which we get to live and which we pass on to those who will follow.

Perhaps we would care more, and care differently, and attend more, and attend differently, if we held in our own minds and hearts what we already deeply know, but usually forget, or haven't developed to the point where it can serve us as a way of being, a way of seeing, a way of truly living wakefully. Perhaps we would know how to stand in our own life, on our own feet, and feel the earth beneath us and the wind in our face and around our body, and know the place as here, and the time as now, and honor the mysterious wisdom that resides within all beings and within our children.

These glimpses are some of what one might see and realize through intensive practice on an extended mindfulness meditation retreat. Retreats are of great and abiding value when we can arrange our lives to go off from time to time to practice in this way. But there are also many times when it may be neither possible nor advisable to go off someplace else for an extended period, especially when juggling the responsibilities of parenting, family life, and work.

This is where the metaphor of seeing the whole experience of parenting as an extended meditation retreat may be useful. It is not that parenting is a retreat from the world, although to some extent a healthy family can buffer the stress of the outer world and create feelings of inner security and peace. It is, rather, that we are using the very circumstances of the world and of parenting, as best we can, and usually under difficult conditions, to help us cultivate mindfulness, look deeply into our lives, and let our doing come out of our being—not just from time to time, but concertedly, as a way of life.

The daily schedule of family life, of course, is much more complex and chaotic than on retreat, dictated as it frequently is to a large extent by the head teachers, who are our children. It will change as they change and grow, sometimes from day to day, sometimes moment by moment. But the practice is always the same: to be fully present, looking deeply, as best we can, and without judging or condemning events or our experience of them. Just presence, and appropriate action, moment by moment. It can be anchored by a daily period of formal practice at a convenient time, but the major commitment will of necessity be the cultivation of mindfulness in everyday life, responding to the call of parenting, allowing each day and each moment to provide the arena for a deepening of awareness.

In this way, waking up in the morning is waking-up meditation. Brushing your teeth is brushing-your-teeth meditation. Not getting to brush your teeth because the baby is crying is not-getting-to-brush-your-teeth-and-taking-care-of-the-baby-first meditation. And so on. Getting the children dressed, getting food on the table, getting them off to school, going to work, diapering, shopping, making arrangements, cleaning up, cooking, everything becomes part of our practice of mindfulness. Everything.

# Meditation: Research and Practical Application

## from *The Meditative Mind*

### by Daniel Goleman

## MEDITATION AND STRESS

While I was in India in 1971, I met a number of Indian yogis, Tibetan lamas, and Buddhist monks. I was struck by the relaxed warmth, openness, and alertness of these men and women, no matter what the situation. Each was the kind of person I enjoyed being with, and I felt nourished when I left them.

There were vast differences in their beliefs and backgrounds. The one thing they shared was meditation. Then I met S. N. Goenka, a teacher who was not a monk, but an industrialist who had been one of the richest men in Burma. Though he had been highly successful, Goenka found that his hectic pace took its toll in the form of daily migraine headaches. Medical treatments at European and American clinics had no effect on his headaches, and he turned to meditation as a last resort. Within three days of his first instruction, his migraines disappeared.

In the 1960s there was a military coup in Burma, and the new socialist government seized all of Goenka's holdings, leaving him nearly penniless. He emigrated to India, where he took advantage of old business and family connections to start a new business. While his new enterprise was getting underway, he traveled throughout India giving ten-day courses in meditation. Some reservoir of energy allowed him to be both full-time meditation teacher and businessman. His example helped me to see that one needn't be a monk to meditate. You can separate the physical effects of meditation from its monastic context.

When I returned to Harvard from India, I found that psychologist Gary Schwartz had begun research into meditation. He had found that meditators reported much lower daily anxiety levels than nonmeditators. They had many fewer psychological or psychosomatic problems such as colds, headaches, and sleeplessness.

My personal experience, and these scientific findings, suggested that meditators were able to roll with life's punches, handling daily stresses well and suffering fewer consequences from them. With Schwartz as my thesis advisor, I designed a study to see how the practice of meditation helps one cope with stress.

I had two groups of volunteers come to our physiology lab. One group consisted of meditation teachers, all of whom had been meditating for at least two years. The other group of people were interested in meditation but had not yet begun to meditate. Once in the lab, each volunteer was told to sit quietly and either relax or meditate. If nonmeditators were assigned to the meditation treatment, I taught them how to meditate right there in the lab. After twenty minutes of relaxation or meditation, the volunteers saw a short film depicting a series of bloody accidents among workers in a woodworking shop. The film is a standard way of inducing stress during laboratory studies, because everyone who watches it is upset by the accidents depicted in the film.

The meditators had a unique pattern of reaction to the film. Just as the accident was about to happen, their heart rates increased and they began to sweat more than the nonmeditators. To get ready to meet the distressing sight, their heartbeats rose and their bodies mobilized in what physiologists call the fight-or-flight reaction. But as soon as the accident was over, the meditators recovered, their signals of bodily arousal falling more quickly than those of nonmeditators. After the film, they were more relaxed than the nonmeditators, who still showed signs of tension.

This pattern of greater initial arousal and faster recovery showed up in experienced meditators whether or not they had meditated before the movie began. In fact, the meditators felt more relaxed the whole time they were in the lab. Rapid recovery from stress is a typical trait of meditators. Even the novices, who meditated for the first time that day in the lab, were less anxious after the film and recovered more quickly than the nonmeditators.

Meditation itself seems the most likely cause of rapid stress recovery. If the rapid recovery among experienced meditators had been the result of some personality trait common to the kind of people who stick with meditation, the novices would have been as slow to recover as were the people who relaxed.

My study may explain the lower incidence of anxiety and psychosomatic disorders among meditators. People who are chronically anxious or who have a psychosomatic disorder share a specific pattern of reaction to stress; their bodies mobilize to meet the challenge, then fail to stop reacting when the problem is over. The initial tensing up is essential, for it allows them to marshal their energy and awareness to deal with a potential threat. But their bodies stay aroused for danger when they should be relaxed, recouping spent energies and gathering resources for the next brush with stress.

The anxious person meets life's normal events as though they were crises. Each minor happening increases his tension, and his tension in turn magnifies the next ordinary event—a deadline, an interview, a doctor's appointment—into a threat. Because the anxious person's body stays mobilized after one event has passed, he has a lower threat threshold for the next. Had he been in a relaxed state, he would have taken the second event in stride.

A meditator handles stress in a way that breaks up the threat-arousal-threat spiral. The meditator relaxes after a challenge passes more often than the nonmeditator. This makes him unlikely to see innocent occurrences as harmful. He perceives threat more accurately, and reacts with arousal only when necessary. Once aroused, his rapid recovery makes him less likely than the anxious person to see the next deadline as a threat.

*Effects of Meditation on the Brain.* The popular appeal of meditation is the promise of becoming more relaxed more of the time. But some highly pressured members of society are not sure that relaxation is a good thing. When Harvard Medical School's Herbert Benson wrote an article in the *Harvard Business Review* urging businesses to give employees time for a meditation break, there was a flood of letters protesting that stress and tension were essential to good business management. A friend of mine, when told to meditate to lower his blood pressure, responded: "I need to take it easy, but I don't want to become a zombie."

Fortunately, meditation doesn't make zombies. The meditation experts I met in India and America were among the most lively people I've met anywhere. Research into the effects of meditation on the brain may suggest why.

Meditation trains the capacity to pay attention. This sets it apart from other ways of relaxing, most of which let the mind wander as it will. This sharpening of attention lasts beyond the meditation session itself. It shows up in a number of ways in the rest of the meditator's day. Meditation, for example, has been found to improve one's ability to pick up subtle perceptual cues in the environment, and to pay attention to what is going on rather than letting the mind wander elsewhere. These skills mean that in conversation with another person, the meditator should be more empathic. Because the meditator can pay sharper attention to what the other person is doing and saying, he can pick up more of the hidden messages the other is sending.

## HEALING PROPERTIES OF MEDITATION

In 1984 the National Institute of Health (NIH) released a consensus report that recommended meditation (along with salt and dietary restrictions) above prescription drugs as the first treatment for mild hypertension. This official recognition was a catalyst in the spread of meditation and other relaxation techniques as treatments in medicine and psychotherapy.

In the early 1970s when I did my dissertation research on meditation and relaxation as antidotes to stress reactivity, this idea was new. I found that meditation lowered anxiety levels and sped the meditator's recovery from stress arousal. The clinical applications for stress disorders seemed obvious.

I was not alone in my findings. The mid-1970s saw a flood of research on meditation, particularly its health benefits. The methodological rigor of these studies was, frankly, uneven. But the thrust of the findings was clear: meditation was helpful in many ways. For instance, the regular practice of meditation lessened the frequency of colds and headaches and reduced the severity of hypertension. Although these medical applications received some attention, the stronger initial welcome for meditation came from psychotherapists who saw it as a way for patients to manage anxiety without drugs, to gain access to otherwise blocked memories and feelings, and as a general prescription for handling garden-variety stress. Meditation was a stress management tool par excellence and was vigorously marketed as such to schools, hospitals, and businesses, along with a variety of other relaxation techniques.

Meditation and relaxation are not one and the same; meditation is, in essence, the effort to retrain attention. This gives meditation its unique cognitive effects, such as increasing the meditator's concentration and empathy. The most common use of meditation, however, is as a quick-and-easy relaxation technique.

Although the Eastern roots of meditation were exotic, it became apparent to investigators that, in terms of its metabolic effects, meditation shared much in common with home-grown techniques of relaxation such as Edmund Jacobsen's progressive relaxation and muscle tension bio-feedback, and with European imports such as autogenic training. Meditation differed from other relaxation techniques in its attentional components, as Herbert Benson pointed out in his best-seller *The Relaxation Response*, but much of its therapeutic quality lay in its effectiveness in getting the meditator into a state of deep relaxation.

As research on relaxation techniques for the management of stress disorders continues, the evidence of their effectiveness has become more compelling. The neuroendocrine changes brought about by becoming deeply relaxed have turned out to be more profound than was first believed by earlier investigators who viewed relaxation techniques mostly in terms of their relief of muscle tension and mental worry. More biologically sophisticated investigations have revealed profound effects on immune function as well as a range of other changes with specific applications.

◆  ◆  ◆

Diabetics, too, can benefit from relaxation. Richard Surwit found that relaxation training improved the regulation of glucose in patients with adult-onset diabetes. Using Jacobsen's progressive relaxation with asthmatics, Paul Lehrer found that the practice lessened the emotional reactions that often preceded attacks and improved the flow in constricted airway passages.

For pain patients, some forms of relaxation offer particular promise. Jon Kabat-Zinn found that mindfulness meditation, coupled with yoga, lowered the reliance on pain-killers and lessened the level of pain in chronic pain sufferers. The causes of the pain ranged from backaches and headaches (migraine and tension) to the various cases seen in pain clinics. Four years after the training ended, the benefits still held.

Relaxation techniques of all kinds are being used by medical patients of different kinds, particularly where stress plays a causative role or exacerbates the problem—and there are few cases where it does not. Some of the more promising applications are seen with the side effects of kidney dialysis and cancer chemotherapy, gastrointestinal disorders, insomnia, emphysema, and skin disorders.

Relaxation is also widely used as an adjunct in psychotherapy, where it has been well accepted far longer than it has in medicine. Even so, there are some problems in applying these techniques. A few people react to relaxation with increased tension and even panic. In these cases, relaxation may need to be introduced after special cognitive preparation or simply not at all.

There are other situations in which meditation may not be appropriate for patients. A schizoid may possibly worsen reality-testing, becoming overly absorbed in inner realities; those in acute emotional states might be too agitated to begin meditation; obsessive-compulsives might on the one hand be too closed to new experience to try meditation, or on the other, overzealous in their efforts.

One task ahead is to sort out the significant differences, if any, between relaxation and meditation techniques in terms of the people and problems for which they will be most effective. But, as the research evidence makes clear, these methods offer a powerful way to tap the inner capacity of patients to participate in their own healing.

# We Wash Our Bowls in This Water

## from *Mountains and Rivers Without End*

### by Gary Snyder

*We Wash Our Bowls in This Water*

*"The 1.5 billion cubic kilometers of water on the earth are split by photosynthesis and reconstituted by respiration once every two million years or so."*

A day on the ragged North Pacific coast get soaked by whipping mist, rainsqualls tumbling, mountain mirror ponds, snowfield slush, rock-wash creeks, earfulls of falls, sworls of ridge-edge snowflakes, swift gravelly rivers, tidewater crumbly glaciers, high hanging glaciers, shore-side mud pools, icebergs, streams looping through the tideflats, spume of brine, distant soft rain drooping from a cloud,

sea lions lazing under the surface of the sea—

> *We wash our bowls in this water*
> *It has the flavor of ambrosial dew—*

•

Beaching the raft, stagger out and shake off wetness like a
   bear,
stand on the sandbar, rest from the river      being

upwellings, sideswirls, backswirls
curl-overs, outripples, eddies, chops and swells
wash-overs, shallows confluence turbulence   wash-seam
wavelets, riffles, saying

"A hydraulic's a cross between a wave and a hole,
    —you get a weird effect.
Pillow-rock's a total fold-back over a hole,
    it shows spit on the top of the wave

a haystack's a series of waves at the bottom of a tight
    channel
       there's a tongue of the rapids—the slick tongue—the
       'v'—
some holes are 'keepers,' they won't let you through;
eddies, backflows, we say 'eddies are your friends.'
Current differential, it can suck you down
vertical boils are straight-up eddies spinning,
herringbone waves curl under and come back.
Well, let's get going, get back to the rafts."
    Swing the big oars,
        head into a storm.

*We offer it to all demons and spirits*
*May all be filled and satisfied.*
*Om makula sai svaha!*


    •


Su Tung-p'o sat out one whole night    by a creek    on the slopes
of Mt. Lu. Next morning he showed this poem to his teacher:

The stream with its sounds   is a long broad tongue
The looming mountain   is a wide-awake body
Throughout the night   song after song
How can I   speak at dawn.

Old Master Chang-tsung approved him. Two centuries later
Dogen said,
  "Sounds of streams and shapes of mountains.
  The sounds never stop and the shapes never cease.
  Was it Su who woke
  or was it the mountains and streams?

  Billions of beings see the morning star
  and all become Buddhas!
  If *you*, who are valley streams and looming
  mountains,
  can't throw some light on the nature of ridges and rivers,

  *who can*?"

# ABOUT THE CONTRIBUTORS

ROBERT AITKEN was introduced to Zen in a Japanese prison camp during World War II after he was captured as a civilian in Guam. He returned to Japan after the war to study Zen. He and his wife Anne established a Zen organization, the Diamond Sangha, in Hawaii in 1959, where he continues to teach and study. He is the author of *Taking the Path of Zen* and *The Mind of Clover*.

JAMES A. AUTRY is an award-winning author, a former Fortune 500 top executive, and a leading business consultant. He is the author of *Life & Work: A Manager's Search for Meaning, Love and Profit: The Art of Caring Leadership*, and the coauthor of *Real Power*.

STEPHEN BATCHELOR, who was educated in Buddhist monasteries in India, Switzerland, and Korea, is Director of Studies of the Sharpham College for Buddhist Studies and Contemporary Enquiry in Devon, England. He is an award-winning author and translator of several books including *Buddhism Without Belief*, *The Tibet Guide*, and *The Awakening of the West*.

CHARLOTTE JOKO BECK teaches at the San Diego Zen Center. She is the author of *Nothing Special: Living Zen* and *Everyday Zen: Love and Work*.

SYLVIA BOORSTEIN is a psychotherapist, a cofounder, and teacher at Spirit Rock Meditation Center in Woodacre, California, and a teacher at the

Insight Meditation Center in Barre, Massachusetts. She is the author of *Funny, You Don't Look Buddhist, It's Easier Than You Think: The Buddhist Way to Happiness,* and *Don't Just Do Something, Sit There.*

JERRY BRAZA, PH.D., who teaches at Western Oregon State College, has taught for over twenty years as a university professor with multidisciplinary training in health and psychology. He is the author of *Moment by Moment: The Art and Practice of Mindfulness.*

KYOGEN CARLSON is a Buddhist priest trained in Soto Zen. He is the Abbot of Dharma Rain Zen Center in Portland, Oregon, and the author of *Zen in the American Grain.*

PEMA CHODRON is an American Buddhist nun and director of Gampo Abbey, Nova Scotia, the first Tibetan monastery in North America established for Westerners. She is the author of *Start Where You Are, When Things Fall Apart: Heart Advice for Difficult Times,* and *The Wisdom of No Escape.*

MIHALY CSIKSZENTMIHALYI is professor of psychology and education at the University of Chicago. He is a writer of fiction and nonfiction, including the best-selling books, *Flow, Creativity,* and *The Evolving Self.*

LAMA SURYA DAS is a spiritual teacher in the Tibetan tradition. He trained with the great Buddhist teachers of Asia and has completed two three-year meditation retreats. Surya Das lectures and teaches meditation retreats worldwide. He is the author of *Awakening the Buddha Within.*

RAM DASS, PH.D., a.k.a. Richard Alpert, has been a contributor to the integration of Eastern spiritual philosophy into Western thought since the 1960s. He received his Ph.D. in psychology from Stanford University and has taught at Harvard, Stanford, and the University of California. He is the coauthor of *How Can I Help?, Be Here Now,* and *The Only Dance There Is.*

MARK EPSTEIN, M.D., is a psychiatrist with a private practice in New York City. He is the author of *Thoughts Without a Thinker* and *Going to Pieces Without Falling Apart.*

RICK FIELDS is the co-author of *Instructions to the Cook*.

ZOKETSU NORMAN FISCHER is a meditation teacher and writer, co-Abbott of The San Francisco Zen Center, Tassajara Zen Mountain Monastery, and Green Gulch Zen Farm. He is the author of the article "On Questioning," which appeared in *Shambhala Sun*.

BERNARD GLASSMAN is abbot of the Zen Community of New York and the Zen Center of Los Angeles, a nonprofit community developer, and teacher. He is the coauthor of *Instructions to the Cook* and the author of *Bearing Witness*.

JOSEPH GOLDSTEIN is one of the founders and guiding teachers at the Insight Meditation Society in Barre, Massachusetts. He studied meditation for many years in India and teaches meditation classes, workshops, and retreats worldwide. He is the author of *The Experience of Insight*.

DANIEL GOLEMAN, PH.D., is a former behavioral sciences writer for *The New York Times* and a former senior editor at *Psychology Today*. Dr. Goleman spent two years in the Far East studying meditation and has taught at Harvard University. He is the author of *Emotional Intelligence*, *Using Emotional Intelligence*, *Vital Lies*, and *The Meditative Mind*.

PAUL GORMAN is Vice-President for Public Affairs and Advocacy at The Cathedral of St. John the Divine in New York City. He was educated at Yale and Oxford, and has taught at Sarah Lawrence College, Naropa Institute, and Omega Institute. He is the coauthor of *How Can I Help?*

VENERABLE HENEPOLA GUNARATANA, PH.D., was ordained at the age of twelve as a Buddhist monk in Sri Lanka. He was a missionary in Malaysia and in India, where he served the untouchable people in Delhi and Bombay. Since 1973, he has been Buddhist chaplain at The American University. He is the author of *Mindfulness in Plain English*.

THICH NHAT HANH is a Vietnamese Buddhist monk, Zen teacher, and poet. He was nominated for the Nobel Peace Prize by Martin Luther King. He is the author of numerous books of prose and poetry including *The Art of Mindful Living*, *Being Peace*, *Cultivating the Mind of Love*, and *The Miracle of Mindfulness*.

EUGEN HERRIGEL was a German professor of philosophy at the University of Tokyo. He undertook a rigorous six-year training discipline with a Zen Master and *Zen in the Art of Archery* is his account of that experience.

PHIL JACKSON was head coach of the six-time national champion Chicago Bulls basketball team. He is one of the most successful coaches in NBA history. Jackson has integrated Eastern and Native American teachings into his coaching philosophy to inspire and guide his team. He is the author of *Sacred Hoops: Spiritual Lessons of a Hardwood Warrior*.

JON KABAT-ZINN, PH.D., is the founder and former director of the Stress Reduction Clinic at the University of Massachusetts Medical Center and Executive Director of its Center for Mindfulness in Medicine, Healthcare, and Society. He is also Associate Professor of Medicine at the University of Massachusetts Medical School. He is the author of *Full Catastrophe Living: Using the Wisdom of Your Body and Mind to Face Stress, Pain and Illness*, *Wherever You Go, There You Are: Mindfulness Meditation in Everyday Life*, and the coauthor of *Everyday Blessings: The Inner Work of Mindful Parenting*.

MYLA KABAT-ZINN, B.S.N., R.N., has worked as a childbirth educator, birthing assistant, and environmental advocate. She is the coauthor of *Everyday Blessings: The Inner Work of Mindful Parenting*.

RONNA KABATZNICK, PH.D., was the psychological consultant to Weight Watchers International for nine years and taught psychology at a number of colleges in New York. She is founder and director of the nonprofit organization Dieters Feed the Hungry and is the author of *The Zen of Eating: Ancient Answers to Modern Weight Problems*.

LES KAYE is abbot of Kannon Do, a Zen meditation center in Mountain View, California. He worked for IBM for over thirty years, starting as a design engineer in 1956 and holding a variety of technical and administrative positions until his retirement in 1990. During his career at IBM he maintained a serious practice in Zen and applied Zen teachings to enhance his work activities at IBM. He is the author of *Zen at Work*.

JACK KORNFIELD, PH.D., who teaches meditation worldwide, was trained as a Buddhist monk in Thailand, Burma, and India. Kornfield, who holds a Ph.D. in clinical psychology, is a founder of the Insight Meditation Society and the Spirit Rock Center. In addition to *A Path with Heart*, he is the author of *A Still Forest Pool*, and coauthor of *Stories of the Heart* and *Seeking the Heart of Wisdom*.

SUSAN GORDON LYDON is the author of *Take the Long Way Home* and *The Knitting Sutra*.

STEPHEN MITCHELL has translated many books, including *Tao Te Ching* and *The Enlightened Heart* and is the coauthor of *Real Power*.

ROBERT M. PIRSIG is the author of *Zen in the Art of Motorcycle Maintenance* and *Lila*.

LARRY ROSENBERG is founder and resident teacher of the Cambridge Insight Meditation Center in Cambridge, Massachusetts, and a teacher at the Insight Meditation Society in Barre, Massachusetts. He is the author of *Breath by Breath: The Liberating Practice of Insight Meditation*.

SHARON SALZBERG is a co-founder of the Insight Meditation Society in Barre, Massachusetts, and the author of *Lovingkindness: The Revolutionary Art of Happiness* and *A Heart as Wide as the World*.

GARY SNYDER is a longtime Zen student and teacher. He is a professor of English on the faculty of the University of California at Davis, and has published sixteen books of poetry and prose. His book *Turtle Island* won the Pulitzer Prize for Poetry in 1975. He was a finalist for the National Book Award in 1992 and has been a Guggenheim Fellow. The book, *Mountains and Rivers Without End*, which is one long poem, took him over forty years to write.

SHUNRYU SUZUKI was an influential Zen master in Japan. As a result of a visit to the United States in 1958, he saw the potential for the development of Zen in America and made a permanent move to San Francisco. He created the first Zen training monastery outside Asia, Tassajara Zen Mountain Monastery, as well as the San Francisco Zen Center and Green Gulch Zen Farm, and was instrumental in bringing Zen practice to America. He is the author of *Zen Mind, Beginner's Mind*.

JOHN TARRANT, PH.D., is a Zen teacher and lineage holder and head teacher of the Diamond Sangha in Santa Rosa, California. He is also a psychotherapist and a member of the faculty of the Program in Integrative Medicine at the University of Arizona at Tucson where he teaches meditation to physicians. He is the author of *The Light Inside the Dark: Zen, Soul, and the Spiritual Life.*

ALAN WATTS was a pioneer in bringing Eastern philosophy to the West. He is the author of many seminal books including *The Way of Zen* and *The Way of Liberation. Talking Zen* is a collection of unpublished essays edited by his son, Mark Watts.

KEN WILBER is a transpersonal psychologist and the author of *No Boundary: Eastern and Western Approaches to Personal Growth, A Brief History of Everything,* and *The Eye of the Spirit.*

GARY ZUKAV is the author of *The Dancing Wu Li Masters* and *The Seat of the Soul.*

# GLOSSARY

*Bodhiharma*  (sixth century) Indian Buddhist who went to China where he established the Ch'an school, which later became known as Zen in Japan.

*Bodhisattva*  One who is dedicated to the liberation of enlightenment and who vows to be a vehicle for the liberation of all sentient beings before fully attaining liberation oneself; one who embodies kindness and compassion.

*Dharma*  (Sanskrit) From a root meaning "to support or sustain;" used to refer to the teachings of Buddha. It is often translated as "the law" or "lawfulness" and carries the meaning "the way things are." It also can refer to a thing or all things, all phenomena.

*Dharma combat*  A playful battle of wits with respect to Dharma. It can be both verbal and nonverbal, traditionally between teacher and disciple; most developed as a form with the Ch'an and Rinzai Zen schools of China, Japan, and Korea.

*Dogen*  (1200–1253) One of the foremost figures of Japanese philosophy and letters. Born in Japan to a noble family, he was orphaned at age seven and ordained a monk at 13. He studied Zen meditation in China under the Zen master Ju-ching from 1223-1227. Returning to Japan, he introduced Zen to Japan and founded the Soto school. His first work was *General Teachings for the Promotion of Zazen* and his primary literary achievement was *Treasury of the True Dharma Eye* which includes over 20 years of his teachings.

*Karma*   (Sanskrit) Literally action or effect of action. The law of cause and effect. Suggesting that the effects of our actions come back to affect one's own present or future life. The circumstances and conditions of birth are said to be caused by actions in previous incarnations.

*Koan*   In Zen a koan is a question, story, or words pointing to fundamental reality. Cannot be understood by logical thinking. For example, "Show me your face before your parents were born."

*Lama*   A Tibetan spiritual teacher or sage.

*Metta*   Lovingkindness (pali word).

*Roshi*   Literally "venerable master." A teacher or spiritual guide who may be a layperson or a monk.

*Samadhi*   A state of intense, one-pointed concentration and absorption. Associated with tranquility, calmness, and stability.

*Sangha*   The community of practicioners of the Dharma.

*Sesshin*   An intensive period of Zen meditation lasting three days to a week. Starts in the early hours of the morning and continues until late at night. Involves instructional interviews with and occasional talks by the Zen master. Literally means "joining of mind to mind."

*Sufism*   The Islamic mystical tradition.

*Sutra*   Literally, a thread on which jewels are strung. A discourse or sermon. Used in Theravada Buddhism for discourse attributed to the Buddha. There are over ten thousand sutras.

*Theravada tradition*    A school of Buddhism prevalent in Sri Lanka, Cambodia, Burma, and Thailand emphasizing the direct teachings of the Buddha on mindfulness.

*Vipassana meditation*    Insight Meditation or mindfulness meditation.

*Zazen*    Japanese term for sitting meditation.

# PERMISSIONS

"The Heart of Practice" and "Judging" from *A Heart as Wide as the World* by Sharon Salzberg ©1997. Reprinted by arrangement with Shambhala Publications, Inc., 300 Massachusettes Ave., Boston, MA 02115.

"Awareness" from *Buddhism Without Belief* by Stephen Batchelor ©1977 by The Buddhist Ray, Inc. and Stephen Batchelor. Reprinted with permission of Putnam Berkley, a division of Penguin Putnam, Inc.

"Bare Attention" from *The Experience of Insight* by Joseph Goldstein © 1976. Reprinted by arrangement with Shambhala Publications, Inc., 300 Massachusettes Ave., Boston, MA 02115.

"Vait a Minute, Vait a Minute" and "The Broccoli Phenomenon" from *Don't Just Do Something, Sit There* by Sylvia Boorstein © 1996. Reprinted by permission of HarperCollins Publishers, Inc.

"The Listening Mind" from *How Can I Help?* by Ram Dass and Paul Gorman © 1985 by Ram Dass and Paul Gorman. Reprinted with permission of Alfred A. Knopf Inc.

"When the Student Is Ready, the Teacher Bites" from *Breath by Breath: The Liberating Practice of Insight Meditation* by Larry Rosenberg © 1998 by Larry Rosenberg. Reprinted by arrangement with Shambhala Publications, Inc., 300 Massachusettes Ave., Boston, MA 02115.

"Three Wondrous Answers" from *The Miracle of Mindfulness* by Thich Nhat Hanh ©1996 by Thich Nhat Hanh. Reprinted with permission of Beacon Press, Boston.

"This Is It," "Cat Food Lessons," "Harmony," "Can Anybody Meditate?" from *Wherever You Go, There You Are: Mindfulness Meditation in Everyday Life* by Jon Kabat-Zinn © 1994 by Jon Kabat-Zinn. Reprinted with permission by Hyperion.

"Discover What Is Asking for Acceptance" and "Training the Puppy: Mindfulness of Breathing" from *A Path with Heart* by Jack Kornfield © 1993 by Jack Kornfield. Reprinted with permission of Bantam Books, a division of Bantam Doubleday Dell Publishing Group, Inc.